RESTORING RELATIONS THROUGH STORIES

Critical Issues in Indigenous Studies

Jeffrey P. Shepherd and Myla Vicenti Carpio
Series Editors

ADVISORY BOARD
Hōkūlani Aikau
Jennifer Nez Denetdale
Eva Marie Garroutte
John Maynard
Alejandra Navarro-Smith
Gladys Tzul Tzul
Keith Camacho
Margaret Elizabeth Kovach
Vicente Diaz

RESTORING RELATIONS THROUGH STORIES

From Dinétah to Denendeh

RENAE WATCHMAN
Foreword by Luci Tapahonso

THE UNIVERSITY OF ARIZONA PRESS
TUCSON

The University of Arizona Press
www.uapress.arizona.edu

We respectfully acknowledge the University of Arizona is on the land and territories of Indigenous peoples. Today, Arizona is home to twenty-two federally recognized tribes, with Tucson being home to the O'odham and the Yaqui. Committed to diversity and inclusion, the University strives to build sustainable relationships with sovereign Native Nations and Indigenous communities through education offerings, partnerships, and community service.

© 2024 by The Arizona Board of Regents
All rights reserved. Published 2024

ISBN-13: 978-0-8165-5035-7 (hardcover)
ISBN-13: 978-0-8165-5034-0 (paperback)
ISBN-13: 978-0-8165-5036-4 (ebook)

Cover design by Leigh McDonald
Cover photo composite from original images by Liam Harison and Johny Goerend, Vasilis Karkalas via Unsplash
Typeset by Sara Thaxton in 10.5/14 Adobe Text Pro with Hadriano Std and Bell MT Std

Publication of this book is made possible in part by the proceeds of a permanent endowment created with the assistance of a Challenge Grant from the National Endowment for the Humanities, a federal agency.

Library of Congress Cataloging-in-Publication Data
Names: Watchman, Renae, 1974– author. | Tapahonso, Luci, 1953– writer of foreword.
Title: Restoring relations through stories : from Dinétah to Denendeh / Renae Watchman ; foreword by Luci Tapahonso.
Other titles: Critical issues in indigenous studies.
Description: Tucson : University of Arizona Press, 2024. | Series: Critical issues in indigenous studies | Includes bibliographical references and index.
Identifiers: LCCN 2023028654 (print) | LCCN 2023028655 (ebook) | ISBN 9780816550357 (hardcover) | ISBN 9780816550340 (paperback) | ISBN 9780816550364 (ebook)
Subjects: LCSH: Navajo Indians—Folklore—History and criticism. | Athapascan Indians—Folklore—History and criticism. | Indian literature—History and criticism.
Classification: LCC E99.N3 W286 2024 (print) | LCC E99.N3 (ebook) | DDC 398/.3550899726—dc23/eng/20231012
LC record available at https://lccn.loc.gov/2023028654
LC ebook record available at https://lccn.loc.gov/2023028655

Printed in the United States of America
♾ This paper meets the requirements of ANSI/NISO Z39.48-1992 (Permanence of Paper).

*Ayóó
ániínishní!*
*With infinite love for
shimásání, Sylvia (Allen) Manus,
dóó sha'áłchíní, Salabiye' & De'Imin-Dezbaa'.*

CONTENTS

List of Illustrations — ix
Foreword by Luci Tapahonso — xi
Preface — xv
Ahéhee' (Acknowledgments) — xxiii

Introduction: "Hózhǫ́ Through Stories" — 3
1. Tsé Bit'a'í: Stories of the Winged Rock — 22
2. Visual Storytelling as Restorative and Relational — 51
3. Reel Restoration in *Drunktown's Finest* — 78
4. Diné Diegesis: *5th World* — 105
5. Denendeh Storytelling: Kinship Restor(i)ed — 126
   Conclusion: Náásgóó nizhónígo bee oonish dooleeł... — 150

Notes — 157
Bibliography — 191
Selected Indigenous Filmography — 211
Index — 215

ILLUSTRATIONS

Maps

1. Dinétah — xxi
2. Dinétah and Denendeh — xxii
3. Denendeh — 129

Figures

1. Tsé Bit'a'í and Dibé Ntsaa — 23
2. Shimásání cheering, in a scene from *Rocks with Wings* — 39
3. Headstone of shimásání Sylvia Allen Manus — 45
4. Highway 491 with Tsé Bit'a'í in the far left-hand corner of a photo formerly on display at the Calgary International Airport — 47
5. Alta Kahn, in a scene from *Navajos Film Themselves* — 59
6. Alta Kahn and Susie Benally, in a scene from *Navajos Film Themselves* — 60
7. Brushing hair with bé'ézhóó, in a scene from *Shimásání* — 66
8. Opening scene of *Drunktown's Finest* — 81
9. Max running on day four of her Kinaaldá, in a scene from *Drunktown's Finest* — 103
10. Aria and Andrei resting near Elephant's Feet, in a scene from *5th World* — 116
11. Aria in traditional clothing, in a scene from *5th World* — 124

FOREWORD

One bright spring afternoon in the 2000s, I attended a lecture by Renae Watchman at the University of Arizona; it's always exciting to learn of work by Diné (Navajo) scholars as Diné studies is now a growing field composed of Navajo academics, unlike past decades when non-Diné scholars posited their theories and facts from outside our culture, language, land, and history. These tenets—culture, language, land, and history—form the basis of Navajo life and are explored by Watchman through the Diné lenses of hané, keyah, ké, and 'ałk'i dáá jiní—wisdom, land, kinship, and stories from time immemorial.

These concepts would come into play that afternoon when we discovered that we are both from Shiprock, on the Navajo Nation. What a lovely surprise that we two Toónii ladies would meet in southern Arizona in a land of saguaro cacti, ocotillo, and javelina—a juxtaposition to a name we are also known by: Toónii, meaning "people of water" since the San Juan River flows through Shiprock and irrigation ditches surround our fields.

We found that I had grown up with her mother, Patti Manus, and her siblings, and that my mother (Lucille Tapahonso) and her maternal grandmother (Sylvia Manus) had been friends and worked at the same government school. Then we found that we are clan relatives: her grandmother is Tódich'íi'nii, which is my father's clan, so she is shinalí asdzą́ą́n, meaning my paternal grandmother even though she is a generation younger than me! When I told my older brother this, he jokingly said, "Now you can ask her for money, and she'll give it to you!"

In any case, this is an example of how our kinship system keeps us connected and cognizant of our responsibilities to others and our families. These complex kinship terms are explained in chapter 3.

Thus, our families spanned generations who grew up seeing Shiprock in the distance, sometimes draped in snow, other times glistening with rain, enveloped in clouds of mist, but most often, her sharp outline is distinct against the vast, blue sky. She takes on soft, muted hues throughout the day: a pale mix of pink and yellow at dawn, a dark-blue purple at midday, and then layers of light red, soft blue, and pink streaks at dusk. Up close, the sharp, jagged peaks are dark brown, then become ocher, and finally, a mix of coral, beige, and gray.

Like many others, Renae and I left Shiprock for college and academic professions. I became a professor and the inaugural Poet Laureate of the Navajo Nation in 2013; my work is in Diné and English. Dr. Watchman has been privileged to teach nationally and internationally; she is now an associate professor of Indigenous studies at McMaster University in Ontario, Canada.

As is a Diné tendency, we seek out Indigenous people wherever we travel, so it's natural that Renae reached out to our Athabaskan relatives in Canada. Many stories, 'ałk'idáá jiní, tell us that we have relatives to the north who speak the same dialect. Even though non-Navajo scholars often postulate that our ancestors migrated to the Southwest using a land bridge from Siberia, Renae shows how the old stories, maintained over centuries, reveal that our communities migrated over this huge land base that is North America and tie together the Diné and Dene through ancestral and linguistic connections.

Though our professions have taken us far from Diné Bikéyah (Navajo land), we are bound to our hometown: Shiprock, Tsé Bit'a'í (Rock with Wings), or Naat'áanii Néez (Tall Leader). In stories told at the dinner table or as we tended animals or plants in the fields, the Shiprock pinnacle is rendered as Nihimá, our mother or protector, a loving sentinel created at the beginning of Diné time.

These stories were considered "hané ííingíí"—hané means wisdom or sacred history, and ííingíí are things of great value, such as "hard goods" (material items such as jewelry, baskets, cars, etc.) and "soft goods" (which include nontangible blessings such as songs, prayers, advice, memories, ceremonial oratory, or words that are "from the heart," wisdom meant to strengthen or encourage us). Hané refers to the body of saad (knowledge) that makes up our history and identity as Diné and outlines our ties to the land, relatives, and all living things. This is known, as well, as "ałki'idáá jiní"—the stories they told us long ago. "They" refer to the ancestors or the Holy Ones who created us and the Navajo world.

Renae Watchman's book explores various versions of "hané ílííngií," covering a range of storytelling (orature and movies) in contemporary Navajo culture as well as Dene literature. She shows how the iconic landform (Tsé Bit'a'í) continues to shape our identities, our sense of ourselves, and our history and how it influences our education and those we educate. It is our connection to the land on many levels and our continuing relationship to water, plants, and animals. Renae also refers to this concept as "hane'tonomy," fusing Diné with philosophic terminology.

As Navajo culture changes and evolves, so do the methods of how hané is shared and how it retains the vast body of saad. This book shows that, albeit altered, traditional thought remains at the center of today's modes of storytelling whether in theater, films, television, or literature. This is further evidenced by the contributions of the various traditional knowledge holders, leaders who are skilled in Western and Indigenous fields, educators, and writers. The works that are surveyed herein reinforce the import of remembering, retelling, and revising the old stories so that they are germane today.

That afternoon in Tucson, it occurred to me that Dr. Watchman embodied the Diné concept of "a'yóo biił illigii"—one who speaks "well," or a person who shares words of wisdom. My father used that term to describe various leaders and medicine people in our community because they were held in high regard.

It's apropos then that his great-granddaughter by clan continues the tradition of restoring harmony, or hózhǫ́, in academia and in our Indigenous communities.

—Luci Tapahonso

PREFACE

Yá'át'ééh shik'éí dóó shidiné'é dóó shik'isóó!¹ [*My relatives, my People, and my friends, everything is good!*] Tódich'íi'nii éínishłį dóó Kinyaa'áanii báshíshchíín. [*I am Bitter Water, born for (in service to my father's People) Towering House.*]² Áádóó Tsalagi (Gv-gi-yv-wi A-ni-tsi-s-qua) éí da shichei dóó Táchii'nii éí da shinálí.³ [*I am Bird Clan from the Cherokee Nation of Oklahoma on my chei's, maternal grandfather's, side and I am from the Red Running Through the Water People on my nálí's, paternal grandfather's, side.*] Naat'áanii Nééz déé' íiyisí naashá. [*My (maternal) family is originally from Shiprock.*] Ákót'éego Diné Asdzą́ą́n nishłį́ [*In this way, I am a Diné woman.*]

Out of respect for my relatives and ancestors, I introduce myself in Diné bizaad (the Diné language) per Diné protocol that recognizes Clan relations.⁴ Diné means "the People," and I use it interchangeably with "Navajo."⁵ Many Diné Clans are toponyms, though oral stories transgress from land-based origins. Ethelou Yazzie, former director of the Rough Rock Demonstration School, underscores that Clans "developed geographically, and ... are place names."⁶ Larry W. Emerson (1947–2017), esteemed Diné scholar and activist, recalls, "In the not too distant past, these introductions also gave indication of where, physically, the individual's family was from. This corroborates the recognition that certain clans predominately populated certain regions."⁷ My Clan affiliations are indeed earth anchored and establish kinship relations with other Diné, and from my chei, with other Bird Clan relatives from the Cherokee. Clan and kinship responsibilities dictate that the Tódich'íi'nii are commonly thought of as philosophers and educators, and the Kinya'áanii are leaders and guides. These foundational teachings are grounded in the Diné episteme of hózhǫ́: the state of harmony, peace, wellness, and balance.

My maternal grandmother was Sylvia Allen Manus from Rattlesnake, New Mexico. Rattlesnake is about seven miles north of the landmark Tsé Bit'a'í (meaning "Winged Rock," "Rock with Wings," and "Wings of Rock," but called Shiprock) and about seven miles southwest of the reservation town also called Shiprock (originally named Naat'áanii Nééz). As a child, she survived boarding school and was eventually sent to Lawrence, Kansas, to attend the Haskell Institute for secretary training. While in Kansas, she met a young soldier, Andrew Manus, who would become my chei (maternal grandfather). He was originally from Tahlequah, Oklahoma. They fell in love, married, and had ten children, nine of whom survived infancy. The first few were born in Tahlequah and the rest were born in Shiprock. Shiprock is home, and Grams only had to scold me once to remind me that I was not from Farmington (the border town where I attended school)! My paternal grandparents were Katherine Mae Keedah Watchman and Lewis Watchman Sr., from Sheep Springs, New Mexico. I am the daughter of Patricia Manus Sandoval and the late Lewison R. Watchman, whose first language was Diné bizaad. I did not grow up under the same roof as Daddy Lew. He fathered me at a young age and struggled with alcoholism and was an insulin-dependent diabetic until he died peacefully in his sleep of his diseases. Though his personal addiction prevented him from keeping a stable job, home, and family, he was an avid reader, brilliant, funny, and had a wealth of cultural knowledge that he shared with me during our cherished visits.

I am a direct descendant of survivors, as are my children and perhaps future grandchildren. My chei's parents were my great-grandma, Edna Gritts, and my great-grandpa, Richard Manus. Great-grandma Edna's mother is listed on the Dawes Rolls as Emma Palone and her father was Philip Gritts. Great-great-grandpa Philip's father was Budd Gritts. My great-great-great-grandpa Bud's mother is listed as Ah-gel-law-hee and his father as Neh-wah-der Gritts. Budd Gritts was born in 1804 in Long Savannah, in what is currently Tennessee, and he died in 1867 in Tahlequah, the Cherokee capital in Indian Territory (currently the state of Oklahoma).[8] How he got there is critical. On October 11, 1838, seven hundred Cherokees who were imprisoned at Fort Cass commenced their journey on the Trail of Tears. There were approximately sixty thousand Indigenous People from various nations that were forcefully relocated and marched the Trail of Tears from 1830 to 1850.[9] The trail that my great-great-great-grandfather walked was called the Bell Route, which began in Charleston, Tennessee, and ended in Evansville (formerly Indian Territory). More than twenty People died on this specific march and route of the Trail of Tears, and those who survived arrived at Indian Territory on January 7, 1839, which took eight weeks and one day.[10] Today, to drive the 666 miles from Charleston, to Evansville, Oklahoma, would take eleven hours and thirty-six minutes, according to Google Maps. Anchoring myself to the storied places of my direct grandparents and theirs facilitates my recognition of the significance of homelands.

I am on the traditional homelands of the Haudenosaunee Confederacy, Anishinaabe, Mississauga of the Credit First Nations, and historically the Erie, Neutral, and Huron-Wendat First Nations. These homelands are included in the Dish with One Spoon Wampum Agreement and adjacent to the Haldimand Tract. The dish represents the territory and the spoon reflects all Peoples who live and share the territory's resources. To share teaches humility, self-restraint, discipline, and communal care to keep the common lands (dish) clean and ready for the next generation and beyond. Although the Agreement originally bound the Anishinaabe, Mississauga, and Haudenosaunee Peoples, subsequent nations and Peoples, including settlers and other newcomers, were invited into the Treaty in the spirit of peace, friendship and respect.[11] These are values and responsibilities that translate well as hózhǫ́, which I practice beyond the four sacred mountains, where I live, work, and learn.[12]

Origins

I initially envisioned this book as *Tsé Bit'a'í (The Winged Rock): Visual & Literary Storytelling* but it evolved into *Restoring Relations Through Stories: From Dinétah to Denendeh*. Through an introduction to, interpretation of, and analysis of oral, literary, and visual hane' (story, narrative, wisdom), this book began as a love song for shikéyah (my homelands), namely for Tsé Bit'a'í, the Rock with Wings, whose pronouns are she, her, and it. I wanted to privilege Tsé Bit'a'í as a literal site, metaphor, and theoretical construct because of my intimate connection to her. Shimásání (my maternal grandmother) taught me stories of Tsé Bit'a'í, which explained the beauty of the sentinel and exposed Grams's historical and cultural knowledge of Diné homelands. As a landmark that distinguishes herself on Diné Bikéyah (Navajo land), I felt obligated to pose critical questions about the cinematic erasure, dislocation, and recolonization of Tsé Bit'a'í and the accompanying traditional stories, resulting in what Boaventura de Sousa Santos calls "the murder of knowledge" or epistemicide.[13] However, I came to realize that by highlighting non-Diné interpretations of stories, I was complicit in that erasure. I expanded my focus to include land-based Diné imaginaries, which are the nexus of the visual and literary stories at the heart of this book.

In 2011, I met citizens from the Tsuut'ina First Nation, a Dene community in Alberta, Canada. Through sharing stories, I came to understand relationality beyond what I had experienced growing up. The Diné are those from the four sacred mountains in Dinétah ("Land of the Diné") in the United States and the Dene are in Denendeh ("Land of the Dene"), in Canada.[14] Since we are ancestral and linguistic relatives, our kinship and relational connections transcend nation-state borders and affirm Diné and Dene kinscapes.[15] Some land-based stories intersect at thematic arcs and select words from our similar languages, revealing Diné and Dene literary kinship, yet in the twenty-first century we are geographically, culturally, politically, and economically distinct.

Prior to moving to Canada, my Diné relatives had mentioned that we have Dene relatives in the Treaty 7 area. Through a serendipitous get-to-know-you tea, I met Elder Bruce Starlight in 2018. As is customary, Bruce and I began by establishing who we were in relation to one another and with our kin relatives. There are circa 350,000 citizens of the Diné Nation, and the odds that I would know or be related to an acquaintance of Bruce was low. When Bruce learned where I was from, the first person he asked me about was Allan Neskahi Jr. I almost fell over because not only did I know him, but we are, in fact, relatives! Allan Neskahi Jr. was my late maternal grandmother's nephew, and he always called my grandma Sylvia by the kinship term "má yazhi," which means "little mother" or auntie. I called Allan "Grandpa Neskahi" and "Mister Neskahi." Bruce was just as astonished as I was that we had uncovered a very close kinship link in my grandpa Neskahi. The Neskahis used to host traditional powwows and gourd dances, and they had ample space on their property on the outskirts of Cortez, Colorado, to welcome and host singers, dancers, healers, spectators, and extended family members. Art Neskahi, one of grandpa Neskahi's sons, wrote about his family and their cultural and spiritual journey, which brought them full circle.[16] So that I could participate in my first powwow, Grams made my first fancy shawl outfit when I was five years old. It was brown and red and made from felt! I have a fond memory of earning my first dollar, which Grandpa Neskahi bestowed upon me for dancing, and Grams was so proud! These early intertribal experiences concretized my participation in the powwow world, which my family encouraged and nurtured. Powwow brought Bruce and my grandpa Neskahi together too.

Bruce said he met Grandpa Neskahi through a Tsuut'ina Elder, the late Jim Dodginghorse. Grandpa Neskahi was the Master of Ceremonies (MC) at the Window Rock Fair in Arizona, and over time, Bruce and Grandpa Neskahi became close friends. Elder Dodginghorse gave Grandpa Neskahi a beaded buckskin outfit as well as a Tsuut'ina name: "Shot Many Times," in honor of one of Dodginghorse's relatives, who was also a warrior. Bruce further shared with me that after Dodginghorse passed away, Bruce made and gifted Grandpa Neskahi a Tsuut'ina feather hat (an eagle feather bonnet). Grandpa Neskahi was a highly respected man, a ceremonial and powwow leader, and he co-wrote the "Gathering of Nations" song with one of his sons, Arlie Neskahi, which was composed in Diné bizaad and continues to be sung every year at the Gathering of Nations Pow Wow on Saturday night by dozens of singers around a drum line. His children, whom I call aunties and uncles, and their children, whom I call cousins, allowed me the great honor to give his eulogy for my maternal grandmother's side of the family when he passed away on January 31, 1998. The feather hat that Bruce Starlight made was lovingly placed on top of his casket and was a powerful image and reminder of our relatives north of the Medicine Line. I had always wondered where the feather hat came from. Twenty years later, I would hear the story that restored our relations. It was such a gift to meet and work with Bruce Starlight, who incidentally has a traditional Diné hooghan (a dwelling called a hogan) on his property on the Tsuut'ina reserve.[17] Knowing our kinship relations, I gained added responsibility to uphold them.

One of my responsibilities is heeding the recommendations of Dene Elders and community members, some of whom strongly encouraged me to include their stories in this book. The new title, *Restoring Relations Through Stories: From Dinétah to Denendeh*, reflects a nascent area of study, where I synthesize and analyze literary and visual stories to encourage reading for restoration. The journey from Dinétah to Denendeh is not literal but literary, to demonstrate the narrative arc of restoration and restorying of relations. Turning to transborder stories models decolonial survivance, ultimately promoting restoration, through hózhǫ́.[18] Recognizing the vast body of Dene literary arts is a direct consequence of the research I originally began, and which Diné filmmaker Sarah Del Seronde's forthcoming documentary will expand upon further. It is "about the relationship between the Diné and Dene Clans and the role of language and oral traditions in the formation of Indigenous identity."[19] Though I do not engage Dene literary or visual artists as a steady throughline in the book, I recognize select Dene authors in chapter 5 as my first step on the journey to restoring relations through stories.

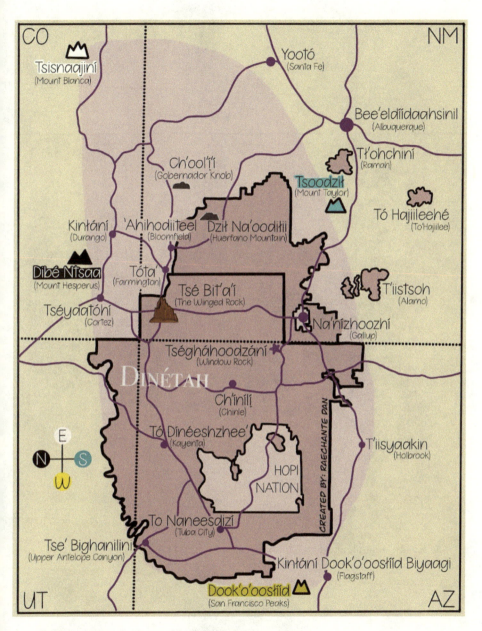

MAP 1 Dinétah. Created by Raechante Dan.

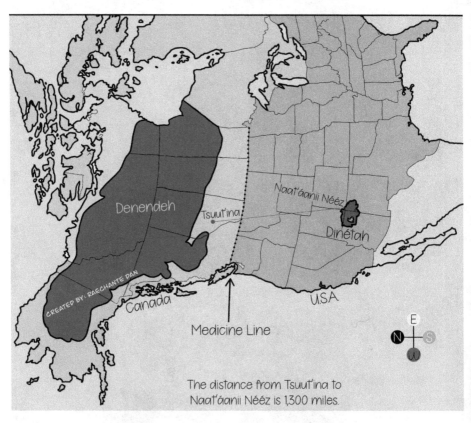

MAP 2 Dinétah and Denendeh. Created by Raechante Dan.

AHÉHEE' (ACKNOWLEDGEMENTS)

Restoring Relations Through Stories: From Dinétah to Denendeh was possible because of unwavering support from family, friends, colleagues, and institutions. My deepest gratitude, ahéhee', goes to Luci Tapahonso, whose verse and prose continue to inspire my thinking. Ahéhee' to Eugene B. Joe, master sand artist and CEO of the Shiprock Historical Society, for sharing stories and resources. Ahéhee' to my uncles Bobby and Casey Watchman, who filled in for my late father (my Diné-language teacher and storyteller). I cannot begin to express my love and appreciation to my uncles, not just for language help but most importantly for the role they took in raising me, housing me, and nourishing me. Along with my uncles, Melvatha Chee is the best Diné-language expert, friend, and mentor, bar none. Baa ahééh nisin, díidí, shik'is. A special note of gratitude to shideezhí, my younger sister, Raechante Dan, whose painting is on the back cover of this book. Grams would be honored to see herself reflected through your eyes.

And to my Dene relatives: Mahsì cho (ahéhee') to Willis Janvier and siyisgaas (ahéhee') to Bruce Starlight and the Eagletail family of Tsuut'ina for your assistance and permission with stories, translations, and support at various stages throughout this process.

I acknowledge other Elders, community members, and family, some of whom have passed on since I began this work. I love and miss my late maternal and paternal grandparents; my late father, Lewison R. Watchman; and two who were father figures: my late uncle Bill Manus and my late stepfather, Ron Sandoval. To my late younger brother, Rylan D. Sandoval, my auntie Karen Manus, my late cousin Denise Manus, and to several relatives we lost during the pandemic, Ayóó'ádajó'nínígíí béédahaniih! May you all Rest in Beauty.

Ahéhee' shik'éí dóó shidiné'é, áádóó ayóó áníínishní. To get home from north of the Medicine Line takes twelve to twenty-four hours, at least two flights, and a long drive. I'm extremely grateful for my kin and chosen relatives for always welcoming me with hózhǫ́, generosity, kindness, laughter, love, and food. My deepest appreciation goes to my siblings Raechante Dan and Ronson Sandoval, auntie Coddie Hengst, and cousins/sisters Shannon Manuelito, Yolonda Yazzie, and Jolene Manus for always sustaining me (especially when not home) with unconditional support, love, and airmailed food from Diné Bikéyah, including Hatch Green Chile, piñons, cedar ash, blue and white corn meal, and dry red chile. Ahéhee' to aunties Cathy Manus, Kelly Curtis, and Joy Manus and to my early childhood caregivers, Dixie Alley, Sandy Williams, and Doris and Klaus Cantzler. To my dear sister, Beth Piatote, Qe'ci'yew'yew'; I am a better human and thinker because of your friendship, kindness, and hózhǫ́, which came with laughter, tears, and mentorship. Ahéhee' to EiRena Begay, Leslie Peabody, and Genevieve Valdez for your enduring sisterhood, friendship, love, and support. As this book is about restoring relations, I acknowledge Patricia Sandoval, Shauna Watchman, and Ryan Watchman, whom I love and hope to repair our ruptures.

I hold close our dear relatives who comforted and supported Rob and I during *that* most horrific January 2020 experience, which obviously halted this work. Kinanâskomitin to Winona Wheeler, Maria Campbell, Louise Halfe, Kim Anderson, Brenda Macdougall, Judy Anderson, Raven Sinclair, Michelle Johnson-Jennings, Derek Jennings, and Alison Green, kia ora.

Ahéhee' to students, colleagues, and friends who offered care, hospitality, teachings, questions, corrections, feedback, ideas, food, and fellowship throughout the years and across the globe: Robert Albricht, Anastasia Arkhipova, Yaw Asante, Holly Atjecoutay, Sharon Austin, Mark Ayyash, Eric Blankenship, Robert Boschman, Sean Carleton, Pua Case, Alexandra Daignault, D. A. Dirks, Kit Dobson, Jane Drover, Soledad Etchemendy, Brenda and John Fisher, Patrisia Gonzales, Liam Haggarty, Leah Hamilton, Aubrey Jean Hanson, Aroha Harris, Richard Harrison, Emily Hutchinson, Ada Jaarsma, Susan Jacoby, Skylar Kay, Carmen Lopez, Hartmut Lutz, Maki Motapanyane, Mary-Lee Mulholland, Scott Murray, NAISA Council, Carmen Nielson, Kirk Niergarth, Karen Pheasant, Leonie Pihama, Gabriele Pisarz-Ramirez, Cherryl Waerea-i-te-rangi Smith, Robyn Tauroa, Linda Tuhiwai Smith, Madonna Thunder Hawk, Sabina Trimble, Mario Trono, Michael Truscello, Gabrielle Weasel Head, and Kimberly Williams.

Librarians Jessie Loyer and Alice Swabey at Mount Royal University are unmatched colleagues and friends who swiftly procured Indigenous, specifically Diné, books, movies, and materials. Additionally, the librarians and staff at the Bibliotheca Albertina Library, especially Sophia Manns-Süßbrich, at the University of Leipzig graciously ordered books not already in their catalog so that I could complete my archival research when I was abroad.

I am indebted to mentors who have helped navigate the academic land mine: Chris Andersen, Russell Berman, Lee Easton, David Hyttenrauch, Barbara Kosta, Tsianina Lomawaima, Jennifer Pettit, C. Mathew Snipp, and Florentine Strzelczyk. Your unwavering support, guidance, and optimistic attitude through various arduous application processes was the steady stability and seasoned experience that I benefited from. Thank you to the sabbatical leave committee at MRU for granting me an academic year to begin drafting this book. I relocated to another country during sabbatical, which was not without its administrative disruptions, but a few key people made the transition less painful: Kitty Pryde, Sue Torres, and Keith Black. The Department of American Studies at the University of Leipzig granted me affiliate status as a visiting research scholar, and I am grateful to Anne Grob, Frank Usbeck, and Crister S. Garrett.

Thank you to Lisa Quinn and Deanna Reder for your initial support of this book. Ahéhee' to Kristen Buckles for your respectful encouragement to see this project to its conclusion. My gratitude goes to the anonymous peer reviewers, and especially to Sheila McMahon, a meticulous copyeditor, who all took the time, with fresh and critical eyes, to help make this a stronger book. Ahéhee' to Chrissy Doolittle for your administrative savvy and my appreciation to Trevor Loken for converting citations under a tight deadline.

Ahéhee' to my new colleagues in the Indigenous Studies and English and Cultural Studies Departments at McMaster University as well as our friend-leagues from other local institutions on these beautiful and storied lands. To commence a job, while in a lockdown, during a worldwide pandemic, was challenging, but I am humbled by your warm welcomes and hospitality (virtual or socially distanced) to feast and visit.

Ayóó áníínishní, I love you, my children, Salabiye' and De'Imin-Dezbaa'. Ahéhee' for your patience and for allowing me the time to work throughout your childhood and into your growing adulthood—you sacrificed so much and I am so very proud of you. Kinanâskomitin nîcimos, ᑭᓇᓈᶯᑯᒥᑎᐣ, shi heart kisâkihitin, Robert Alexander Innes, for your fierce and fun love, unequivocal support, and gentle encouragement to pick this project back up after a long period of dormancy. I love you (ayóó áníínishní) and I thank you (ahéhee').

I take full responsibility for omissions and errors in this book.

RESTORING RELATIONS THROUGH STORIES

Introduction

"Hózhǫ́ Through Stories"

> This morning, the sunrise is a brilliant song. . . . The world responds, stretching, humming. The sunlight is Diyin, sacred beams. . . . Again, as a Diné woman, I face east on the porch and pray for Hózhó one more time. For today, allow me to share Hózhó, the beauty of all things being right and proper as in songs the Holy Ones gave us.
>
> —LUCI TAPAHONSO, *BLUE HORSES RUSH IN*

This opening epigraph is from "A Birthday Poem," by Luci Tapahonso, the 2013 inaugural and revered Poet Laureate of the Navajo Nation.[1] I write this on February 3, 2022, my child's sixteenth birthday. With hózhǫ́ in my heart, I offer Tapahonso's words, which render Diné origins, presence, and restoration, to commence this book in the proper way.

"Hózhǫ́ Through Stories" consolidates my previous, ongoing, and future research. Hózhǫ́ is a complex Diné worldview and philosophy that cannot be defined with one word in the English language. Hózhǫ́ means to continually strive for harmony, beauty, balance, peace, and happiness, but most importantly we have a right to it.[2] Hózhǫ́ is "Diné-centered decolonization," according to Larry W. Emerson.[3] Ethelou Yazzie, an early Diné studies cultural advocate, argues that hózhǫ́ is the "one right way—the way of harmony and beauty."[4] Vincent Werito says the primary principles of hózhǫ́ weave the mental, physical, emotional, and spiritual facets of living and learning to culminate in coming to a state of hózhǫ́. He emphasizes holism, respect, and dynamism; as Diné, we say that we are always in pursuit of "becoming hózhǫ́," which ultimately culminates in restoration:

> The principles of hózhǫ́ are encapsulated in the cognitive (mental), physiological (physical), psychological (emotional), and intuitive (spiritual)

aspects of human development and growth—or holistic living and learning. . . . Two important Diné cultural values that I believe my parents have taught me are contingent upon the principles of hózhǫ́: (1) having reverence and respect for nature, for myself, for others, and for the land and (2) nurturing my spiritual faith. . . . In reflecting on my childhood, I realize now that as I learned the literal meaning of the word "hózhǫ́" and its associated concepts, I also internalized it into my thinking. For example, when the word "hózhǫ́" is used now to describe the beauty and peacefulness of a place or the good attributes of a person . . . it reminds me of when I was in a similar place or state of mind; . . . I now realize that while the essence of the meaning of hózhǫ́ could be interpreted as a fixed or constant idea to imply a state of peace and harmony, it can also be interpreted and understood as an ever-changing, evolving, and transformative idea, especially in how an individual applies and interprets its meaning to her or his life.[5]

Like the dynamism and kinetic facets of hózhǫ́, the work herein takes us through many landscapes, places, sites, and stories (oral, literary, and visual) in search of becoming hózhǫ́ and restoring relations. I begin with an overview of stories that bring a monolith to life, I introduce the dynamic field of Indigenous film, I closely analyze two distinct Diné-directed feature-length films, and I introduce Dene literatures. As a literary scholar, I use textual analysis, archival research, oral history, visual and film analysis, and discourse analysis. To receive the gift and honor of Indigenous narratives about the land necessitates protocols of reciprocity, tobacco offerings, honoraria, and simply visiting with Elders and other knowledge holders.[6] Prior to the pandemic, I turned to my aunties, who connected me with community members through email, snail mail, and cell phone. As a Diné woman, I approach the "texts," which includes the material relayed through orators and storytellers, with respect and an interpretive lens informed by hózhǫ́ to preserve the continual passage of Diné or other Indigenous epistemologies and frameworks.

Methodology

Restoring Relations Through Stories: From Dinétah to Denendeh is informed by scholarship in Diné studies, Indigenous studies, Indigenous film studies, Indigenous literary studies, and ecocriticism.[7] These are inter- and transdisciplinary areas; though I have learned from non-Indigenous and Indigenous scholars, where relevant, I privilege Indigenous scholars' analyses, theories, and interpretations. Cree scholar Margaret Kovach's *Indigenous Methodologies* (2009) outlines what constitutes Indigenous scholarship: "In assessing Indigenous scholarship, I look for distinctive qualities such as engagement with tribal knowledges, colonial implications, purpose, integration of narrative component, and considered discussion of what has been learned through the research."[8] She also discusses the inseparability and importance of Indigenous stories and epistemologies to Indigenous sovereignty, writing that "tribal epistemologies are the centre of Indigenous methodologies."[9] Harmonizing artistic and creative works with research and Indigenous epistemologies is the future of rigorous and nuanced scholarship. To read stories (oral, literary, and filmic) through Indigenous knowledge systems is to recover and restore Indigenous presence and kinship as an act of hózhǫ́. Uncovering and applying Indigenous epistemologies allows scholars to think about comparative connections to other Indigenous Nations' philosophical worldviews as renascent methods to approaching everyday experiences, struggles, and achievements, constituting meaningful Indigenous engagement. Restorying and retelling oral stories—like those about Tsé Bit'a'í (Shiprock Peak)—reclaims and reframes the significance of Indigenous land, landscape, landmarks, and homelands and is an act of privileging a Diné epistemic methodology. Furthermore, throughout the book and when appropriate, I share personal anecdotes, which is reflective of oral tradition. Much of my analytical framework is informed by oral stories. Vine Deloria Jr. (Lakota, Standing Rock) was an early advocate for this practice. In *Red Earth, White Lies: Native Americans and the Myth of Scientific Fact* (1997), he writes: "The non-Western, tribal equivalent of science is the oral tradition, the teachings that have been passed down from one generation to the next over uncounted centuries. The oral tradition is a loosely held collection of anecdotal material that, taken together, explains the nature of the physical world as people have experienced it and the important events of their historical journey."[10] As I argue for the restoration of stories and relationships, orality is a fundamental approach in my book. Finally, I deploy many Indigenous-centered theories by Indigenous scholars, but having a knowledge of Diné bizaad influences and guides my interpretations and analysis, which is emblematic of Diné worldviews and knowledge systems.

Although *all* my grandparents spoke their languages fluently and my late father's first language was Diné bizaad, I am not a fluent speaker. Despite this, I demonstrate restoration of Diné language and teachings to convey how our knowledge systems animate our presence and kinship culminating in hózhǫ́. As I am still a learner, I have undoubtedly made mistakes.

Three interrelated Diné bizaad concepts that guide and organize my analysis are hane', 'ałk'idą́ą́' jiní, and kéyah. They are active and living words in the creation of knowledge production. Heeding the works and teachings about hane', 'ałk'idą́ą́' jiní, and kéyah dictates my nitsáhákees (thinking, reasoning, and analysis), nahat'á (planning and developing), iiná (living and implementing), and siihasin (reflecting and assuring). These four respective principles come from Sa'ąh Naagháí Bik'eh Hózhǫ́ǫ́n, "the Diné traditional living system, which places human life in harmony with the natural world and universe," and underscore my methodology.[11] Diné poet, playwright, politician, and Medicine Man Rex Lee Jim (Kin Łichíi'nii, born for Táchii'nii; his chei is Kin Yaa'áanii, and his paternal grandfather is Naakaii Diné'é) unpacks Sa'ąh Naagháí Bik'eh Hózhǫ́ǫ́n:

> Literally, *sǫ* means old age, *ah* means beyond, *naa* means environment, *ghái* means movement, *bi* means to it, *k'éh* means according, *hó* means self and that sense of an ever-presence of something greater, *zhóón* means beauty, *nishłóó* means I will be, *naasháa doo* means I walk. This may be stated in the following way. "May I walk, being the omnipresent beauty created by the one that moves beyond old." Now all we know that we are born into this world and we live for some time and then we all die.[12]

Diné-language fluency animates complex worldviews that take a lifetime to learn and understand. Daily, seasonally, and throughout our life stages, we renew this learning and build upon the previous day, season, and life stage to live with goodness, to achieve "an ever-presence of something greater."

Hane' (Story, Narrative, Wisdom)

The principles of Sa'ąh Naagháí Bik'eh Hózhǫ́ǫ́n honor a Diné worldview of hane', which is the Diné bizaad (Navajo language) word for story, narrative, and wisdom and the first concept that informs my analysis. Hane' (which is both singular and plural) encompass fiction and nonfiction stories and are oral, alphabetic, or literary (including songs, creation epics, novels, prose, or poetry): "the descriptive hane' na'ach'ąą (designed stories) is also used [for poetry]. Hane' encompasses the spoken poetry as well as the traditional Diné narratives like coyote stories and emergence stories—and can incorporate song."[13] Coyote stories are "Ma'ii [Mą'ii] joodloshí baa hane'," and emergence stories are "Hajíínéí hane'."[14] Volume 1 of *Navajo Children's Literature, Álchíní Bá Hane'*, covers the following genres: "Origin Stories: Hodeeyáádą́ą́' Baa Hane'; Animal Stories: Naaldooshii Baa Dahane'; Personal Stories: Diné Baa Dahane'; Biographical Excerpts: Diné Ła' Ádaa Dahalne'; Frightful Tales: Yíiyá Baa Dahane'; Stories That Teach: Na'nitin Hane'; Humor: Baa Dlohodilchíhígíí Hane'."[15] In addition to these genres, there are stories that are restricted to the winter months called "haigo hane'," which differ from stories about winter, or "haigo bahane'." In this book, I use Diné bahane' (not italicized), which means "story of the People," as well as *Diné bahane'* (italicized), which specifically references the book by Paul G. Zolbrod about the journey narratives of Navajo creation.

In addition to oral, alphabetic, and literary wisdom, hane' also captures the genres of visual stories and visual storytelling (including television shows, documentaries, short and feature-length fiction films, and material cultural items). Visual hane' can be read from beadwork, "cane baskets, wampum belts, birchbark scrolls, gourd masks, sand paintings, rock art, carved and painted cedar poles, stones and whale bones, culturally modified trees, and so on. While serving many cultural and ceremonial purposes, these items also communicate stories and ideas.... Our literary traditions [are] broadly inclusive of all the ways we embody our stories in the world."[16] Hane' are also Indigenous epistemai, and outside of Diné worldviews, stories are widely discussed for their historical relevance, everyday community prevalence, and future dynamics.[17]

Hane' reflect a Diné body of knowledge. Almost three decades ago, Tapahonso wrote "Singing in Navajo, Writing in English: The Poetics of Four Navajo Writers." She said of hane':

> This body of knowledge is referred to as *saad*—which encompasses stories, songs, prayers, ritual oratories, and instructions or teachings. It is said that a person who is raised well and taught this knowledge is wealthy. To Navajos,

a person's worth is determined by the stories and songs she or he knows, because it is by this knowledge, that an individual is directly linked to the history of the entire group.... The elements of these stories and songs include the proper use of rhythm, meter, symbolism, concrete diction, and imagery. Other aspects include *a sense of place* and heavy use of repetition.[18]

A Navajo person's cultural and literary wealth is demonstrated through saad, which Rex Lee Jim defines as "language and voice."[19] Restorying saad elevates Diné being, marking one as a good relative and descendant. Tapahonso—whose Clans are Tódik'ozhi, born for Tódich'ii'nii; her chei is Deeshchii'nii and her paternal grandparents are Kinlichii'nii—begins her essay by positioning herself within the winter storytelling months, when Navajo oratory is permitted, and she retells different iterations of a story to demonstrate how "differences depend on geography, dialects of the Navajo language, or the individual oration style of the storyteller. The essence of the story . . . retains the original format" and "doesn't discount other versions, but rather adds to the body of knowledge being exchanged."[20] As a body of knowledge, wisdom, and ideas, hane' live in tandem with saad, supporting restoration.

Nehiyaw, Saulteaux, and Métis scholar and citizen of Cowessess First Nation Robert Alexander Innes argues that "historically, traditional stories governed peoples' interactions. . . . [They] express certain values central to the culture."[21] Together these arguments affirm that "stories are who we are."[22] Kovach recognizes that one's (Indigenous) story anchors their work and methods in ways that Western research models cannot.[23] Cherokee scholar Daniel Heath Justice adds that the role of stories "help[s] us find ways of meaningful being in whatever worlds we inhabit, whatever contexts we've inherited," but in particular, he advocates that hane' enables us to "imagine otherwise."[24] Choctaw scholar LeAnne Howe and Padraig Kirwan describe stories as powerful "verbal art."[25] Tłı̨chǫ Dene (Dogrib) writer and storyteller Richard Van Camp shares, "It's through stories that we've come to know each other. We trust each other because we've trusted each other with our stories. We know each other through our stories. Storytelling = connection = community = joy and comfort = health and survival."[26] This exemplifies becoming hózhǫ́. Through this constellation of knowledge, hane' encourage resurgence and Indigenous cultural harmony and are restored in Indigenous languages or translated into English. Colonial interference and governmental policy contributed to the loss, erasure, and minimizing of the value of Diné bahane'. When storying and living stories are silenced, this is epistemicide: "Indeed, without those stories, without the teachings about the *who*, *how*, and *why* of us, something is profoundly, almost existentially amiss. We don't need to speak them to live them; even those not given voice are inextricably embraided in our sense of self. We know ourselves *only* through stories."[27]

Early on in my research, my auntie Coddy (Kathy Hengst) put me in contact with Eugene B. Joe, CEO of the Shiprock Historical Society (founded 2010), whom I met with on August 30, 2016. The Shiprock Historical Society is a nonprofit, volunteer group whose aim is to preserve and share cultural, historical, and political stories of the community. Joe complimented and encouraged me to persevere on my "precious learning journey." He was happy that I came back home in search of more answers. He said home is "where your nest, roots, foundation, where your blood flows, the four winds, the sun, moon, and the stars sing."[28] I was honored to have had some time with Joe. He told Alysa Landry, "Navajo stories traditionally were shared orally.... Everyone has a story that relates to our collective past, but if you look at stories individually, they're not the full picture. They're just parts. Everyone's version of the story has different details, making the whole story richer. We're bringing those stories back, piece by piece."[29]

Many of the stories I share are also piecemeal, but this is deliberate. Sharing ceremonial oral stories is not without controversy.[30] I do not have the years of apprenticeship training to restory the Diné traditional and oral stories. Some stories are told only within the confines of a sweathouse or only during the snow-covered earth months, when it is cold, aptly called haigo hane' (winter stories) in the Navajo context. Out of respect for Diné and Dene storiers, and because the act of telling stories can be linked to ceremony or to the weather, I do not share oral stories that have not been previously published. I reference printed and published accounts of oral Diné journey narratives (referred to in the literature as creation stories) as they relate to the texts I analyze. Where appropriate I integrate family stories with respect.

I also listen to Diné poet laureates Luci Tapahonso and Laura Tohe, who have carved out space for re-creating Diné stories, while also expressing their hesitation for rendering the traditional Diné narratives outside their ceremonial contexts. To do so would not be in the best interest of the

Diné and is culturally disrespectful. Tapahonso approaches the topic of writing down traditional stories with caution: "I don't do that. I can write about . . . [a] ceremony . . . but it's just surface; I won't go beyond that. . . . I would never take a creation story and rewrite it or re-tell it. I don't think that's my place to do that. . . . A lot of things are alluded to."[31] Tohe explains: "You're not supposed to take any of the Navajo stories, or any of the Native American stories essentially, and pull them out of their ceremonial context."[32] In 2008, she was invited by the Phoenix Symphony and composer Mark Grey to assume the role as the librettist for *Enemy Slayer: A Navajo Oratorio*. Tohe consulted Diné Elders to rework the stories to convey a twenty-first-century perspective of the Navajo Hero Twins, Naayéé Neezghání and Tó Bájísh Chíní, without giving away "secrets of the Navajo deities."[33] While this was initially Grey's idea, Tohe prioritized working with other Diné creatives, like filmmaker Blackhorse Lowe, to make the oratorio evoke a return to hózhǫ́, as evidenced by this chorus:

> Shiyázhí, there is a natural order in the world (trans: beloved one)
> You must return to it
> You have walked away
> from the corn pollen path
> Shiyázhí, t'áá shòòdí (trans: beloved one, please!)
> You have purpose for your existence
> You are our child and a child of the Holy People.
>
> Return to the path of hózhǫ́
> Return to the Beauty Way
> In the world there is
> evil and beauty,
> sickness and health,
> disorder and harmony,
> light and darkness
> Balance must always be restored
> Éí bik'eh nanína, shiyázhí (trans: follow that path, my child)
> Follow the corn pollen path of life
> Follow the corn pollen path of life
> Follow the corn pollen path of life
> Follow the corn pollen path of life.[34]

Introduction

To encourage the beloved one to follow the corn pollen path of life does not betray intimate, ceremonial secrets. In fact, this oratorical script exudes hózhǫ́ in its very creation, the literary aesthetics of dual languages, and the respectful message of hope and restoration, which is intended for other listeners and includes the audience in attendance. While these words are sung in the style of a ceremonial prayer, the message is not meant solely for ceremony and extends beyond ceremony. That this, like many published accounts featuring Beauty Way messages, is for wide consumption is telling of the inclusivity of Diné thought.

Jennifer Nez Denetdale, the first Diné Nation citizen to earn a doctorate in history, provides a nuanced, thorough, and rich account of the years leading up to 1863 from the perspective of a Diné descendant. Her book *Reclaiming Diné History: The Legacies of Navajo Chief Manuelito and Juanita* (2007) respectfully and astutely weaves histories of family, Diné, and U.S. colonialism. She is Tł'ógi (Zia or Weaver) Clan, born for 'Áshiihí (Salt) People. Her chei is Kin łichíí'nii (the Red House) Clan and her paternal grandfather is Tó 'aheedlíinii Water Running Together (or Water Flowing Together) Clan.[35] Denetdale writes, "I have deliberately chosen to rely on published creation narratives, especially those by Navajo writers. Like other native scholars, I find divulging information about the sacred stories and ceremonies from my family, kin relations, and medicine people a violation of ethical and responsible research. I consciously did not inquire about sacred knowledge from my grandparents, and if references were made, I did not include them in my publications. Many members of the Navajo community practice the values found in the traditional stories."[36] Denetdale, Tohe, and Tapahonso are respected matriarchs and have been deeply influential to me. I honor their words and actions on how to conduct Diné-centric, ethical research.

In addition to the ceremonial and seasonal constraints of retelling oral stories of creation, there are oral histories of family survival during the Navajo Long Walk era and of their internment at Bosque Redondo that can be off limits. Diné bahane' have power to trigger. This catastrophic historical event lasted from 1863 to 1868. About the Long Walk, Denetdale writes, "In 1863, the Americans instigated an all-out war against Navajos. Under James Carleton, the Indian fighter Kit Carson literally scorched Navajo country, forcing Navajo surrender. As prisoners of the U.S. military, in 1863, Navajos were exiled to Fort Sumner, New Mexico, where they were imprisoned from 1864–1868."[37] In "Chronology of Important Dates in Diné Political and Literary History," she adds: "1864: Many Navajos died during the Long Walk, which was actually a series of forced marches—at least fifty-three, between 350 and 450 miles—to the reservation at the Bosque Redondo."[38] Bosque Redondo is called Hwéeldi (or Hwééldi). Tohe cautions,

> While the people might know stories, they could choose to not tell them because they are too horrendous and could cause harm when remembered. One must carefully use thoughts and words, for they have great potential. I came to learn that this might have caused the People to withhold stories of the Long Walk; the pain and suffering the ancestors endured was so nearly unbearable that they named Fort Sumner, where they were starved, raped, exploited, and killed, *Hwéeldi*: the place of extreme hardship where the Diné nearly took their last breath.[39]

This powerful analysis succinctly clarifies Diné ethics and methodologies that trump entitled Eurocentric Western attitudes that all knowledge should be accessible. While we don't want to elevate and centralize suffering, Tohe asks: "What is *Hwéeldi Bééhániih* and why should it be remembered? *Hwéeldi Bééhániih* speaks of mythic ties and informs the Diné of their past and their connections to tribal sovereignty. We must learn the stories and we must remember them."[40]

Luci Tapahonso wrote "In 1864," a creative nonfiction prose piece, and introduces it with this prologue, which describes how thousands of Diné ended up in Hwéeldi: "8,354 Navajos were forced to walk from Dinetah to Bosque Redondo in southern New Mexico, a distance of three hundred miles. They were held for four years until the U.S government declared the assimilation attempt a failure. More than 2,500 died of smallpox and other illnesses, depression, severe weather conditions, and starvation. The survivors returned to Dinetah in June of 1868."[41] While actual numbers of Diné and Apache who perished are estimated to be around ten thousand, and the distances varied between 350 and 450 miles one way by foot, depending on the route, Tapahonso's prologue captures the atrocities that our ancestors endured over several years before being allowed to walk back home in 1868, to the confines of the four sacred mountains. Twenty-first-century Diné existence is testament to Tapahonso's homage: "There were many who died on the way to Hwééldi. All the way we told each other, 'We will be strong, as long as we are together.' I think that was what kept us alive. We believed in ourselves and the old stories that the holy people had given us. . . . This is why we are here. Because our grandparents prayed and grieved for us."[42] Our existence is because our grandparents survived, as did theirs. Diné survival is directly connected to the survival of hane'. While many Diné hid from the military to avoid capture and imprisonment during this time, Tapahonso reminds us that thousands died, but the songs and stories did not perish. In 1868, when the Diné were allowed to journey home by foot for the Second Long Walk, they sang "Shí Naashá" (I am walking) and cried tears of joy upon recognizing the four sacred mountains. During my junior year of high school, I studied abroad in Rellingen, Germany, as a foreign-exchange student. After ten months away, I felt a similar anticipation and joy of returning to familiar landmarks. This is not to equate a study-abroad program with forced internment, but I could relate to the return to homelands. Knowing that Tsé Bit'a'í would greet me upon my return home, like the four sacred mountains did for our ancestors who walked back from their internment at Hwéeldi in 1868, was a stark reminder of our continued survivance. Immediately following Diné and Apache imprisonment, Hwéeldi was meant to describe a "place of suffering." Hwéeldi is now also recognized as a "place of survival."[43] Memorialized into our collective memory throughout Diné Bikéyah (Navajo land) and beyond, the signing of the Treaty of 1868 signaled the end of the Long Walk era and an end to the suffering and commenced a "New Navajo Beginning."[44]

Finally, apart from direct quotes, I avoid designating hane', or oral traditions, as "myth," "ritual," "folklore," and "legend." Gregory Younging (1961–2019; from Opaskwayak Cree Nation) locates the origins of inappropriate terms that uphold a hierarchy that negates Indigenous systems of literary genealogy and historiography. Younging writes, "the terms imply that Oral Traditions are insignificant, not based in reality, or not relevant."[45] This story-gathering journey has brought me closer to one of my languages and to my homelands, piece by piece.

'Ałk'idą́ą́' jiní ("a long time ago, they said")

Diné stories begin with the phrase "'ałk'idą́ą́' jiní," which is the second concept that guides my analysis. 'Ałk'idą́ą́' jiní brings attention to an imminent learning and listening moment: "a long time [ago], they said."⁴⁶ Laura Tohe recites,

> In the people's memory are the stories
> This we remember:
> Ałkidą́ą́' adajiní nítę́ę́'.
> They say long time ago in time immemorial:
> the stories say we emerged from
> the umbilical center of this sacred earth into the Glittering World.⁴⁷

Irvin Morris's fictionalized autobiography *From the Glittering World: A Navajo Story* (1997) offers the Diné journey stories as a referential foundation, to position himself as a Diné man.⁴⁸ The epic of the organization of Mother Earth and subsequent Diné creation tells of a series of ascensions from worlds below the current one, the Fifth or Glittering World.⁴⁹ Morris begins the story of Hajíínéí (The emergence) with the expression "alk'idáá' jiní" and resumes to translate, "It happened a long time ago, they say. Alk'idáá' jiní is the Navajo-language equivalent of 'Once Upon A Time.' In the beginning there was only darkness, with sky above and water below."⁵⁰ Jake Skeets (Tsi'naajínii or Black Streak Wood, born for Tábąąhá or Water's Edge, also Edgewater), a Diné poet and assistant professor, offers this clarification of ałk'idą́ą́, as a

> Diné . . . marker of time when storytelling. . . . *Dą́ą́* is the reference to time. However, the words before *dą́ą́* don't mean "once upon." . . . I conclude now that there is no neat translation of *ałk'i-*, but through its broken components, we can piece together an idea of how time is constructed in Diné. *K'i* is related to planting, perhaps referencing the way plants grow from the ground up or a planting of a thing that took place in time, and this story is the harvest. Like "once," the *Ł* takes center stage in this phrasing. . . . The *Ł* connotes a deep space that has the capacity to possess an entity within it, like time. . . . The *Ł* in *ałk'idą́ą́* then becomes a reference to a story being conjured from a deep space and time.⁵¹

Skeets's philosophical dissection of time adds to the growing discourse on how Diné bizaad shapes the collective and historical conscious of theorizing about and the telling of stories. Additionally, his thinking conveys what he has coined Dinétics, or Diné "aesthetics and poetics."⁵² The hane'

I analyze are inspired by Diné origin stories, Diné bahane'. Morris's novel acts as a précis, observing that when the sky and water encountered each other, Diné creation was set into motion. This First World was a powerful, ancient place where only Nílchi'i Dine'é (Mist People), Hasch'ééh Dine'é (the Holy People), and other spiritual beings existed.[53] Over time, Nílchi'i Dine'é caused disharmony, betrayal, and chaos and their punishment was banishment, which they disobeyed. The Nílchi'i Dine'é were then aggressively pursued by a great flood, which scared them—encouraging them to flee the First World.[54] They ultimately found a place in the east to ascend into the Second World, where their actions again resulted in their banishment. They headed south to emerge into the Third World, where again they caused disharmony, betrayal, and chaos and were told to leave. They headed west and "entered into the Fourth World through a winding entrance hole."[55] When they emerged into the Fourth World, they saw the four sacred mountains that define contemporary Diné Bikéyah.[56] They also found several other beings and deities, who after some time put their skills together to create the first superhuman beings, Áltsé Hastiin and Áltsé Asdzą́ą́n, who gave birth to twins. The first-born twin children were nádleeh.[57] Áltsé Hastiin and Áltsé Asdzą́ą́n produced four more sets of twins, and over several years, there was a vibrant superhuman community (from the Holy People) that also saw the creation of Mą'ii (Coyote), who introduced his mischief. Eventually, Áltsé Hastiin and Áltsé Asdzą́ą́n had an argument, which resulted in the well-known story about the separation of the sexes. After four years of being separated, and with the help of the nádleeh, everyone reunited, which was mostly celebratory. During the feasting, Mą'ii stole one of Water Monster's children, which caused another huge flood.[58] Before they escaped the rising flood waters, the animal beings and others collaborated to figure out a plan of escape. Two supernatural beings gathered soil from each of the sacred mountains and planted some reeds, which eventually grew into the savior reed that ascended into the present: the Fifth or Glittering World.[59]

This highly abridged excerpt of traditional Diné origin stories, passed down from Diné oral history, demonstrates the oeuvre's complexity as a body of Diné literary arts and affirms the People as being from Diné Bikéyah. Klara Kelley and Harris Francis's *A Diné History of Navajoland* (2019) illustrates that "oral tradition makes a bond between the land and the people. [Oral history is like] the batter of the Kinaaldá alką́ą́d [alkaan] (a girl's coming-of-age- ceremonial corn cake), . . . [it] holds the other ingredients together. It nourishes people with lessons about living today."⁶⁰ The relationship between land and the People is critical. The alkaan is baked underground, in the earth and protected by corn husks. Without the land, there would not be alkaan. Kelley and Francis frame their argument with a simile that starts with "the batter," but the preparation of Kinaaldá alkaan is not at all simple. There is no direct-from-the-shelf insta-box mix, where you "just add water" or "just add an egg (or oil) and water." There is an exhaustive list of hard-to-find, expensive supplies and materials required in addition to an array of human labor needed, as well as a knowledgeable Hataałii to lead the songs and ceremony. Families begin saving and preparing for years prior to a young girl's Kinaaldá, which takes four days, or at least ninety-six hours of nonstop work. Once the corn kernels are procured, traditionally the girl grinds the corn into a powder using a grinding stone (tsé dashjéé', or the base stone) and tsé dashch'iní (the top grinder).⁶¹ The ground-up corn is then transferred into large buckets of hot water and stirred with traditional Navajo stirring sticks. Once the batter is finally made, raisins are sometimes added to it, and some teachings, 'ałk'idą́ą́' jiní, dictate to add salivary enzymes from chewed cornmeal.⁶² Finally, the batter is poured into a shallow, wide circumference in the earth and literally baked in the ground, which was dictated in the stories of creation. Enacting this creates an unbreakable earth/land bond to oral stories and oral history.

The comparison to alkaan evokes temporal, economic, cultural, and kinship responsibilities that establish the complexity of oral history. I extend Kelley and Francis's batter allegory to demonstrate that these variations of ingredients—similar to variants of oral stories—ultimately result in alkaan, 'ałk'idą́ą́' jiní. The process is long, laborious, and out of a deep love for the young Kinaaldá. This comparison is very meaningful as I understand how complex the sustained bond is between oral stories, the People, and Diné Bikéyah (Navajo land). The phrase "'ałk'idą́ą́' jiní" invites reasoned and critical thinking and reflection of hane'.

Kéyah (Land)

The final concept that informs my analysis is kéyah, or land. Diné and other Indigenous epistemologies of origin, survival, restoration, and sovereignty are storied in the land, as Seneca scholar Mishuana Goeman argues: "Native nations . . . had and still have their own claims on the land, beginning with creation stories."[63] Land and stories are inseparable, across miles and across distinct cultures. Diné land- and place-based stories reflect resiliency, contain teachings and knowledge, outline traditional laws and governance, and mark the Diné—and Indigenous—continuum into the future; as such, they are illustrative of survivance. Kéyah encompasses Nahasdzáán (Mother Earth), mountains, landmarks, landscape, flora, rocks, place, (sacred) space, and home. My thinking about kéyah comes primarily from Diné authors.

> *Nahasdzáán.* She provides for all living things; she sustains life. We are her children, *biyázhí daniidli.* The Diné philosophy teaches that we humans depend on *Nahasdzáán* and that she must be cared for and respected; our survival depends on it. After the umbilical stem falls off the baby, it is buried in the earth near the child's home. This ensures that the child will never become lost, that the child will remain tied to *Nahasdzáán.* These beliefs remained in the minds and hearts of the people who were forced out of the homeland. Even though they were imprisoned hundreds of miles away, the land within the four sacred mountains was still there for them. It held their birth stems.[64]

In this passage, Tohe emphasizes human and other-than-human dependence on Mother Earth (Nahasdzáán). Diné honor teachings and restore/restory them: like burying our umbilical cords, leaving a physical trace of Diné being, seeded in Navajo land, marking that soil as home. Hane', Diné journey narratives (Diné bahane'), remain rooted in Dinétah, as originating within the four sacred mountains, through ascensions from below. The Diné oeuvre of traveling and migration narratives has ties to the land that are repeated by other neighboring Indigenous Peoples, indicating our footprints and birth stems have a timeless presence on the land.[65]

Kéyah encompasses landmarks, and Morris's words resonate with my experiences: "I have seen these landmarks every morning of my life, whether or not I am actually home. These mountains and formations are as real and as alive for me as are the stories that animate them. Better than anything else, they tell me who I am."[66]

Diné geobotanist Arnold Clifford finds explanations of the kéyah not only through the hane' but also through astronomy. He demonstrates their interdependence:

> The Four Sacred mountains are embedded in Haa Jih Naah Haa Neeh [Hajíínéí hane'] (Emergence tales).... The Sun, Moon, and Stars were placed in the heavens, according to a grand plan. Groupings of stars made up different celestial constellations where Navajo laws, codes of morals and ethics were written, so Navajos can live a well-structured life.... Traditional tales also stress the importance of sacred mountains in the interior of the Four Sacred mountains. The sacred central mountain is Dzil Nah Oh Diilthii [Dził Na'ooditii] (revolving mountain).... From the mountain top, the Earth's land surface and river courses were re-established, the land surface was revegetated, the sacred mountains replaced, the Sun, Moon and Stars restored, and the early foundations of leadership, family values, cultural tales, the moral and ethics of living in a state of Hozhjo and the Beauty Way of life emerged.[67]

Clifford's overall thesis is to acknowledge the importance of mountains, of kéyah, and while his knowledge comes primarily from Diné thought, he worked with Navajo mathematician Vernon Willie to conduct research on the placement of the mountains as they relate to the stars and the solstices, all of which are told in the Hajíínéí.

Denetdale explains the relationality and kinship aspects of land as follows: "Pointing out the sacred dimensions of the relationships between people and land, many Native people see the land as a living entity that has provided sustenance for all living beings, and is therefore known as Mother."[68] The sustenance provided by our Mother includes crops that can survive desert conditions (corn, squash, melons, peaches), medicines (tea, tobacco, sage, and cedar), and lush and verdant foliage like piñon trees. This southwest nourishment is unique, and I was fortunate to have grown up amid this abundance.[69]

The Southwest is host to dozens of Indigenous cultures. Esteemed Kiowa author and Pulitzer Prize awardee N. Scott Momaday lived on Navajo land and praised Keith H. Basso's *Wisdom Sits in Places: Landscape and Language Among the Western Apache* (1996) with the following blurb: "Place may be the first of all concepts; it may be the oldest of all words."[70] Dudley Patterson, an Apache Elder and cultural mentor, told Basso the land "can make people wise."[71] When Basso asked him what wisdom is, Patterson replied, "It's in these places.... Wisdom sits in places."[72] Though he struggled with defining and confining place, Basso focused on Nadene meaning making of places and names, which offers insight into Nadene epistemology. Like the Dene, the Nadene are linguistic relatives to the Diné. Momaday asserts the foundational importance of *place*, as the oldest of all words, in *The Man Made of Words* (1997) and *The Names: A Memoir* (1976). He writes: "A prayer from the Night Chant of the Navajo begins with homage to *Tsegi'*, 'place among the rocks,' place of origin."[73] Such stories that seek to locate a place's origin are prominent in the Diné storied narratives. Tsé Bit'a'í is a monolith featured in the journey narratives, and essentially, it is a mountainous rock. Paul Zolbrod, respected settler scholar of Navajo culture, history, and stories, writes in *Diné bahane': The Navajo Creation Story* (1984) that rocks are alive in Navajo country: "the 'inner forms' occupy rocks, hills, mountains, and even the sun and the moon."[74]

Kéyah, land, also evokes the counterdiscourses of displacement, dislocation, alien(nation), disconnection, and relocation. These oppressive and genocidal counterdiscourses are firmly planted in the historical and cultural consciousness of Indigenous Peoples. For example, the atrocities of nineteenth-century long walks displaced the Diné and the Nadene (Apache) from their safe places to Hwéeldi, an "anti-place" that marks land as unimportant, according to American philosopher Edward S. Casey.[75]

Navajo thinking is how I approach my analysis. The three Diné-language concepts at the center of my book—hane', 'ałk'idą́ą́' jiní, and kéyah ("stories," "a long time ago, they said," and "land")—are interrelated. Here I provided context and synthesized the discourses about their place in Diné thought, but they are more than contextual. Hane', 'ałk'idą́ą́' jiní, and kéyah also serve as my analytical framework; they are embedded within the Diné philosophy and epistemology of hózhǫ́. Hózhǫ́ through stories punctuates Diné perspectives without ignoring other Indigenous-centered theories on the topics. Innes writes, "Indigenous cultural knowledge can be employed as a theoretical framework as a means to explain Indigenous peoples' views, thoughts, and motivations."[76] I approach the literary journey from Dinétah to Denendeh with these tools to explain, describe, and analyze from a Diné perspective, which is my theoretical framework. Because Indigenous literary and visual stories, philosophies, and critical thought are written and/or translated into English, Indigenous knowledges are accessible.

While each chapter has its own argument, combined they demonstrate my book's overall argument that hane' (oral, literary, and visual stories) are restorative for relationships—broadly defined. Though all chapters are not solely about Diné content, *Restoring Relations Through Stories: From Dinétah to Denendeh* offers a Diné-focused analysis of hane', supported by Indigenous literary criticism from across multiple disciplines. I view non-Diné, Indigenous works through Diné-centered epistemologies to demonstrate a decolonial analysis.

* * *

Chapter 1, "Tsé Bit'a'í: Stories of the Winged Rock," introduces my relationship to the iconic storied monolith. The translation of Tsé Bit'a'í is "Winged Rock," "Rock with Wings," and "Wings of Rock," but it is known to locals as Shiprock (Peak). In my youth, I saw Tsé Bit'a'í every day, but it was not until I was far from home and saw her on the big screen that I had a deep appreciation that prompted homesickness. Tsé Bit'a'í demarks a site that continually draws me home, as I once drew it from memory. I trace the origins of the monolith as well as the role the rock and the site play, according to oral accounts that are now published. Through Tsé Bit'a'í's literary and filmic casting, I interrogate Tsé Bit'a'í's erasure, presence, and othering by non-Diné filmmakers and image producers. By introducing the various stories of Tsé Bit'a'í, my aim is to emphasize the significance of the geomorphic landform and argue for her restoration.

Chapter 2, "Visual Storytelling as Restorative and Relational," adopts a cornstalk and cornfield analogy to illustrate the vibrant and ascending field of Indigenous visual storytelling in film and on television. Visual storytelling by Indigenous creatives has sought to restore by privileging Indigenous aesthetics and narrative autonomy, which I advance as hane'tonomy. Indigenous screen presence has deep roots with early work by Indigenous creatives who had few resources and learned the craft through lived experiences, in tandem with Indigenous community input and support. This facet of relationality can rupture when ethical Indigenous filmmaking is breached by way of fraudulent claims of Indigenous identity. The chapter also offers a trajectory of Diné hane'tonomists and argues that it is strong enough to constitute its own field within the greater field of Indigenous visual storytelling.

Chapter 3, "Reel Restoration in *Drunktown's Finest*," focuses on the 2014 feature film by Sydney Freeland (Diné). While her lens captures the lives of three archetypes in attempts to rectify the bruised nickname of her hometown, Gallup, New Mexico, I argue for an engagement with the ground beneath their feet. The film's opening utterance longs to know why People stay in such a place, given the reeling realities of its citizens. I analyze the film through the Diné philosophy and epistemology of hózhǫ́. In tandem with an analysis anchored by hózhǫ́, the chapter aims to uncover how Diné traditional stories propel the film's narrative and provides context for understanding the intricacies of contemporary Navajo lives and places, which Freeland renders as reeling with chaos, sickness, despair, and disconnect, or hóchxǫ́ (the opposite of hózhǫ́). Through the recognition of Diné cultural and political identities, their aversion to Navajo land pivots to restoration, acknowledgment, acceptance, and 'ayóí 'ó'ó'ní (love).[77]

Chapter 4, "Diné Diegesis: *5th World*," offers a Diné-centered analysis of Blackhorse Lowe's first full-length feature film, *5th World* (2005). Lowe engages cinematic filmmaking techniques that give verisimilitude to this intimately Diné storyline. I look at the multiple levels of Diné filmic narrative and cultural stories and argue that this epitomizes in what I am framing as a "Diné diegesis," which is a culmination of a Diné-centric worldview and episteme that has borrowed from Western literary, classical, theoretical, and cinematic understandings of narrative, framing, and sound. Lowe's visual images, complemented with voice-over narration in both Diné bizaad and English, convey saad, a Diné diegesis and epistemology that exhibit sonic sovereignty and hane'tonomy.

Chapter 5, "Denendeh Storytelling: Kinship Restor(i)ed," is an exploratory introduction to storytelling in Denendeh ("Land of the People"), in the far north of the Medicine Line. I argue that story and narrative affirm Diné and Dene relationality and literary reciprocity across kinscapes and colonial and political borders. Stories are the nexus of kinship and restoration when viewed through the lenses of Dene law and hózhǫ́. The four sections in this chapter demonstrate a literary journey. I provide an overview of "The Dene of Denendeh," introduce "Dene Oratory," analyze "Contemporary Dene Storytelling," and conclude with "Dene Yati and Dene Language Restoration." The stories and storytellers in this chapter reflect only a few stars in the brilliant constellation of Dene literary arts.

CHAPTER 1

Tsé Bit'a'í

Stories of the Winged Rock

> In the west, Shiprock looms above the desert. Tsé bit'a'í, old bird-shaped rock. She watches us. Tsé bit'a'í, our mother who brought the people here on her back. Our refuge from the floods long ago. It was worlds and centuries ago, yet she remains here. Nihimá, our mother.
>
> —LUCI TAPAHONSO, *SÁANII DAHATAAŁ*

This epigraph is from the prose poem "The Motion of Songs Rising," by Luci Tapahonso. It tells of the enduring significance, personhood, and relationality of Tsé Bit'a'í, "Nihimá, our mother," who is revered with she/her pronouns. Nihimá's magnificence is reduced by many as simply an inanimate, albeit outstanding, geological landmark. The "old bird-shaped rock" stands out because of her enormity and beauty and is more than a land sentinel. Tapahonso's and my family's homelands are watched over by Tsé Bit'a'í, a site whose presence is acknowledged in stories. Tapahonso's poetics personify Tsé Bit'a'í as a matrifocal monolith, demonstrating a Diné literary aesthetic, "a native literary aesthetics of survivance," of being actively present.[1]

Like my grandmothers Manus (née Allen) and Watchman (née Keedah), who wove storied rugs and textiles that articulated cultural epistemologies, I aim to weave and unveil a tapestry that argues for the cultural, epistemic, and legal restoration of Tsé Bit'a'í through the rematriation of her stories. This chapter is guided by Diné theories and epistemologies and is organized into four sections that center Tsé Bit'a'í, or Shiprock Peak. The first section, "In Beauty It Begins," initiates Tsé Bit'a'í with a discussion on names. The next section, "The Hane'," presents about ten storied fragments that feature Tsé Bit'a'í from the traditional journey narratives,

FIGURE 1 Tsé Bit'a'í and Dibé Ntsaa. Courtesy of the author.

including published, contemporary Diné accounts. They are retold from Diné worldviews and are both well known and unfamiliar. The retellings lay the foundation for the next section, "Tsé Bit'a'í's Dislocation," which places us in contemporary, non-Diné storytelling contexts. I critique and analyze one feature film: Walt Disney Studios Motion Pictures' *John Carter* (2012), exposing Tsé Bit'a'í's visual dislocation and othering her as foreign and enemy, resulting in epistemic erasure. The chapter ends with "Restoring Tsé Bit'a'í, Honoring Hózhǫ́."

"In Beauty It Begins"

Per Diné protocol, I open with a decolonial Diné approach, "kodóó hózhǫ́ dooleeł," translated as "it begins in beauty" or "in beauty it begins."[2] Situated in northwest New Mexico, within the four sacred mountains, Tsé Bit'a'í means "Winged Rock," "Rock with Wings," or "Wings of Rock," but is called Shiprock Peak (or just Shiprock). Tsé Bit'a'í is located on the outskirts of a reservation town formerly known in Diné bizaad (the Navajo language) as Naat'áanii Nééz ("tall leader"), but it is now called Shiprock too. The town is a flourishing reservation metropolis on the northern edge of the great Diné Nation, which spans the states of Utah, Arizona, and New Mexico. Locals are primarily Diné. Historian Jennifer Nez Denetdale explains, "We call ourselves the Diné or The People. We also name ourselves Náhookah Diné (Earth Surface People) and Bilá' ashdla' (Five-Fingered Ones)."[3] Shiprock (the town) prides itself as the "Naashjizhii' Capital of the World." Naashjizhii' is dried steamed corn. This designation of Diné culinary pride is featured on the cover of every issue of the annually published *Shiprock Magazine*, edited by Eugene B. Joe. The magazine is organized by the Shiprock Historical Society (est. 2010), whose aim is to preserve "the cultural significance of the town, the annual Northern Navajo fair and the historical growth of the community."[4]

Existence, presence, being, and places are reliant on names, but whose version of a place-name, whose toponym, matters? Shiprock is an English name that eclipses two distinct Navajo names: one a landmark, Tsé Bit'a'í; and the other a nearby reservation community, Naat'áanii Nééz.[5] In N. Scott Momaday's *The Names: A Memoir* (1976), he makes a grave error. He refers to "Shiprock, which is called in Navajo Naat'aaniineez [*sic*] (literally 'tall chief'; the town takes its name from the great monolith that stands nearby in an arid reach of the San Juan Basin). The name Shiprock, like other Anglicizations in this region, seems incongruous enough, but from certain points of view—and from the air, especially—the massive rock Naat'aaniineez resembles very closely a ship at sea."[6] The tendency for settlers to claim and name lands that they are unfamiliar with is not surprising; however, Momaday lived in Shiprock from 1936 to 1943. That he would retell a settler's account of the anglicization of Tsé Bit'a'í is surprising. This demonstrates the prominence of settler narratives eclipsing Indigenous ones. Furthermore, Momaday misunderstands the meaning of Naat'áanii Nééz, which does not literally mean "tall chief." It literally means "tall leader" or "tall one who speaks." In the context of Shiprock, the town's name meant "tall boss," to describe the height of William Taylor Shelton (1869–1944), who in 1903 was assigned as superintendent for the San Juan Indian Agency by "President Theodore Roosevelt to go to

New Mexico and establish the Shiprock Reservation for the Navaho [*sic*]."⁷ Momaday also attributes the wrong Navajo name to the pinnacle and does not acknowledge the Diné name Tsé Bit'a'í. Even more troubling is that he completely ignores the traditional Diné stories about Tsé Bit'a'í and privileges an "incongruous" colonial version. In 1860, prior to the Navajo Long Walk to Fort Sumner, Captain J. F. McComb called Tsé Bit'a'í "The Needle." The Needle was replaced by the English name Ship Rock (two words) in 1870 because non-Navajo settlers believed that it resembled a nineteenth-century "full-rigged sailing schooner."⁸ This renaming reflects an unimaginative and nonsensical nautical nomenclature that further stripped Tsé Bit'a'í of her origin stories. Place naming, and naming in general, is significant to Diné and other Indigenous Peoples. A narrative of "place links present with past and our personal self with kinship groups. . . . Our knowledges cannot be universalized because they arise from our experience with our places. This is why name-place stories matter: they are repositories of science, they tell of relationships, they reveal history, and they hold our identity."⁹ Margaret Kovach's observations are relevant to Tsé Bit'a'í and the stories of her presence.

Georges Erasmus is Dene, or Tłı̨chǫ (Dogrib), from Behchokǫ̀ (which means "Big Knife" and replaced the town's former name, Rae-Edzo) in the Northwest Territories. He advocated for restoration of Dene place-names and turned to Dene literary autonomy: "We made our own history. Our actions were based on our understanding of the world. With the coming of the Europeans, our experience as a people changed. We experienced relationships in which we were made to feel inferior. . . . They began to define our world for us. They began to define us as well. Even physically, our communities and our landmarks were named in terms foreign to our understanding. We were no longer the actors—we were being acted upon. We were no longer naming the world—we were being named."¹⁰ This instance of Tsé Bit'a'í's place-name is a case in point. This act of replacing and renaming our storied places interrupted the process of becoming hózhǫ́, affecting communities on both sides of the Medicine Line. If recognized at all, our stories have been dismissed as quaint storytelling and mythologizing. In thinking about Tsé Bit'a'í, my maternal family's hometown mother, I am grappling with how the regenerative hane' responds as a corrective.

The Hane'

The following hane' are retold by Diné (and in one instance by a Dene family from the Tsuut'ina First Nation in Canada). I begin with excerpts from the Diné journey narratives shared with me by my late maternal grandmother Sylvia Manus and my late father, Lewison Watchman.[11] These family stories are supported by published accounts from Diné knowledge holders. Tsé Bit'a'í is a place wherein Diné "knowledges are bound," reflecting their potential for restoration.[12] Indigenous stories and teachings continue to recover from ongoing colonial violence; I have honored and respected storytelling protocols, guided by the Diné philosophy of hózhǫ́, as defined by Vincent Werito (see the introduction).

Just seeing Tsé Bit'a'í or the storified evidence scattered hundreds of miles throughout the kéyah, the land, that makes up the Navajo Nation conjures up hane' from Navajo journey narratives. The oral, published, and archived creation narratives featuring Tsé Bit'a'í are complex, nuanced, and diverse. There is no definitive version of the oeuvre, exemplifying narrative storytelling autonomy, or what I call hane'tonomy.

When I was a child and throughout my youth, my grams, aunties, and uncles raised me communally. I would spend summers, weekends, or long stretches with them in Shiprock. Grams worked as a dorm maid for the now closed Shiprock boarding school. I grew up seeing Tsé Bit'a'í every day, because at 1,583 feet (which is taller than the Eiffel Tower) she is visible for miles.[13] Tsé Bit'a'í is a twenty-seven-million-year-old monolith. Grams would tell stories about how Tsé Bit'a'í came to be at her present location. I have vivid memories of going to meetings with Grams, an active citizen of the Shiprock community. To keep me quiet and busy, she would sit me down with a sheet of paper and a pencil. She would announce to whomever would listen: "You have to see how my granddaughter can draw! She draws Shiprock really good!" I could draw Tsé Bit'a'í, Nihimá, from memory and from all cardinal directions, which encouraged my artistic proficiency. When not in meetings, Grams would take me with her on errands or longer road trips from one community to another. Her recollection of Diné bahane' would be triggered by places.[14] Our location would determine which part of the epic she would retell, and she would point out the storified remains found on the kéyah. To Diné, like the Apache of Basso's study, "what matters most . . . is *where* events occurred, not when."[15] For instance, the blood of the monster giant, Yé'iitso (or petrified lava), is evidence of the Navajo Hero Twins' victories and critical role in saving humankind from "monsters who roamed freely and devoured both animals and humans."[16] The defeated and slain giant's blood as well as his fossilized appendages are now permanently scattered up to 155 miles away from Shiprock, near Grants, New Mexico.

Tapahonso's words at the beginning of this chapter introduce a telling of the great bird, Nihimá, our mother, who now rests as Tsé Bit'a'í, and how she carried our relatives on her back. In the Shiprock region, proud recitations of the hane' inform us that "there was once a great bird that came *from the north* and she carried our relatives on her back. This bird crash-landed at its current site."[17] The evidence of the crash landing is the site of Tsé Bit'a'í because she resembles a great bird's exposed and fossilized wing. The essence of this story endures, but in my youth, I only heard the story from my positioning as a young Navajo girl in present-day Dinétah, Navajo land. It never occurred to me that this familiar version retold among the generations was one-sided. While there might be some minor variances in details of the story, the constant was that a great bird brought our ancestors *from the north*, but to my young mind, *the north* meant Colorado or Wyoming!

In 2010, I moved from Tucson, Arizona, to a place currently called Calgary, Alberta, Canada, which is in Treaty 7 territory. These are the storied and traditional homelands of the Niitsitapi (Blackfoot Confederacy) from Siksika, Piikani, and Kainai, the Îyârhe Nakoda (from Bearspaw, Chiniki, and Wesley First Nations), and the Tsuut'ina First Nation. Calgary is known to the Niitsitapi as Moh'kinstsis, to the Îyârhe Nakoda as Wîchîspa, and to the Tsuut'ina as Kootsisáw.[18] In translation, all these words mean "elbow" and describe the water route where two rivers meet. The Elbow River was a prominent meeting place where stories, food, and goods were traded. The land was also once shared with the buffalo and replete with berries, flowers, and healing plants. It is the significance of this storied Indigenous place that I draw attention to in the link between stories that connect kin, establishing relations. I quickly learned that my former employer, Mount Royal University, was adjacent to a Dene community. The Tsuut'ina (which means "a great number of People") are Dene speakers, hence ancestral relatives of the Diné.[19] According to a 2017 *Navajo Times* report, there were 171,000 fluent Diné speakers.[20] In grave contrast to this, the Tsuut'ina language is spoken fluently by only twenty-nine People, according to esteemed Tsuut'ina Elder Bruce Starlight.[21] In spite of ongoing colonialism, where Indigenous languages struggle for restoration, stories and our histories have persisted. Like many Indigenous Nations, the Diné have hane' and the Dene have honi (oratory and stories) about how our relatives were separated.

In the fall of 2011, I was visiting and feasting with the Eagletail family from the Tsuut'ina Nation and my storied universe grew. I finally heard the story of Tsé Bit'a'í's origin from a Dene (Tsuut'ina) position, bringing the entire story of the monolith's creation, death, and continual existence to completion. Upon hearing I was from Shiprock, the late Tsuut'ina Elder Fred Eagletail said,

> We have a story of how our People divided. Our People tell of a time of struggle between families. During the frigid cold of winter, one family was feuding and could not resolve their issues. Half of this family decided to summon a great bird. They climbed atop the bird that carried our ancestors on its back. They also took with them the base of a pipe and left the stem in the north. This bird carried our People to the south, where Navajos now call home. Some say this great bird was a Thunderbird, which after days of flying, crashed-landed, which caused its death, but miraculously, the People were spared. The great thunderbird, our relatives, and the base of the pipe were never seen again. Up here in the north, we still have and use the stem of the pipe and the Navajos in the south still use just the base.

I was floored that I had never heard the beginning of this story, which I have been granted permission to share by Hal Eagletail, son of Fred Eagletail.[22] This Tsuut'ina migration story complements the Hajíínéí, the Navajo emergence stories, that are part of our epic cosmology about Diné bahane', and taken holistically they emphasize Diné and Dene survivance. While not explicit, their hane' begins 'ałk'idą́ą́' jiní, in "the frigid cold of winter," signaling storytelling time and permission for the story to be told for generations to come.

Diné orature recounts that the Diné were created within the confines of the four sacred mountains. Through a series of ascensions from underworlds (outlined in the introduction), the hane' situate us currently in the Fifth World, or the Glittering World, explaining that Diné did not come from elsewhere. The hane' illustrate our celestial ancestors as travelers, explorers, defenders, and experiential teachers in a Dinétah-centric universe. Peter Nabokov ridicules the Diné bahane' as strategic: "to claim the southwest as their [Navajo] motherland was to smother it with stories. Few American Indian nations have produced such a crowded atlas of place names and localized narratives. One wonders if a certain insecurity may lie at the root of this tendency to leave no site untitled or unstoried, and whether the impulse to stake spiritual claims becomes stronger when those of historical residency are weaker."[23] The Tsuut'ina migration story offers one explanation for Dene and Diné separation, which negates Nabokov's claim of "localized narratives" while also providing some merit to migration theories.

Jessica Z. Metcalfe, an archaeological scientist, led a team of researchers in a study that unearthed material cultural items that are evidence of trans–Turtle Island travel and not necessarily evidence of migration. The findings of "preserved organic remains, including moccasins, basketry, and cordage," challenge mid- to late twentieth-century anthropological claims that the Diné are relative newcomers to the Southwest who ostensibly borrowed Pueblo thought, cultural practices, and stories.[24]

The distance from the present-day Dene community of Tsuut'ina to the Diné community of Shiprock is about 1,300 miles. Metcalfe's study "suggests Dene ancestors migrated farther south than previously thought."[25] Their excavation site is in northern Utah, but they "would not be surprise[d] if late thirteenth-century Promontory cave occupants had connections with regions as far south as northern Arizona.... Promontory-style moccasins have recently been identified near Mesa Verde, supporting the idea of a connection with the Southwest."[26] That preserved "fragmentary faunal remains" date back eight hundred years and can be traced to Athapaskan-language communities is testament to precontact travel and trade, which expanded oral stories, histories, and relationships to kin and land.[27] Elder Eagletail's Thunderbird-turned-Tsé Bit'a'í story emphasizes the difference in traditional pipes used by the Dene and the Diné, and, in fact, traditional Navajo pipes do not have a long stem. Together, these material cultural items reflect Diné and Dene "historical residencies" as dynamic and enduring, as opposed to fabricated, recent, and weak. Nabokov's ire about Diné placemaking is curious, given that his book is devoted to stories from Indigenous Peoples and their homelands in all four cardinal directions. Is Nabokov projecting his own insecurities about his place in the world?[28] In *If This Is Your Land, Where Are Your Stories?*, J. Edward Chamberlin instructs, "It is an assumption that understanding sophisticated oral traditions comes naturally to the sympathetic ear. It doesn't. Just as we learn how to read, so we learn how to listen."[29] What I heard and understood of Eagletail's sophisticated hane' is an explication of Tsé Bit'a'í's origin. It was initiated because of conflict and the desire to live in peace, or hózhǫ́. The characters (a feuding family) think (nitsáhákees) about their situation and how to come to a resolution; they plan (nahat'á) and delegate by dividing People and assets; then they implement (iiná) action and board their Thunderbird relative, living and surviving atop until she crash-lands; and ultimately the People reflect (siihasin). Siihasin transcends temporalities: in long-ago time ('ałk'idą́ą́' jiní), the survivors reflect upon what became of their "spared" relatives (k'é) and pipe, while contemporary Dene also reflect upon our separation. Oral literary arts, coupled with material cultural items, contribute to restoration and restorying, or hózhǫ́. Eagletail shared a version of the Tsé Bit'a'í, Shiprock Peak, origin story, which includes a nuanced beginning that dissolved borders and united kinship, despite being a hane' of separation. The Tsé Bit'a'í origin story is one that I had heard repeatedly, but never from a Dene perspective. Siyisgaas, ahéhee'!

Returning to Dinétah-centric stories about the Winged Rock's origins, Diné author Irvin Morris renders a poetic account of Tsé Bit'a'í and begins in medias res. The Winged Rock existed in its present dormant form yet still took flight. 'Ałk'idą́ą́' jiní, "*It is said that long ago, in some primordial time, the people were in danger and fled to the rock for safety. Like an enormous bird, it rose up and flew away with them. It settled here, its gigantic wings spread to the north and south. Some say it will come to life again, should the need arise.*"[30] This fragment does not tell where the ascension took place, but the purpose of Tsé Bit'a'í was to lift the People to safety. The danger that threatened them is not explicit; however, Morris's autobiographical novel iterates many floods of creation—as does Tapahonso's quote—that led to the repeated ascension from worlds below and to the evolution of life as we now know it.[31]

Another Tsé Bit'a'í' origin story, retold by Harrison Lapahie, describes coming to being by dry, earthen waves. Tsé Bit'a'í was thus created and existed as a safe site of refuge for the People until lightning destroyed a footpath, stranding many atop. 'Ałk'idą́ą́' jiní, the Diné were hard pressed by their enemies. One night their medicine men prayed for their deliverance, having their prayers heard by the Gods. They caused the ground to rise, lifting the Diné, and moved the ground like a great wave into the east away from their enemies. It settled where Shiprock Peak now stands. These Navajos then lived on the top of this new mountain, only coming down to plant their fields and to get water. For some time all went well. Then one day during a storm, and while the men were working in the fields, the trail up the rock was split off by lightning and only a sheer cliff was left. The women, children, and old men on the top slowly starved to death, leaving their bodies to settle there. Therefore, because of this story, the Navajos do not want anyone to climb Shiprock Peak for fear of stirring up the ch'iidii [ch'į́įdii], or to rob their corpses.[32]

Lapahie's rendition ends by illustrating the taboo to climb Tsé Bit'a'í (ch'į́įdii are spirits of the dead). The didactic moment in this story is sufficient to discourage traditional Diné not to climb Tsé Bit'a'í; however, non-Navajos began climbing the monolith as sport in 1939, and climbing her has been illegal since 1970.[33] According to Morris, "Before it was finally closed to climbers, many *bilagáanas* lost their lives on its treacherous heights because of unpredictable winds, crumbling rock, rattlesnakes, and fatigue."[34] The Navajo Nation's Parks and Recreation Department website says, "DO NOT desecrate Navajo lands and violate the trust of the Navajo people by discarding cremated human remains on tribal lands. Please respect our tribal beliefs. NO ROCK CLIMBING on Navajo Land. Please abide by the humble religious requests of the Navajo people and do not climb the Monuments. 'Navajo law will be strictly enforced on this issue,' Parks Department Manager."[35] While Tsé Bit'a'í is not part of the official Monuments (of Monument Valley), nor does it fall under Navajo Park designation, it is Diné land. Therefore, such rules and policies clearly are in place to restrict non-Diné access to protect Tsé Bit'a'í from rock climbing and desecration and to respect Diné sovereignty and beliefs.[36] The Diné laws and permit requirements have not deterred climbers. The deliberate rejection of Diné law illuminates the collective, neocolonial attitude of holding Indigenous sovereignty insignificant and irrelevant. Climbing Indigenous sacred sites further exemplifies settler ignorance and privilege and vilifies mountain, land, and water protectors who work to restore Indigenous sovereignty.[37]

In Lapahie's iteration, Tsé Bit'a'í's formation was paramount as a site of safe refuge for the People from enemies in the west and is unlike the Dene migration story, where Tsé Bit'a'í' is personified as a matriarchal great bird used as a vessel to carry a family from the north to the south, restoring harmony and ceasing dissension. Once the monolith was settled, it featured prominently in the journey narratives of the epic Diné Hero or Warrior Twins, Naayéé Neezgháni and Tó Bájísh Chíní, who were born to Asdzą́ą́ Nádleehé (Changing Woman).[38] Larry W. Emerson clarifies and corrects the English translation of their names, Naayéé Neezgháni and Tó Bájísh Chíní. He says that Naayéé Neezgháni's name does not directly translate to Monster Slayer, as I (and several others) commonly translate it. Emerson encourages the description of Naayéé Neezgháni as a protector and explains that Naayéé does not exactly mean "monster"; it means "adversity, chaos, and tribulation."[39] Neezgháni does not directly translate to "Slayer" or "Warrior" (as there is not a real Diné bizaad equivalent). Emerson says that Neezgháni means "to overcome; [specifically] to overcome adversity, chaos, and tribulation."[40] Emerson also explains that Tó Bájísh Chíní ("born for—and *of*—water") alludes to the waters of childbirth in which the child was born; the child was "birthed from a woman; a peacemaker."[41] These distinctions evoke a more powerful understanding of the teachings as they relate to contemporary times, and if we normalize the twins as Protector and Peacemaker, as opposed to Monster Slayer and Child Born for Water, we might be better equipped to achieve hózhǫ́.[42]

As children of Jóhonaa'éí and Asdzą́ą́ Nádleehé and grandchildren of the Holy People, the Hero Twins were endowed with supercelestial powers and were fully grown after four cycles of four days' time, in which they had to prove their strength and endurance by competing in various tests against the Diné deities or the Holy People.[43] These tests were preparing them for their biggest challenge, which was to kill the various monsters, who were feasting on southwest Indigenous People and causing disruption and disharmony. The monsters' origin is part of a separate cycle of hane' from the traditional Navajo journey oeuvre. Jóhonaa'éí said, "*Yé'iitsoh* the Big Giant devours our people, and *Déélgééd* the Horned Monster devours them. *Tsé nináhálééh* the Bird Monster feasts upon us, and so does *Bináá'yee agháni*, who kills with his eyes."[44]

Tsé Bit'a'í, Shiprock Peak, is significant because it was the home of Tsé Nináhálééh and his family. Prior to his passing in 2012, my dad and I attended a N'da' ceremony, which took place right near the base of Tsé Bit'a'í.[45] At the N'da', the origins and context of the ceremony and the site's significance were sung to life in Diné bizaad. The location initiated storytelling time, as my dad was flushed with memories about Tsé nináhálééh. My dad did not disclose anything to me while we were in the ceremonial hooghan; he summed up an English translation out of respect for the host family. He translated the lyrics of the songs, which affirmed the story he had previously been taught. Tsé Nináhálééh is both singular and plural and is translated as Bird Monster, Rock Monster Eagle, Rock Bird Monster, or Winged Monster. Tsé Nináhálééh is said to have terrorized the People from atop Shiprock Peak. There was a total of four winged monsters, including two giant bird monsters who raised their young at the top of Tsé Bit'a'í.[46]

In stark contrast to Lapahie's version that marked Tsé Bit'a'í as created in a precontact time, the following hane' depict Tsé Bit'a'í in a post–Spanish contact temporality. Tsé Bit'a'í is where the nest of Tsé Nináhálééh, the monster bird, was built. Some versions of this story say there was only one giant bird, and Johnny Rustywire's father said "the Tsé Nináhálééh—Winged Monster birds, they were like dragons in a way, but not like them in other ways, they would fly around and look for men. They would pick them up no matter where they were and carry them away."[47] He continued:

> In those days there were just the Indian people living here, no one else was here then, all of the people were afraid . . . tribes wore their own tribal outfits fitted with jewelry, sash belts, silver and turquoise beads. The bird flew to Laguna and took a man from there and brought him back to the rock, and then threw him down on the rocky pinnacle of Shiprock and he would be shattered, his turquoise jewelry would fall off and fly all over. The bird also flew to Zuni and those Indians were afraid of them. Those birds flew all over Dinetah-Navajoland where Navajos lived looking to eat anyone they found. There was no safe place.[48]

Despite noting only "Indian people living" in Dinétah, Rustywire's story exposes postcontact tribal names as well as the fact that they adorned themselves with materials that were acquired through trade with non-Indigenous Peoples. The overlap between Holy People time and contemporary time is also revealed in a variant told by Navajo Elder and storyteller Reginald Nabahe, who calls the Monster Eagle "One That Would Turn to Stone."[49]

> There was the One That Would Turn to Stone. Now this One That Would Turn to Stone was also killing people. Now that Shiprock Pinnacle that's over there, that's where she had her offspring. She had two offspring, one was a boy and the other a girl. Now this One That Would Turn to Stone was an eagle, a very large one. Back then there were Navajos present, also Zunis and Pueblo Indians, they were present in that area. Now this large eagle would pick up these people and take them back to Shiprock, where her offspring would eat these people.[50]

This story conflates the stories of two different monsters, One That Would Turn to Stone and Tsé Nináhálééh. The premise of these stories is that humans were being hunted as prey from the top of Tsé Bit'a'í, and the oral journey narratives relate that Naayéé Neezgháni, the Protector, was on a quest to destroy the monsters. The other Warrior Twin was on standby in the event Naayéé Neezgháni needed assistance.

Naayéé Neezgháni "traveled across the plain, leaving the mountains far behind him. Until he saw *Tsé Bit'a'í* the Rock with Wings in the distance. It was a great black rock towering high above the desert plain surrounding it. And it resembled a bird with outspread wings ready to take flight."[51] Accounts about how Naayéé Neezgháni and Tsé Nináhálééh engage in the grand battle differ slightly: "Monster Slayer camouflaged himself by wearing hide skin and a part of the horn itself from Déélgééd; he also placed two sacred feathers under his arms. He walked around Shiprock until the Monster Bird picked him up."[52] Rustywire's dad's account differs in how Naayéé Neezgháni (the Protector) along with the Peacemaker reached the summit of Shiprock: "The Twin Heroes set out for Shiprock and through the power of walking on rainbows they were able to run to the top of the Shiprock pinnacle."[53] Whether Naayéé Neezgháni was captured by Tsé Nináhálééh or they used a rainbow bridge to ascend to the top of Shiprock, the oral stories illustrate that the great battle of Naayéé Neezgháni and Tsé Nináhálééh took place directly on Tsé Bit'a'í.

In 2011, Diné scholar Lloyd L. Lee (Kinyaa'áanii, born for Tł'ááshchí'í; his chei is 'Áshįįhi and his paternal grandfather's is Tábąąhá) says Naayéé Neezgháni killed both monster bird parents from their large nest atop Tsé

Bit'a'í. In some versions, while battling Tsé nináhálééh, Naayéé Neezgháni was thrown off the top of the peak and used protective eagle feathers to soar safely to the ground, where they were able to shoot and kill Tsé Nináhálééh with a bow and arrows of sheet lightning gifted by Jóhonaa'éí. In other versions, Tsé Nináhálééh swooped down from the east, then from the south, then from the west, and finally grabbed Naayéé Neezgháni with his talons as he came in from the north and "lifted him off the ground, bore him high into the sky, and carried him all the way to the topmost ledges of *Tsé Bit'a'í* and beyond."[54] These hane' illustrate why the Hero Twins were responsible for saving the Náhookah Diné (Earth Surface People) from the monsters. Tsé Bit'a'í's twenty-seven-million-year-old presence is ancient, contemporary, and the avowal of our continued, future existence.

Although the Protector and the Peacemaker decimated monsters, humans could not live in peace and harmony among each other, and other monsters manifested and persist today in the Glittering World. Avery Denny and Michael Lerma developed two visual models that identify six twenty-first-century Naayéé. They are "social ills harming people today. *Yaa'*, or lice, involves cleanliness, *Dichin* is hunger, *Dibáá* is thirst, *Bił* is sleep, *Łe* is jealousy, and *Té'é'į* is poverty."[55] These monsters align with Emerson's clarification that Naayéé are "adversity, chaos, and tribulation."[56] Other monsters are introduced by colonialism and capitalism (diabetes, cancers, mental illnesses, and alcoholism). Because of the imposed reservation system, the Navajo Nation has become a food desert, and many homes do not have running water or electricity; therefore, the sheer remoteness of some communities has restricted access to mental, physical, and spiritual health resources. En masse, this environment feeds the metaphorical monsters.

With the outbreak of the worldwide pandemic came the arrival of yet another Naayéé.[57] Diné Elders, leaders, healers, community members, and scholars call this Dikos Ntsaa'ígíí-Náhást'éíts'áadah, which translates to the "Big Cough Nineteen" and describes the novel coronavirus, COVID-19.[58] Sunny Dooley, a Diné storyteller, explains, "We have every social ill you can think of, and COVID has made these vulnerabilities more apparent. I look at it as a monster that is feasting on us—because we have built the perfect human for it to invade."[59] Just weeks after the world went into lockdown in March 2020, the Navajo Nation saw an overnight surge of positive cases. This prompted Navajo Nation governance to enforce mandatory masking, distancing, curfews, checkpoints, and lockdowns. Because of the many barriers to access healthy food, clean water (which is precious and not ample to handwash excessively as encouraged to do so by medical professionals), and personal protective equipment (PPE), many Diné community members initially struggled. The director of the Navajo Nation Community Health Representative (CHR) program, Mae-Gilene Begay, shared how they collaborated with local authorities early in the pandemic to offer Navajo-language education, support, and information to combat Dikos Ntsaa'ígíí-Náhást'éíts'áadah, or COVID-19.[60]

In May 2020, activist and Diné citizen Allie Young organized the movement called Protect the Sacred, which amplifies the motto "Diné Bidziil," or "Navajo Strong."[61] She mobilized celebrities and then president of the Navajo Nation, Jonathan Nez, to encourage Diné youth, health-care workers, and all citizens to be the modern-day Protectors, or Monster Slayers, evoking hane' to protect the Diné community. The viral YouTube video "#NavajoStrong" begins and ends with a visual image of Tsé Bit'a'í. Young's voice-over narration introduces the stories of the Hero Twins from the Navajo journey stories. Her creative variation of the Hero Twins' story is unique and refreshing because she depicts the naabaahii (warrior) Hero Twins as Navajo women warriors in battle. I have tried to honor this depiction throughout this book, as I find it relevant and an act of restoration and Diné-centered decolonization by positioning women as warriors.[62] Young says that to slay the twenty-first-century Naayéé (monster) coronavirus, we need to do so in a way that exudes hózhǫ́ǫ́jí, "cherishing hope, love, and the Beauty Way of our people."[63] Her campaign went viral as Mark Ruffalo and Marisa Tomei (Marvel movie heroes) downplayed their superhero status to applaud and recognize the Diné superheroes, the naabaahii in actual life. With support from other celebrities across the globe, the momentum continues.

When news broke in March 2020 of the new twenty-first-century monsters, there were no reported cases. Almost two years later, on January 4, 2022, there were 41,779 confirmed cases, 39,586 recovered, and 1,590 Diné citizens who died from the virus.[64] With the introduction of vaccines, and more importantly with community buy-in to get vaccinated, the cases have not returned to former devastating levels. On June 30, 2023, there were 84,206 confirmed cases and 2,162 deaths.[65] The seemingly never-ending pandemic has taken a toll and affected every family on the Diné

Nation, and mine is no exception. On my maternal and paternal sides, I have lost five close and distant family members. Two of these deaths were not COVID-related; and more than sixteen close family members have recovered from the virus. The pandemic has prevented us from gathering to mourn the deaths as a family, which leaves a gaping void that is in need of hózhǫ́: healing and restoration.

The examples of Begay's and Young's approaches highlight the importance to honor k'é responsibilities with respect and care. New virus variants are appearing, and the Navajo Nation continues to play a prominent and proactive role to combat this monster. Lee's astute observations of the ways naabaahii were successful in defeating monsters, according to the Diné bahane', include selflessness and "lessons of service, teamwork, using appropriate tools, setting goals, [evoking] compassion, preparation, adaptability, discipline, belief, consistency, organization, and following a spiritual approach."[66] In addition to medical science, adequate financial resources, and supported frontline warriors and community health representatives, we turn to and elevate hane', traditional Diné stories. To achieve restoration, hózhǫ́, we have to be Diné Bidziil, Navajo Strong.

Through the Diné stories, Tsé Bit'a'í's voice emerges; she is a conduit to restore relations and affirm being through her existence. In direct contrast to the cultural and traditional stories of Tsé Bit'a'í that elevate her as a cultural and historical marker of the longevity, survival, and continued existence of contemporary Diné are Hollywood's narratives.[67]

Tsé Bit'a'í's Dislocation

Due to the allure of the landscape, the Diné Nation has been a haven for film production crews. Additionally, the entire state of New Mexico has attracted Netflix, which purchased ABQ Studios in Albuquerque, just a few hours southeast of Shiprock.[68] New Mexico Film Office director Amber Dodson explained, "Netflix understands the unique assets New Mexico has to offer—a talented and hardworking crew base, landscapes, production businesses and infrastructure, film-friendly community and competitive film tax incentives."[69] Not only are the financial and environmental benefits among the best in the country; so are Indigenous land and landscapes, where non-Diné storytelling erases, replaces, and displaces. There are Diné laws for filming on Dine Bikéyah (Navajo land). These are regulated through fee-based permits issued by the Navajo Nation. The Navajo Nation Office of Broadcast Services hosts the Navajo Nation Film Office (est. 1974) and the Navajo Nation TV & Film Office. Additionally, the Navajo Nation Parks and Recreation office issues permits for still photography, cinematography, and commercial filming on all areas of Dine Bikéyah. Filmmakers and crews have clear policies to adhere to when they want to stage Navajo land and the Land of Enchantment. The beauty, solitude, and grandeur of our enchanted lands welcome harmonious acts of reciprocity. When Diné laws and protocols are abided, not only is Diné sovereignty recognized, but these actions actively restore relations among neocolonial production companies and local Indigenous Peoples. To disregard Indigenous, specifically Diné, sovereignty by circumventing the law is an act of epistemicide culminating in disenchantment that resets the cycle of restoring relations.[70]

Tsé Bit'a'í, the Shiprock pinnacle, has attracted global attention and earned celebrity status because she has been cast in at least twenty-eight documentaries and motion pictures.[71] What follows is a brief overview of select feature films, directed by non-Diné filmmakers.[72] I then focus on one Disney feature film. In many movies, Tsé Bit'a'í was photographed simply because she was a sight to behold on the way from here to there, like when Tsé Bit'a'í was driven past in *Pontiac Moon* or *Natural Born Killers*, both released in 1994.

Tsé Bit'a'í is featured in the documentary *Rocks with Wings* (2001), by Rick Derby. The focus is not on the peak but on the Shiprock Lady Chieftain's basketball team and their coach, Jerry Richardson. Coach Richardson molded a winning squad from 1980 to 1992, and under his leadership, they won the state basketball championships in 1988, 1989, 1990, and 1992. Women's basketball brought communities together and home games were always sold out. Incidentally, the film captures a scene where my grandmother Sylvia Manus and my great-auntie Angie Sells are featured in two distinct close-up shots. Along with 3,998 others, they are in the stands of the Pit (the basketball gymnasium of Shiprock High School) cheering wildly, supporting our hometown team!

Rocks with Wings took Derby thirteen years to complete, and though Tsé Bit'a'í inspired the name, it's a descriptor for the players who became powerful, like rocks, and under Richardson's coaching were empowered to use their wings to soar.[73] The meta story of Tsé Bit'a'í did not appear in

Tsé Bit'a'í

FIGURE 2 Shimásání cheering. Film still from *Rocks with Wings*, directed by Rick Derby.

the documentary's narrative arc, but Tsé Bit'a'í's iconic image is visible on the gymnasium floor, a subtle invitation for players and fans to acknowledge her presence.

The Tsé Bit'a'í' stories depict a great bird in flight. Ironically, one can see this storyline displace Shiprock Peak. Tsé Bit'a'í' makes a cameo appearance in Michael Bay's 2007 feature *Transformers*, distributed by Paramount Pictures. *Transformers* dislocates Tsé Bit'a'í as war-torn Qatar, the site of enemy territory in the present-day Middle East, which was influenced by the real-life U.S. invasion of Iraq. The analogies of this characterization are chilling.

The Host (2013), directed by Andrew Niccol, spotlighted Shiprock Peak as a primary filming site. The *Albuquerque Business First* morning edition reported on Tsé Bit'a'í's prominence in the film, which was adapted from the novel by Stephenie Meyer.[74] *The Host* features Tsé Bit'a'í as a place of refuge for humans who are hiding from aliens who have colonized Earth. The aliens, who have committed genocide of humankind, use human bodies as hosts, erasing their minds. The only Indigenous actor in the film is my Chinle cousin, Tatanka Means (Diné, Oglala Lakota, and Omaha), who plays a chopper pilot. Means's physical body is host to one of the genocidal aliens. Those hiding from the aliens are known as the resistors and occupy the belly of Tsé Bit'a'í, which they have outfitted to become a self-sustaining, agricultural hideout, complete with thermal baths and multipurpose caves. Mainstream film's cultural domination is central to neocolonization and imperialism by transgression, which we see here with the desecration of Shiprock Peak.

Shiprock Peak is also cast in the 2014 Lionsgate film *Beyond the Reach*, directed by Jean-Baptiste Léonetti. In *Beyond the Reach*, the sentinel and the Navajo Nation are sites of the deadly, inescapable Mohave desert.

In 2019, Dwayne Johnson and Kevin Hart were on the Navajo Nation filming the blockbuster sequel *Jumanji: The Next Level*.[75] Hart rode a camel through the town of Shiprock, dislocating the Diné Nation as an unknown place of entrapment in a perilous adventure game. Dwayne "The Rock" Johnson took selfies at a local celebrity rock, Tsé Bit'a'í, and posted his appreciation for his Four Corners hosts, saying that "the spirit and the mana are so real."[76] His heartfelt gratitude, kindness, and reciprocity left a very positive impression. While Tsé Bit'a'í's role in *Jumanji* (2019) was minor, the actors and their engagement with locals modeled hózhǫ́.

A road movie that takes place in a dystopic, postapocalyptic future is the 2021 sci-fi feature *Finch*, starring Tom Hanks and directed by Miguel Sapochnik. I found it refreshing that the only place where the sun's deadly ultraviolet rays do not harm Finch (played by Hanks) or his family dog, Goodyear, is at the base of Tsé Bit'a'í, where he eventually dies in peace surrounded by the beauty of Nihimá. This film does not reduce the pinnacle to an otherworldly other but rather casts her as an aesthetic presence to behold.

The first time I became aware of Tsé Bit'a'í's force in a blockbuster film was in 2012, when she was featured in a trailer for a film by Walt Disney Pictures. I sat in a movie theater and saw Tsé Bit'a'í and the Navajo landscape glide into view via an aerial, panoramic long shot. The shot evoked the soaring of the northern great bird, and the experience was magnified by THX audio, as the narrator introduced Disney's *John Carter*. As a prominent and storified landmark that I grew up seeing daily, Tsé Bit'a'í' brought immediate Diné pride that was instantly muffled by the voice of God, which described what I witnessed as "a world away." To see Tsé Bit'a'í featured on the big screen was at once overwhelmingly meaningful yet also confusingly offensive. The grandeur of the monolith was breathtaking, exasperating, and heartbreaking as I experienced profound homesickness at the sight of the pinnacle. At the same time, I quickly realized this particular movie had cast Tsé Bit'a'í as a featured landmark on Mars, homeland to Disneyfied aliens as enemies to be annihilated.[77] To see Nihimá staged as an abandoned locale on Mars whose original inhabitants are extinct rather than as a site of Diné and Dene survival, resilience, and presence as told in the oral stories prompted me to ask questions that have not been addressed in the scholarly discourse.[78]

Directed by Andrew Stanton, *John Carter* is a sci-fi Western that takes place "a world away." The film's fictional world incorporates the binaries of savage and civilized by pitting two alien races against each other. Furthermore, it contributes to the tired cliché of a white savior who rescues an "Indian princess," common in Hollywood Westerns.

John Carter is an adaptation of the science fantasy novel *A Princess of Mars*, by Edgar Rice Burroughs (1875–1950). It was initially published in 1912, one hundred years prior to the Disney film, as the first in the Barsoom series and later published as a hardcover in 1917. My focus is on a few key scenes from Disney's cinematic adaptation and not on the published book, but for context I turned to historian Richard Slotkin's chapter on Burroughs in *Gunfighter Nation*.[79]

Burroughs's sci-fi writings were heavily influenced by his own professional experiences and failures while living in a blatantly racist United States. Slotkin identifies how Burroughs based the novel's alien characters on the binary of pitting Indigenous and white people against each other. He does so through an unimaginative, albeit confusing, color scheme: "The first two races Carter meets define the range of difference and the inevitability of 'savage war' that results from it. The Green Martians of the Red Planet correspond to the redskinned Apaches of Earth, the Green Planet; the highest Barsoomian race, which corresponds to the whiteskins on Earth, are the Red Martians."[80]

In the serial and novel *A Princess of Mars*, Burroughs depicted the Green Martians of the Red Planet (Mars) as heathen-like (referring to the Apache) and called them Tharks. The Red Martians had technology, were literate, and were portrayed in the Disney film as the Heliums and Zodangas. Burroughs was proud of his settler colonial lineage, which he could trace all the way to signatories of the Declaration of Independence, and he wrote the lead protagonist, John Carter, to reflect this.[81] Burroughs departs from his lineage and creates a character that is distantly descended from Matoaka (1596–1617), the most famous Indigenous matriarch. According to Slotkin: "Although Carter clearly embodies the 'masterful' qualities of the Anglo-Saxon, Burroughs also links his heredity to the American Indians. As a descendant of the First Families of Virginia he is not ashamed to include the blood of Pocahontas in his lineage, and he has lived with the Sioux as a warrior among warriors."[82] The ultimate goal of this self-identification is to enact Indigenous erasure while simultaneously leveraging Indigenous claims to space and place.

Disney's adaptation is ultimately about saving Barsoom (Mars) from dying from environmental extraction. Two Red Barsoomian (Martian) kingdoms, the resistant Heliums and the predatory Zodangas, have been at war for more than a century. Scenes of their warfare open *John Carter*, emphasizing the power-hungry leader of the Zodangan, Sab Than, accepting an otherworldly gift from three celestial Therns (shape-shifting, white aliens with long life spans). Cutting to a parallel time, but on Earth, to New York City in 1881, the film shows the protagonist John Carter trying to get away from a mystery man who is following him. Carter is a veteran of the Confederate army and described as a "wonderous storyteller." He suddenly dies after summoning his only nephew by express telegraph. Carter's nephew, Ed (named Edgar Rice Burroughs in the movie), inherits all of Carter's possessions, including his personal diary, which holds secrets that propel the plot forward. As Ed reads the diary, we flash back in time. The superimposed titles say the setting is now Fort Grant Outpost, 1868.[83]

The year 1868 is historically momentous for the Diné, as June 1, 1868, marked the end of a yearslong violent military campaign against the Navajo and Mescalero Apache, which I outline in the introduction. Much like the lived historical experiences of Diné relatives, ancestors, and kin in 1868, Disney's John Carter finds himself in a war zone in Fort Grant and surrounding territories. Unlike the U.S. military campaign against Indigenous Peoples on Earth, Carter is accused of "going Native" because he refuses to take sides or to fight against the "hostile Apache." Due to Carter's resistance, he is suspected of being anti-American and unpatriotic, so he is imprisoned. He makes a daring escape with guards in hot pursuit.

Carter rides through Indigenous homelands and runs squarely into the Apache, with whom he converses in the Na-Dene language.[84] Since the Confederate guards are chasing him, led by Colonel Powell, the Apache come to Carter's aide. A pistol fight ensues between the Apache and the cavalry and Powell is shot. Carter and the injured colonel seek refuge in a cave. The keen Apache track them yet stop suddenly and do not pursue Carter and Powell further into the cave. At the cave's entrance, the camera tilts up, shifting the Apache gaze upward, fixing on a spiderweb symbol carved into the stone. After a moment of paralysis and fear, the Apache slowly back up and flee. The cave holds valuable gold and the walls contain evidence of literacy, through ancient petroglyphs. These glyphs are understood to be alien and not Indigenous petroglyphs, however. Suddenly, out of nowhere, appears a Thern who possesses a medallion that dematerializes Carter and teleports him from Earth (Jarsoom) to Barsoom (the Red Planet of Mars).

Back on Barsoom, there is a princess named Dejah Thoris who is also a regent and scholar. She has fled from her kingdom, Helium, because her father wants to marry her off to the enemy nation of Zodanga as an act of peace, which can ultimately save Barsoom. While the two Red nations on Barsoom continue their hundred-years' war and fight for power, the Green alien nation schemes. A Green Tharkian warrior called Tars Tarkas nonchalantly states, "Let Redmen kill Redmen until only Tharks remain." In a reversal of the familiar anti-Indigenous trope that Hollywood smothered their stories with, Tarkas flips the genocidal death wish onto the civilized. Tarkas, as a reflection of the "heathen Apache," shares his desire to be free of both Heliums and Zodangas, or "Redmen" who were originally characterized by Burroughs as the "highest Barsoomian race, which corresponds to the white-skins on Earth."[85]

After the battle, in which Carter played a large role in the victory, he ultimately saves the Red Princess, Dejah Thoris. The Tharks praise his warrior skills and make him an honorary Thark. Carter rejects the honors the Tharks bestow on him; together with the princess and the Thark Sola, he goes on a three-day journey to find the fabled Gates of Iss, which Carter needs to get back to Earth. Their journey takes them just past an ancient, abandoned city whose former inhabitants are now extinct. This lifeless, abandoned city is depicted by the landmark Tsé Bit'a'í, Shiprock Peak. Carter, the white savior, fights for the Red Princess's love and for her nation, and in the end, the Red Princess marries him. Their marriage ceremony is marked by the sharing and consumption of holy water contained in one sole vessel that they each drink from, which is eerily similar to the practices of traditional Navajo weddings. Also parallel is how the new groom moves in with his bride's family. Because Carter marries a matriarch, he relocates to the Red Planet of Barsoom (Mars), which is her traditional homeland. Deja Thoris is played by Viola Lynn Collins, who claimed to be of "Irish and Cherokee Indian" ancestry.[86] While her Indigenous identity claims are without merit, the casting choice is relevant to Burroughs's original intent of the character. Slotkin says that Princess Thoris is "Burrough's solution to the classic 'miscegenation' problem of American literary mythology" but goes further and "makes her oviparous."[87] Slotkin continues, "Dejah Thoris is a perfect reconciliation of the contradictory values attached to women in the Frontier Myth. Her Indian qualities make her an appropriate object for the indulgence of erotic fantasies, while her aristocratic lineage and status as both virgin and Indian captive identify her as a 'redemptive' White woman and an appropriate mate for the White hero."[88] The race relations of the 1912 novel translated onto the 2012 film and are magnified by the setting. Burroughs's racist ideologies about Indigenous/white relations resulted in the erasure of Indigenous sovereignty by placing the action in outer space. Unlike his own ancestors who were complicit in Indigenous land dispossession by forcing Indigenous Peoples off their homelands, Burroughs's literary rendering dispossessed Indigenous characters entirely off planet Earth! A century later, and in a manner of four seconds, Tsé Bit'a'í was staged on the Red Planet as an ancient, abandoned city—abandoned because the original Peoples were extinct—which is a tacit form of colonization.[89] In the end, neither Shiprock nor the Diné Nation were listed in the film's credits, and of all the Indigenous extras on set, only an Apache Leader, Apache #1, and Apache #2 were credited. Tsé Bit'a'í is an unnamed and unacknowledged landmark as well as a site of transgression.

Restoring Tsé Bit'a'í, Honoring Hózhǫ́

In early 2004, I got the devastating news that my maternal grandmother had passed away. I was in my third year of a doctoral program at Stanford University. In addition to my grief, I had kinship responsibilities to uphold

FIGURE 3 Headstone of shimásání Sylvia Allen Manus. Courtesy of the author.

to honor hózhǫ́. However, my accountability to my family was measured against my graduate student responsibilities, which are incongruent. I was discouraged from abandoning my graduate seminars to return home to mourn. I refused to put graduate education ahead of my family, which did not register with some of my superiors. I journeyed home to attend the services, where I had the honor of leading her eulogy before we ushered Grams out of this world. To honor Grams's love of Tsé Bit'a'í, the Diné bahane', and the greater Shiprock community, my auntie Coddy selected a headstone that is engraved with the iconic image of Nihimá (our mother), Tsé Bit'a'í. This memorialization is a recognition of hane', Diné thought and knowledge, and models Diné-led restoration. We have access to the stories and their significance, which teaches how to strive for hózhǫ́.

Tsé Bit'a'í is at the cultural and storied center of the ancient Anasazi and the contemporary Diné and is also a prominent landmark of the state of New Mexico, or the Land of Enchantment, that has attracted international fame beyond the sacred mountains. The image of Tsé Bit'a'í has been appropriated by non-Diné mainstream media. Similar to how *John Carter* failed to acknowledge Tsé Bit'a'í in the credits, there are countless examples of Tsé Bit'a'í's likeness on items that reflect an empty, meaningless, dormant volcano plug. Irvin Morris muses that Tsé Bit'a'í "has been featured on innumerable postcards, calendars, and magazines, its twin craggy peaks silhouetted against a red-and-purple sunset."[90] Because her craggy peaks are so photogenic, Shiprock was bestowed the honor of *USA Today*'s "America's Best Geological Formation" in 2016 by 10Best and *USA Today* readers.[91] One souvenir that is popular among tourists is a mug from the YOU ARE HERE collection (2017), distributed by the Starbucks Coffee Company. The state of New Mexico Starbucks mug depicts the Land of Enchantment through iconographic images, namely Tsé Bit'a'í along with a hot-air balloon, a chile pod, a yucca plant, a roadrunner, and pueblos.

Twenty-seven miles east of Shiprock is the border town of Farmington. On January 28, 2002, the print edition of the *Farmington Daily Times* changed its masthead from a bonsai-looking piñon tree to a sketch of Tsé Bit'a'í, Shiprock Peak, that is centered prominently between the words "Daily" and "Times." When I emailed the *Daily Times* editor Sammy Lopez on March 9, 2016, he said the change was made to the masthead because "[Shiprock] is a dynamic structure that represents the area." The online edition, however, lacks the iconography of Shiprock Peak; Lopez was not able to tell me why. The Farmington Public Library offers a library card with the image of Shiprock on it, among a selection of other images a patron can choose from.

Across the New Mexico state border, Arizona marketing experts created a postcard that proudly appropriates the image of Tsé Bit'a'í, with the words ARIZONA printed boldly on top. They claim Tsé Bit'a'í as an Arizona landmark. What both New Mexico and Arizona do not seem to understand is that Tsé Bit'a'í does not belong to either of these places. She is older than statehood, and Diné stories give her image meaning.

North of Shiprock, 1,278 miles according to Google Maps, is the Calgary International Airport (YYC). Prior to YYC renovations in 2016, the restricted customs area was located directly beyond the ticketing counters. After snaking through the stanchions, all departing passengers were greeted by a centrally mounted panoramic photograph of Dinétah, my homeland. The image was of Highway 491, positioned northbound from Gallup to Shiprock, New Mexico, with the Tsé Bit'a'í monolith offset to the west and in the background.[92]

My maternal family is from Shiprock, and my paternal Watchman family is from Sheep Springs, New Mexico, which is halfway between Gallup and Shiprock on Highway 491, which is well traveled as it directly connects

Tsé Bit'a'í

FIGURE 4 Highway 491 with Tsé Bit'aí in the far left-hand corner of a photo formerly on display at the Calgary International Airport. Courtesy of the author.

Shiprock and Gallup. I know this stretch of road very well. To see this panoramic flanked to the right by a less prominently sized image of the U.S. Capitol made me smile. This oversized panoramic was one of twelve images that told stories of the nation: the U.S. Capitol, the foggy atmosphere surrounding the Golden Gate Bridge, the Statue of Liberty, Mount Rushmore, and other iconic images of baseball and wheat fields. I found the panoramic photograph of Diné Bikéyah comforting, as it was featured prominently at the YYC international airport, and even interpreted it as a significant link to home because of the stories this image held for me. Who, besides the Diné and Tsuut'ina, know the stories that speak volumes in this panoramic? My gaze and ideological interpretation focus on the unspoken stories held in the landscape, particularly by the monolith in the far distance. The image depicts a seemingly never-ending open road in the so-called Wild West, which may have been the intention of the photo's selection.[93] The customs officials I spoke with did not know where this image was geographically located, yet they were able to name ten of the other images featured in their workspace at the YYC international airport. While unknowable to the majority of passers-through, the panoramic connects two Indigenous stories whose origins are anchored in the earth as Tsé Bit'a'í, the Winged Rock. Its unknown-ness is emblematic of epistemicide.

Reversing the devastation of epistemicide is possible. Restoring Tsé Bit'a'í and enacting hózhǫ́ necessitates recognition of hane'. Our hane' and sacred mountain songs say we come from the land and the earth is our mother, yet she is vulnerable because she has not been granted personhood status. To seek hózhǫ́, or restoration of our mother to our homelands, will necessitate a movement that encourages and empowers Diné to know and honor the stories and songs. Furthermore, it will require that Diné critically connect with Tsé Bit'a'í, and the four sacred mountains, as protectors and enforce Diné sovereignty and traditional legislation over our lands, stories, and epistemologies.

I am encouraged by other examples around the globe, where Indigenous land, landmarks, and places like mountains and waters have been granted personhood status with human rights. Such movements have been led by Indigenous communities and activists.[94] Perhaps if Tsé Bit'a'í, the hane', and cultural understandings associated with her were protected by similar legislation and recognition, then our Winged Rock might be safe from extractive people and cinematic projects with her integrity restored.

In Quebec, for instance, the Muteshekau-shipu (Magpie) River was recognized with legal personhood status. In Aotearoa (meaning "long white cloud," and the Te Reo Māori, or Māori-language word to refer to New Zealand), Taranaki Maunga and the Whanganui River have also been afforded this level of respect and recognition. Jacinta Ruru, a law professor at the University of Otago and co-director of Nga Pae o te Maramatanga, says, "Maori people have always spoken about rivers or mountains 'as being their ancestors and that we must be respecting them, that their health and wellbeing is totally interrelated to the health and wellbeing of us as people and our community.'"[95] The hózhǫ́ of the People demands that hane', kéyah, and Diné bizaad be retained, spoken, and protected; these are directly tied to the hózhǫ́ of Tsé Bit'a'í. New Mexico could learn from these precedent-setting examples and legally recognize Tsé Bit'a'í with personhood status. Tsé Bit'a'í will always be a storied matriarchal ancestor, Nihimá to the Diné, but a legal acknowledgment of her personhood might facilitate hózhǫ́ and restoration. Despite many stories that clearly position her as protector of the People, colonization, rapid assimilation, and visual storytelling have dislocated and reduced her down to myth and othered her. To restore Tsé Bit'a'í with respect and the care for her longevity ensures Diné and Dene survivance.

On July 2, 2019, I was humbled to receive a traditional moko (tattoo), ink-wrapped around my left wrist by moko artist Christine Harvey and her daughter Tamāhine o te Kohu Harvey.[96] Their Iwi are Moriori, Ngāti Mutunga o Rekohu, Kai Tahu, Te Ati Awa, and Ngāti Toa Rangatira. On her father's side, Tamāhine's Iwi are Tuhoe and Ngāti Whare o Te Urewera. They attended a community Kōrero that I was invited to in Taranaki (New Plymouth), Aotearoa.[97] My talk "Looking to Mountains and Stories for Hózhǫ́" was sponsored by Tū Tamawāhine o Taranake. I respect Māori pepeha (introductory speech) protocols, so I learned how to introduce my maunga, my river, and my Iwi. My maunga is demarcated by Tsé Bit'a'í, not a mountain in the sense of the Rockies but akin to Taranaki Maunga as they share characteristics recognized by both of our Peoples and communities. I spoke about Tsé Bit'a'í's stories and their significance, as they are related to achieving hózhǫ́. My talk resonated with Christine and she immediately knew what moko I would leave Aotearoa with. She sketched the moko onto my wrist freehand with a yellow highlighter, prior to making it permanent with ink. My moko art depicts the Taranaki Maunga on the top side of my left wrist, flanked by other symbolic images, inspired by the local landscape. It is a continual, infinity wrist tattoo that evolves into a stylized, Māori rendering of the image of Tsé Bit'a'í on the underside, culminating in a genius circumfused balance of art and hózhǫ́. Christine lovingly pronounced that I would always have the Dine bahane' with me, no matter where I go. I am deeply grateful for this treasure; kia ora, Christine! I ultimately fully beaded a purse of my moko; to bead mountain stories was my pursuit of hózhǫ́. As a gift and to mark my solidarity with Kanaka 'Ōiwi mountain protector Auntie Pua Case, I beaded a necklace that is a "visual metaphor" of a lei supporting three storified mountains: Mauna a Wākea (Mauna Kea), Tsé Bit'a', and Taranaki Maunga.[98] Advocacy to protect our land-anchored kin brought us together. The love and support exemplified by the beaded floral lei (Pacific Island aesthetics) renews and restories the mountain hane'.

The oral and published stories about Tsé Bit'a'í give historical and cultural context of Diné and Dene becoming, being, and persistence. Stories of matriarchal monoliths and mountains are universal to global Indigenous identities, connecting communities across colonial borders and waters, upholding sovereignty, and enacting the tenants of hózhǫ́. The commodification of Tsé Bit'a'í through postcards, library cards, billboards, mastheads, and coffee mugs ironically contributes to her epistemic erasure. That states and border towns co-opt Shiprock Peak's image can be interpreted as honoring, but it is iconographic land theft, as the empty image is dispossessed of Diné knowledge through hane'.

The hane' teachings are restorative, despite external ills and monstrous attempts of erasure. My critique of non-Dine, non-Indigenous visual storytelling introduces why Indigenous visual storytelling through television directing and filmmaking is vital to the reclamation of stories, ideologies, worldviews, and knowledges, which is the focus of the next chapter.

CHAPTER 2

Visual Storytelling as Restorative and Relational

> We are creating our national cinema, just like any other country. We have radio and print, but this is the next frontier. We're contributing to something bigger.
>
> —NANOBAH BECKER (DINÉ), QUOTED IN LANDRY, "HUMANITY AND COMPLEXITY"

Following the landscape narratives of Tsé Bit'a'í (Shiprock Pinnacle) from chapter 1, which traced oral and literary stories grounded in Diné worldviews to their alienation in feature films by non-Indigenous filmmakers, this chapter acts as an introduction and overview to the landscape of Indigenous visual storytelling, or Indigenous film and television.[1] I do not analyze other forms of visual storytelling like woven tapestries, sandpaintings, storyteller jewelry, still photography, billboards, postcards, or artworks. These have been marketed by and for Indigenous Peoples, indeed, but all have historically vexed relationships because of their commodification. It was because of movies that I became aware of the complete erasure of Diné traditional stories, which led me to explore if Diné filmmakers specifically, and Indigenous filmmakers in general, turned inward (to traditional stories of families, communities, or kinship relations) to honor restoration and relationality in their creative works. This journey of tracing stories (oral, literary, and visual), from Dinétah to Denendeh, that seek to restore relations necessitates a brief overview of the field of Indigenous visual storytelling.[2]

In thinking of an analogy for Indigenous film and TV, I envision a field of corn, not just for the imagery it evokes but mostly because of the cultural significance of naadą́ą́' (corn) to the Diné and to other Indigenous Nations.[3] Corn nourishes, sustains, is restorative, and, according to Diné cultural practitioner Galen Ben, "represents the journey of life."[4] Corn is also directly connected to the journey narratives. Like corn, visual storytelling is growing, thriving, and on an upward journey. Diné film, as a stand-alone category in the burgeoning field of Indigenous film, is made up of living, blossoming, and thriving stalks. One corn stalk produces leaves and one to two ears of corn; therefore, one stalk does not make a field. For a field to flourish, it must be nourished by fertile ground, sunlight, air, and water and be protected from invasive species and pests. Each stalk is anchored by roots, the Elders and cultivators of visual storytelling. The leaves and ears are the creatives, whose works can be signified by the individual kernels. The tassels, corn silk, and pollen are all part of the analogy of nurturing, restoration, and growth toward new breath, new voices, and new life: the up-and-coming creatives. The industry is continually growing with exciting visual storywork currently underway. Diné traditional teachings dictate that song and protocol strengthen what is to come. John E. Salabye Jr. and Kathleen Manolescu's story "The Navajo Beginnings of Corn" tells of a grandson who acquired some corn seeds; as he planted them in the field, he sang: "Łeeyashjí' Anáá' óshjááh nisin. Łeeyashjí' Abikéé'. He sang, 'I am putting seeds into the ground according to my thinking. These are the footprints in the ground.'"[5] Thinking is the first philosophical tenant of Sa'ąh Naagháí Bik'eh Hózhǫǫ́n.[6] Thoughts are brought to life through song, and footprints as foundational for corn's grown are analogous to the Elders of visual stories and storytelling.

While an analogy is meant to be theoretical and pliable, I have attempted to honor the corn stalk as a roadmap throughout this chapter. A field (whether of corn or of an academic discipline) could not be possible without roots—Indigenous roots. In the endnotes, I point to key Indigenous film criticism to date. From the roots emerges a stalk that nourishes leaves and ears of corn, serving as an introduction to a stand-alone field of Diné film. Herein I offer my emergent conceptualization of visual narrative autonomy, as hane'tonomy. There are hundreds of Indigenous filmmakers, which is beyond the scope of this book, so I offer a snapshot of pathbreakers, engaging in the discourse of how to define Indigenous film. I also argue for the importance of authenticity and legitimacy of Indigenous identity, in support of Indigenous creatives. The chapter concludes—at the top of the stalk, as it were—with a brief overview of the burgeoning futures of Diné visual storytelling in television. Throughout, the work is guided by the metaphorical act of offering tádídíín (corn pollen), as it is embodying the practices of becoming hózhǫ́ and restoring relations.

The Roots and Relations of Indigenous Visual Storytellers

Indigenous film has ascended from erroneous depictions out of Hollywood to diverse self-representations by active cinematic creatives around the globe.[7] Indigenous bodies were early targets of modernity and continue to be influential in contemporary cinematic narratives.[8] While contemporary creatives are in demand as directors, they follow in the footsteps of several prominent filmmakers and creatives, whose works trace back to the era of silent films.[9]

During the silent era, Indigenous actors had presence, but they had very little agency to self-represent in ways that corrected the way we dance, love, laugh, resist, "live, look, scream, and kill."[10] Chickasaw filmmaker Edwin Carewe (born Jay John Fox) directed fifty-seven movies between 1912 and 1934.[11] Because Carewe's filmic output did not privilege Indigenous actors, creatives, content, or aesthetics, he is usually overlooked as a pioneer of Indigenous film.[12]

Though there were early Indigenous creatives, the practicality and feasibility to take up cameras in our hands was not continual. Life circumstances on Turtle Island were legislated and restricted (on both sides of the Medicine Line during the twentieth century due to Federal Indian Policy on the U.S. side and Indian Act constraints and amendments on the Canadian side). This would change with global advocacy by Indigenous, Black, and other Peoples of color for civil rights and recognition. These historic and often tumultuous periods during the twentieth century would reflect anti-Indigenous bias through non-Indigenous lenses and newsreels. When cameras were firmly in Indigenous care, filmmakers restoried these events from Indigenous perspectives.[13] In addition to documentary Indigenous filmmaking, Māori filmmaking is foundational to Turtle Island Indigenous self-representation and visual storytelling through decolonization tactics.[14] The impact of Merata Mita (1942–2010), of the Iwi Ngāti Pikiao and Ngāi Te Rangi, and Barry Barclay (1944–2008), of the Ngāti Apa Iwi, remains powerful and groundbreaking to global Indigenous visual storytelling autonomy.[15] Throughout his lifetime, Barclay championed Indigenous filmmaking by insisting on elevating a Māori lens.[16] In "Celebrating Fourth Cinema," a speech delivered on September 17, 2002, and published in 2003, he coined the category of Fourth Cinema to mean Indigenous film.[17] He said, "The camera ashore, the Fourth Cinema Camera, is the one held by the people for whom 'ashore' is their ancestral home."[18] His speech was a strong evocation to promote filmmaking by Indigenous creatives and telling Indigenous stories to silence imperial, colonial, and genocidal narratives that have spoken on behalf of Indigenous Peoples for more than a century.[19]

On October 13, 2022, Mi'gmaq filmmaker Jeff Barnaby died after a yearlong battle with cancer. He kept his illness private; as such, the news of his death was devastating. Barnaby redefined Indigenous cinema in the twenty-first century. Between 2003 and 2019, he directed two feature films, a documentary short, three short films, and a music video. From the musical soundtracks to the overall aesthetics, Barnaby was a gifted visual storyteller who reflected everyday Indigenous verisimilitude. He unapologetically depicted a residential school narrative in *Rhymes for Young Ghouls* (2013) with humor and horror. The protagonist was named Aila, played by Kawennáhere Devery Jacobs (Mohawk). Barnaby said the character Aila was long-past due; she was "a strong female Native character that doesn't have anything to do with ancient spirits or sacred trees or any of that bullshit. She's just badass. That's it."[20] Though Aila gets beaten, is nearly raped, and has lost her parents to death and incarceration, Barnaby effectively restored Indigenous women's autonomy, resilience, and humanity, which demonstrates restoring relations through visual storytelling. His second feature film, *Blood Quantum* (2019), is about zombies, but with a Barnaby aesthetic and storyline. His penchant for humorizing horror is unique and original. While those with Indigenous blood are immune to becoming zombies, they are outnumbered by white/settler zombies, but the film ends imagining the future (decades beyond the historical timeframe it is set in). The space he has created is monumental and his cinematic seeds are firmly and deeply rooted in the field. He modeled fierce, powerful, and forward-living Indigenous self-representation through restorative visual storytelling autonomy.

Indigenous filmmakers deploy Indigenous aesthetics.[21] Hózhǫ́ is a term I turn to throughout this book, and it is rightly understood as a strictly

Diné aesthetic, or as Skeet's coined, Dinétics, that reflects and conveys beauty—but not in the Western understanding of the term. I further cognize Indigenous literary and filmic aesthetics to include (and these may or may not be captured on the screen) acknowledgment of Indigenous Peoples' land and place; adhering to local community protocols; narrating in Indigenous languages; restoring imbalance and resolving conflicts through Indigenous worldviews and philosophies; incorporating the work of Indigenous artists, beadworkers, tailors, chefs, and other behind-the-scenes essential creatives; and acknowledging traditional Laws of the People, which can mean ignoring or resisting mainstream film or literary conventions in favor of traditional storytelling motifs, humor, songs, arcs, and practices. Indigenous aesthetics are things that those on the "inside" of the culture would not question. Items like wardrobe, props, film sets, mise-en-scène, and pre- and postshooting protocols are/have become Indigenized, reflecting Indigenous aesthetics. Indigenous aesthetics are also not limited to the visual. Sound, the soundtrack, or resistance marked by silence also signify aesthetic autonomy from Indigenous perspectives in film and television. Indigenous aesthetics, whether artistic, literary, or filmic, has the power to benefit Indigenous communities and to support the restoration of relationships and relationality.

Indigenous self-representation on the screen directly benefits Indigenous People. Diné filmmaker Sydney Freeland observes, "Those moments of viewers recognizing themselves in the characters are crucial, and it's made possible when minorities aren't just in front of the camera, but when they are behind the scenes too."[22] This evokes the power and privilege that the underrepresented have been forced to contend with on screen. Her inclusive language (using *minorities* instead of Diné or Indigenous People) transcends ethnicity and race, gender, socioeconomic status, or education levels and illuminates how the power of presence and recognition is healing and restorative and is a result of decades of Indigenous self-representation, frequently called narrative, cinematic, or visual sovereignty.[23] Mapping the historical genealogy and trajectory of discussions about self-representational film work by Indigenous creatives has been undertaken at several moments in the twentieth—and ongoing into the current—century.[24] Advancing creative sovereignty as narrative, cinematic, or visual has a long and healthy debated history, but overusing the term *sovereignty* has negative implications to true decolonial and anti-colonial work.²⁵ Jolene Rickard (Tuscarora Nation, Turtle Clan from the Hodinöhsö:ni Confederacy) urges scholars to remain committed to Indigenous political sovereignty and fuse (or hybridize) it with arts-focused discourses in "Sovereignty: A Line in the Sand" (1995). Similarly, Brendan Hokowhitu (Ngāti Pukenga) writes:

> While Māori Television employs genres and formats borrowed from mainstream commercial television (e.g., news, sports, lifestyle programs, reality TV, documentaries), the product is a hybrid televisual text, which departs from the discursive regiments that govern mainstream commercial television. The presentation of the weather, for instance, in the typical format following the news, becomes indigenized by using a map that "renames the nation" employing Māori place names. Such "renaming" may be considered tokenistic, yet to literally view "the nation" through Indigenous mapping on a daily basis is epistemic.²⁶

In a similar vein, Jo Smith expresses that "Indigenous peoples have their own terms for describing authority and self-determination (tino rangatiratanga in the context of Aotearoa) but must work within Western-defined paradigms of sovereignty in order to effect social change and achieve social justice."²⁷

In response to this, I turn briefly to Diné discourses on creative works and sovereignty. Colleen Gorman's "Navajo Sovereignty Through the Lens of Creativity, Imagination, and Vision" and Larry W. Emerson's "Diné Sovereign Action: Rejecting Colonial Sovereignty and Invoking Diné Peacemaking" are just two of ten chapters in *Navajo Sovereignty: Understandings and Visions of the Diné People* (2017), edited by Lloyd L. Lee. Gorman asserts that "language is essential to Diné sovereignty and identity."²⁸ Emerson advances this thought and writes, "The term *sovereignty* has *Bilagáana* origins rooted in imperialism, conquest, control, power, and wealth, and therefore is detrimental to Indigenous ways of knowing, being, and becoming."²⁹ To replace the English term *sovereignty*, Emerson suggests a "decolonized, Diné culturally and linguistically relevant [one] ... hozhóójí naat'á," which means peacemaking.³⁰ In a conversation Emerson had with an Elder, they discussed sovereignty and concluded that "sovereignty is a process of achieving a state of ... *hózhǫ́*. ... Diné peacemaking processes ... offer Diné an opportunity to embark on a healing journey that restores and revitalizes a sense of hózhǫ́ and k'é."[31] To think about peacemaking over sovereignty aligns with my thinking of centering Diné principles as theory and analytic. In the contexts of arts-based or creative ways of onscreen self-governing and self-representation, I see Indigenous visual storytellers actualize hózhǫ́ through k'é. Because I want to invite others into the dialogue, I have been thinking of how to discuss storytelling sovereignty. Cherokee scholar Liza Black writes, "Sovereignty continues to be invoked, contested, and reformulated in the field, often by adding an adjective to create an art-based idea of sovereignty."[32] I return to the Diné word *hane'* (story, narrative, or wisdom) and hybridize (as Gorman, Hokowhitu, and Rickard propose) it with *autonomy* for *hane'tonomy*. Hane'tonomy is an attempt to capture decades of thinking about narrative/cinematic/visual sovereignty through a fusion of Diné bizaad and English. Diné bahane' evoke k'é (kinship and relations) and are kincentric, supporting Emerson's theorizing. This return to my roots is a small way to introduce a concept that elevates the power of stories, narrative, or wisdom (hane') while honoring the importance of creative self-representation. My choice of privileging the word *autonomy* (read: individual) over *sovereignty* (read: collective), then fusing it with a Diné bizaad concept, is my attempt to challenge thinking that has been dominated by Eurocentric terminology. Indigenous communities continue to advocate for sovereignty, for self-governance in the political and legislative realms, as there are long-standing systemic and human issues for survival that need immediate attention. If Indigenous creatives' works (artists, filmmakers, and writers) do not directly benefit Indigenous Peoples, their homelands and communities, and their futures, then the output cannot be broadly stroked with a metaphorization of being narratively, cinematically, or visually sovereign. To metaphorize sovereignty is to nullify it. Hane'tonomy is not restrictive. It is storytelling autonomy and should span all genres and imaginations.

Diné Hane'tonomists

In "The New Navajo Cinema: Cinema and Nation in the Indigenous Southwest" (2010), Randolph Lewis recognizes a distinct nationalist Navajo cinema, albeit "still in its infancy."[33] He argues, "Although it may seem premature to label a few dozen projects as a budding national cinema, . . . a quiet nationalism can be found in the cinema of the indigenous [sic] Southwest."[34] He recognizes valid challenges for Diné-centered filmmaking to be categorized as its own field. The hurdles he observed in 2010 were few Diné filmmakers, "no state support, a few vibrant commercial networks to facilitate its production and distribution, and little to no public recognition."[35] Yet, through a sustained focus on three Diné filmmakers (Nanobah Becker, Blackhorse Lowe, and the late Bennie Klain), Lewis convincingly argues for the possibility of a "New Navajo Cinema." The new in this articulation is important, as that implies an old: the seedlings in the field of Diné film, allowing for future growth. The act of seeding constitutes thrivance (or Indigenous ways of being, knowing, and doing).[36]

In 2023, there are more than forty Diné filmmakers, three of whom Lewis identified in 2010. Forty-plus (Diné) corn stalks represent Diné directors in this flourishing field, accompanied by hundreds of international Indigenous creatives, as distinct stalks that produce all colors of ears of corn. While there are now state and international funds available through a competitive process, there are no targeted funds allocated by local Diné media organizations. In terms of public recognition, the Navajo Nation's TV & Film entity was established in 2018; it "proudly serve[s] the Navajo Nation through the Navajo Nation Film Office, NNTVF Productions, and the NNTV5 Television Station. . . . [NNTV5 is] the only Tribally-owned, funded and operated TV STATION in the United States."[37] I could not establish if the Navajo Nation TV & Film conglomerate offers funding specifically for Diné filmmakers, though it supports media work in a variety of ways. In January 2020, the New Mexico Film Office established the Senator John Pinto Memorial Filmmakers Fund, which awarded $100,000 to Indigenous filmmakers in the state in its initial year.[38] The late senator was a former Navajo Code Talker. The Sundance Institute offers $25,000 grants for short documentary films for "Native and Indigenous Storytellers."[39] With the explosion of Diné filmmaking, it demonstrates that stable and sustained funds are sorely needed. These two pots of money are not strictly reserved for Diné filmmakers, minimal amounts are granted per awardee, and they are not guaranteed, creating a competitive process.

Diné citizens have been making films since the 1960s. Seven silent short films were made in 1966 by talented young learners; all but one hailed from the Pine Springs community. They are Elders and ancestors in the field: Mike Anderson, Al Clah, Susie Benally, Alta Kahn, Johnny Nelson,

Mary Jane Tsosie, and Maxine Tsosie. Their work was not independent, nor did they continue filmmaking beyond the summer season. They were subjects in an anthropological study conducted by Sol Worth and John Adair, who outline their rationale, methods, and observations in two subsequent publications.[40] Their aims were to put cameras and one hundred feet of film in Diné hands "to communicate their view of their world"; as such, Worth and Adair are prized for their contributions to early visual anthropology.[41]

After learning how to use film equipment, the students created short films as practice. Their foci were everyday, mundane objects and activities (Anderson's *The Piñon Tree* and *The Ants*; Nelson's *The Summer Shower* and *The Navajo Horse*; the Tsosie sisters' *John Adair Hangs Out the Laundry*; Maxine Tsosie's *The Boys on the Seesaw*; Clah's *The Monkey Bars*; Benally's *The Swing*).[42] After a week of training, the students ventured into making "full-length films."[43] Six of these were nonfiction, actuality films and one evoked a story from Navajo literary history. The nonfiction films are *Old Antelope Lake* by Mike Anderson, *A Navajo Weaver* by Susie Benally, *Second Weaver* by Alta Kahn, *The Navajo Silversmith* and *The Shallow Well*

FIGURE 5 Alta Kahn. From *Navajos Film Themselves* trailer.

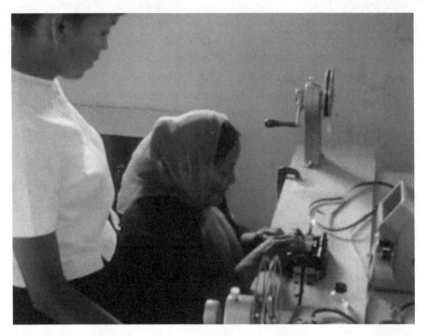

FIGURE 6 Alta Kahn and Susie Benally. From *Navajos Film Themselves* trailer.

by Johnny Nelson, and *The Spirit of the Navajo* by sisters Mary Jane and Maxine Tsosie. The creative fiction film, *Intrepid Shadows* by Al Clah, also includes a poetic "soundtrack" that he read while the film was screened.[44] The students organized a "World Premiere" of their films for a community screening, on July 25, 1966, which attracted about sixty people.[45]

Though the filmmakers were given ostensible freedom to capture whatever they wanted, Worth and Adair's ever-presence as researchers loomed large, and the Diné "view of their world" did not align with their expectations on many fronts, which is reflected in their published account of the endeavor. Their biased, hierarchal, patronizing views about the Diné in 1966 are not worth repeating here, but in an insightful, handwritten note, Clah provides insight into their mutual understanding. He writes that Worth "had a marvelous time teaching ah Injuns how to put moving objects on the magic tape."[46] Clah was the only filmmaker who was not from the community of Pine Springs; he was studying at the Institute of American Indian Arts in Santa Fe. He was an artist, poet, and scholar, and his handwritten note reflects the researchers' ignorance through a witty reversal using "Tonto-speak" and pan-*indian* stereotypical tropes to reflect their simple-minded racism that they cast onto the Diné "subjects." Clah's note was sarcastically signed "Chief AL."

Almost twenty years later, in 1986, Arlene Bowman's *Navajo Talking Picture*—a documentary that featured her nonconsenting grandmother—premiered to mixed reviews. She is considered "one of the first Native filmmakers in the United States."[47] Because of Bowman's approach (namely ignoring her grandmother's wishes to not be the subject of the film), *Navajo Talking Picture* was not well received on the Navajo Nation.[48] Despite Bowman's tactics, she persevered, and her work carved a space in the field, against Diné cultural expectations.

Lewis's 2012 book *Navajo Talking Picture: Cinema on Native Ground* focuses on Bowman and her project. His first chapter, "A Brief History of Celluloid Navajos," provides a long, comprehensive history from 1906 to the early 2000s of non-Diné-directed films, filmed on Navajo land, that extracted Diné bodies, homelands, stories, languages, and voices. It begins chronologically, starting in 1906 with Edward Curtis's *Yebechai Dance*. Lewis uncovered evidence of a lost werewolf movie, "*The Werewolf* (1913), which featured a Navajo woman-turned-monster."[49] He corrects the oft-cited error that John Ford was the first to film in Monument Valley by pointing us to Zane Grey's 1925 film *The Vanishing American*.

"A Brief History of Celluloid Navajos" begins with a focused critique on the movie *The Dark Wind* (1991), directed by Errol Morris and executive produced by Robert Redford. Lewis's scathing critique says that *The Dark Wind* is "a symbolic failure of Hollywood's continuing inability to honestly engage Navajo culture; it's unwillingness to cast Navajo actors in Navajo roles; it's lurid theatricality about Navajo spirituality . . . ; and its reliance on a white popularizer, Tony Hillerman, for source material."[50] Redford and Morris did not have a common vision, and Redford reportedly disagreed with Morris's directorial autonomy.

Victor Masayesva Jr. directed the documentary *Imagining Indians* (1992), which contains interviews from actors hired (and mistreated as well as ignored) on big studio sets like *Dances with Wolves* and *The Dark Wind*. In his sharp critique of *The Dark Wind*, Masayesva includes footage from a Hopi community council meeting wherein they are vehemently opposed to filming on Hopi land, usurping Hopi ceremonial acts. To further demonstrate their opposition, they do so in the Hopi language, and the non-Hopi film team are left to trust an interpreter. The non-Hopi film team look defeated and embarrassed, yet the final cut of the feature film still contains the scenes in question. *The Dark Wind* also recruited Diné cast and speakers, one of whom was my late father, Lewison R. Watchman. He was in Long Beach during the making of *The Dark Wind*. Through the moccasin telegraph, he heard they were looking for Navajo speakers, so he showed up one day and offered his time and voice. He was compensated a few hundred dollars as an ADR (Automated Dialogue Replacement) and is miscredited as Lewis Watchman. He shared with me that all he had to do was speak Navajo; they did not care what he said. He was able to preview the scene for context but otherwise had autonomy for what he could say. What made it into the final cut is at 1:03:30–1:03:54, when officer Jim Chee (played by Lou Diamond Phillips) arrives at the Tuba City Truck Stop Café, where a large sign on the wall proclaims, "Best Navajo Taco in the Southwest!" Chee is late to his meeting with his Hopi counterpart, Cowboy Albert Dashee, played by Gary Farmer (Cayuga from Six Nations), and as he rushes in to sit at the table, in the background you hear my dad speaking Diné bizaad for a bit longer than twenty-four seconds. What is audible is quickly drained out by Chee and Dashee's conversation. The English translation of what my dad said is "There's no more baking powder, so just overwhelm it with salt!"[51] This is hilarious, given that all the customers could hear this (Chee and Dashee), if they actually understood Navajo. On this day, the café's "best Navajo taco" will be made with fry bread that is way too salty and won't rise. Knowing my dad, he saw the sign and took the opportunity to employ his hane'tonomy and sabotage the scene with humor and wit. I miss you, dad; ahéhee' for these laughs.

Over the next thirty years, Redford supported other Hillerman adaptations, and he collaborated with Chris Eyre to create the 2002 PBS film *Skinwalkers*. Redford continued to believe in the potential that Tony Hillerman's novel *The Dark Wind* (1982) could be done respectfully. Redford took the time needed to build relations and collaborate with a team that would address the controversies that the Errol Morris feature caused in the 1990s and to redress them. Chris Eyre outlines the production trajectory, highlighting the personal and serendipitous intersections of the foundational backers.[52] Along with Redford and Eyre, George R. R. Martin, author of the series A Song of Ice and Fire that has come to life as

HBO's *Game of Thrones*, was one of these key executive producers who believed in the story. In 2019, Graham Roland (Chickasaw) stepped forward as series creator and executive producer of season 1 of the newest iteration, called *Dark Winds* (2022), produced by AMC Networks. Season 1 has six episodes, and the show was renewed for a second season. Under the direction of Eyre (who directed four episodes), and with the support of an all-Indigenous writers' room (two of six are Diné) and featuring a cast of A-list Indigenous actors as leads (three supporting roles are played by Diné actors), the television series has taken great care to restore and restory.[53] *Dark Winds* fuses two Hillerman stories: *Listening Woman* (1978) and *People of Darkness* (1980). The Indigenous creatives, however, elevate and underscore Diné oral stories, language, nuances of culture, land, aesthetics, and relationality. The titles of each episode are significant. The first two are in English, and the last four are in Diné bizaad and articulate meaning to culturally informed viewers. On their own, each title pays homage either to a significant character from the Hajíínéí, Dine bahane', or to distinct Diné worldviews through language. Taken together, they form intricate and circular layers of relationality, with the third and middle episode, "K'e" [k'é], meaning kinship. The centrality of "K'e" (or k'é) was envisioned by co-scriptwriters Maya Rose Dittloff (Mandan, Hidatsa, and Blackfeet) and Razelle Benally (Diné). Their vision carried the episode and the embedded narrative of the Kinaaldá (which I discuss in chapter 3), which emphasizes for Diné the critical importance of women, namely that of Asdzą́ą́ Nádleehé (Changing Woman, our primary deity, whom all Diné women are taught to emulate). The visual stories interwoven in "K'e" went beyond the base plot of death and crime by highlighting love, support, and community. Dittloff and Benally, along with the Diné actors featured in the episode (Deanna Allison and Elder Ann Tsosie), were clear leaders in the direction of "K'e" (directed by Sanford Bookstaver).

Another writer on the *Dark Winds* writing team is Billy Luther (Diné, Hopi, and Laguna Pueblo), who directed *Miss Navajo* (2007) as well as other shorts and television shows, and is in postproduction of his first feature film, *Frybread Face and Me*. He is proud of their work on the show, as an example of reclamation of stories. He clarifies that at the time of Hillerman's writing, there were very limited options to see Dinéness in media. This reminds me of the kinetoscope actualities of the late nineteenth century; viewers had to peep in to see Indigeneity. Hillerman's writing was tolerated, read, and praised by Navajos, though we were still squinting to get a peep of ourselves depicted. This has improved. The creatives of *Dark Winds* depicted Navajoness in ways that some contemporary Diné (and those of the 1970s) can relate to. Luther is cognizant that viewers are astute: "It's a lot of weight to carry as writers in the room with something so new to an audience. There are only a few Native TV shows out there, so I know we're all under a microscope."[54] Indeed, *Dark Winds* has been critiqued, and not all Diné condone the writing or identify with the characterization and events in the show.[55] What is noteworthy is that we are now on an entirely different level of Indigenous film and television critique. Not only have creatives evolved, whereby Indigenous creatives are in charge, but the audience has also evolved. We have moved beyond representations of Indigeneity in general, to zoom in and note critical nuances that outsiders will miss. Luther and Eyre and the creative team deliberately withheld overt explanation of actions and everyday Diné lifeways as well as cultural appropriative facets. If one is in the know, there was no need to explain, or worse to become palatable for a non-Diné viewership. Despite their proactive and respectful efforts, privileging community (Diné) consultation, some viewers were vocal online.

The Facebook fan page of *Dark Winds* is one venue where Diné fans chime in to voice their grievances with Navajo-language inconsistencies (spoken by non-Navajo, albeit Indigenous, actors) or with scenes that depict culturally sensitive events. On this fan page, there is relative empathy and support for Diné grievances. In response to these vocal critiques, the creatives are committed to improving and correcting facets for the second season.[56] There are, of course, a few fans who want to emphasize creative license and remind viewers that the show is "not real." The Facebook banter highlights the tensions that are at the heart of why ethical Indigenous filmmaking and visual storytelling matter. Additionally, it also revealed an insider/outsider debate that Robert Alexander Innes examined in his 2009 article, "'Wait a Second. Who Are You Anyways?': The Insider/Outsider Debate and American Indian Studies."

The observations of Innes, writing about Indigenous research, can be tailored for visual storytelling screening critiques. He says, "The critics of insider research have asserted that insiders' closeness to their research community clouds their views and leads to biased research findings. Insiders counter that their positioning provides a contextual understanding of the community that outsiders do not possess."[57] Diné insiders advocate for respectful onscreen representation, yet this falls on deaf ears as well as on blind eyes to outsiders who do not possess Diné cultural and contextual knowledge. An example of scholarship that lacks cultural context, resulting in an incomplete reading and incoherence, is by Denise K. Cummings, who analyzed Diné filmmaker Blackhorse Lowe's short *Shimásání* (2009). As an outsider, Cummings missed everyday Diné cultural signifiers and Dinétics in "Visualities of Desire in *Shimásání* and *Sami Blood*" (2019).[58] She charges Lowe's establishing shot as simply a "hogan, a primary Navajo dwelling, set against an austere background with *no notable topography*."[59] That Cummings does not *see* the landscape as a character, or even make deeper connections about the significance of the earth and plant medicines within the four sacred mountains, is an oversimplified reading of the opening scene. She also did not offer insight about the types of hooghan, which would have enriched her interpretive and critical analysis. Cummings dismisses Lowe's creative editing and Diné aesthetic as "confusing," without considering the oral Diné storytelling and traditional stories that informed the visual one. Throughout Lowe's film, there are allusions to Diné cultural texts and contexts. Without saying anything explicitly, these signifiers are placed in the film, and for those on the inside, an explanation is not necessary. For Cummings, the wind just whirrs, vocables are mere accoutrements, and the sun just rises. The wind, sound, and sun are critical protagonists in our Hajíínéí hane' that could have been treated with more nuanced analysis. The work of analytic interpretation for literary and film scholars is to identify and explain cultural signifiers to unlock deeper meanings that are being conveyed. I can relate to being a cultural outsider when it comes to biblical hermeneutics. When a common symbol recurs in a text, it might convey a story that I will need to uncover in my formal analysis. Does the writer or director focus in on something? If so, why? At five distinct moments in her chapter, she points out the presence of Blue Bird flour bags but simply calls them props without the recognition of them as signifiers of contemporary survivance, pride, and humor.[60] Here is an instance where Lowe integrated multiple layers of meaning, but to an outsider they have no significance. Cummings does not unpack the cultural significance of the symbolism of the blue bird; for insiders, we understand its reverence and restorative power. There is a song we sing on the final dawn of the Shiprock Ye'ii Bi' Chei, namely the Blue Bird song, which "celebrates the happiness and peace that the blue bird symbolizes."[61] Flour was a ration that has a complicated history; it served to sicken us, but once we mastered how to manipulate flour, it became a source of Diné survival. A local and beloved brand is Blue Bird flour. The salvaged Blue Bird flour bags at one time clothed our People out of necessity, but today they are used to design contemporary wearables by Diné designers as both nostalgic and futuristic fashion statements. Cummings betrays her outsider status by only seeing poverty and modernity with the staging of the Blue Bird flour sacks as curtains. This is not to say that outsiders can never learn or analyze cultural products; these are learnable and take time. Another layer that Lowe integrated of insider Diné cultural understanding is about the significance of hair and of our hairstyle, the tsiiyééł. Cummings missed another opportunity to engage on a deeper level (evidence she did not tie her own hair in a tsiiyééł, or hair bun), which for insiders is common knowledge. The stories that inform the Diné hairstyle, the tsiiyééł, explicate why we use yarn to tie the tsiiyééł. She actually misreads the film and says the hair is tied up with white ribbon—and the ribbon was a prop (not connecting the significance of yarn to sheep as a postcontact staple and hence of Diné livelihoods). Finally, she refers to the Diné hairbrush (bé'ézhóó' or be'ezho) as a "straw implement" and thus instantly nullifies the teachings attached to the brush and to tł'ohtsohzhóó', the plant used to make it; the bé'ézhóó' is rendered insignificant without deeper engagement.[62] The traditional hairbrush is used to comb a Diné girl's hair on the final day of her Kinaaldá ceremony; hence, it is directly tied to traditional oral stories of creation. Cummings's non-Diné lens mistakenly reduces this

FIGURE 7 Brushing hair with bé'ézhóó. From *Shimásání* trailer.

homage to our stories as a revelation of domesticity. Lowe's short film is rich and beautiful (in the Diné understanding of the term). It allows the audience to think deeply and critically, but Cummings's analysis is a simplified reading that reinforces outsiderness, missing restorative Diné cultural nuances.

Ignoring insider feedback is an act of ongoing erasure and "diminishes insider perspectives."[63] This is testament to why inclusion of creatives behind and in front of the camera is mandatory, and in this case nation specific. Diné filmmaker Ramona Emerson says that creatives from their own communities should be telling their own stories—not Tony Hillerman![64] Emerson has directed documentaries and shorts and is also a forensic videographer. These experiences are reflected in her debut novel, *Shutter* (2022), which she wrote because discussion of death is forbidden for traditional Diné. She had more creative license with literary storytelling than she does with scriptwriting and cinematography. If she were to make a film where a strong Diné woman deals with death on a daily basis, she knows she would get criticized from within the Diné community, like the creatives have been for the Hillerman adaptations. She said that unlike Hillerman's works, her novel does not contain sensitive Diné knowledge. She understands her responsibilities of respect and putting the community first. As an insider with cultural knowledge, she does not abuse it. Emerson's cultural context of place and being Diné herself equip her to be a respectful literary and visual storyteller, while also engaging in hane'tonomy.

In 2015, the National Museum of the American Indian hosted "Humanity and Complexity: Diné Spotlight: A Showcase of Navajo Film," which featured Diné creative works that spanned "love stories to science fiction to the gritty, hard-hitting stories of modern life on the reservation."[65] The filmmakers spotlighted were Angelo Baca, Nanobah Becker, Klee Benally, Princess Benally, Christi Bertelsen, Christopher Nataanii Cegielski, Velma Kee Craig, Shonie de la Rosa, Sarah Del Seronde, Sydney Freeland, Melissa Henry, Daniel Edward Hyde, Bennie Klain, Blackhorse Lowe, and Donavan Seschillie. According to a *Navajo Times* article, "With 14 filmmakers' work showing in New York and countless others making films on the reservation, [filmmaker Nanobah] Becker believes the Navajo people are establishing a cinematic record that is unique to the tribe."[66] This impressive lineup adds to the constellation of Diné film creatives and visual storytellers. One attendee, Teresa Montoya, was a doctoral student during the 2015 Diné film showcase and had previously directed a short film in 2013 called *Doing the Sheep Good*, a tribute to the 1966 Diné filmmakers. Montoya captured the restoration of their work, as the films returned to the four sacred mountains for a screening decades after they took up the cameras. Montoya completed her doctorate in 2019 in anthropology with a filmmaking certificate. On Diné filmmaking, she says, "It's powerful to use creation stories to not just think about the past, but also the future."[67] One such oral story turned visual story was restoried by Nanobah Becker.

Becker, whose words commence this chapter, sees the realization of a national, Navajo cinema. She is a contributor to Diné visual storytelling as a director, producer, and writer for music videos and short films. Her sci-fi short *The 6th World: An Origin Story* (2012) adds to the literary oeuvre of Diné journey narratives by putting our stories and ancient survivance plant—corn—literally in the next frontier, on another World, in space. Becker imagines and extends our oral journey narratives to include a Sixth World. In what has been passed down, the worlds of ascension stop at this one—the current one I am writing from and you are reading from—and there are no other worlds beyond this, the Glittering World. To see the continuance of our epic Hajíínéí (emergence) in ways that imagine us living and thriving through hane'tonomy, while also retaining the essence of oral traditions, is restorative: on the path toward becoming hózhǫ́.

The New York City Diné filmmakers showcase spotlighted young, Diné talent; however, Lewis argues that non-local Dinétah attention needs to be supplemented by support from within the four sacred mountains. In the years since his plea, there have been one-off Navajo film festivals, like the 2011 Rock with Wings Film Festival, the Shiprock High School "Navajo Filmmaker Film Festival," and the Navajo Film Festival, which screens films that are solely in the Navajo language. Students who are exposed to filmic opportunities are the pollen in my cornfield analogy but not in the ceremonial or spiritual sense invoked by tádídíín. Diné author Esther G. Belin shares that she once took a class that "enabled [her] to voice [her] concerns though the moving image. Once given the opportunity to re-create images, to re-tell stories, [she] utilized that medium to produce five videos and help found the Women of Color Film and Videomakers Collective."[68] Collectives and film festivals are abundant for the broader field of Indigenous visual storytelling, and support for Diné-centric film is welcomed by filmmakers whether these are on Navajo land or beyond.[69] Indigenous film festivals have now become more accessible than they were thirteen years ago, and many offered virtual streaming during the worldwide pandemic. Online streaming continues in 2023, like the Vision Maker Film Festival, alongside in-person screenings as the world cautiously resumes gathering. There is growing industry support for Indigenous filmmakers and creatives, beyond those that are targeted for southwest talent as previously mentioned.[70] Taken together, it is not surprising that Diné film is on a steady rise. The "heuristic function" that Lewis evoked appears to have broken the bubble that he saw Diné film trapped in.[71] While the concerns that Lewis brought forward in his 2010 essay about the improbability of a feasible, sustainable "New Navajo Cinema" are being put to rest, we are witness to the flourishing field of Fourth World Cinema that has ample space for national cinemas to take root, as Diné filmmaking has.

In addition to the feature films I discuss in chapters 3 and 4, other Diné filmmakers include Andee and Shonie De La Rosa, who directed *Mile Post 398* (2007), and the 2022 film *A Winter Love*, by Rhianna Yazzie. There are dozens of Diné-directed short films and documentaries; some are included in the filmography.

Restoring Ruptured Relations

> Indigenous films need to be made by Indigenous People.
> —LISA JACKSON (ANISHINAABE), INTERVIEWED
> ON CBC'S *THE NATIONAL*

Relationships are key to who is in front of and behind the camera. This leads to a discussion on the lack of relationships, where breaches of restorative kinship and trust threaten the integrity of Indigenous film—like invasive species and weeds that threaten the crop.[72]

What makes a film Indigenous? Do Indigenous directors, Indigenous executive producers, Indigenous writers, Indigenous actors, Indigenous collaborators, or Indigenous homelands make a film Indigenous? In 2018, Anishinaabe journalist Duncan McCue had a conversation on CBC's *The National* with Lisa Jackson (Anishinaabe), Alethea Arnaquq-Baril (Inuk), and Jesse Wente (Ojibwe). Jackson and Arnaquq-Baril are film directors and Wente is the director of the Indigenous Screen Office. While McCue did not ask them about every facet of filmmaking, the question "What makes a film Indigenous?" cannot be answered with those facets (director, writers, actors, collaborators, or place) in isolation. In fact, the question stems from a Eurocentric way of thinking as opposed to a collaborative, community-focused perspective that marks Indigeneity. McCue asked them "the *Dances with Wolves*" question, which considers a movie to be Indigenous because it has Indigenous content (in this case, the cast included Indigenous actors and the Oscar-winning movie was set during the Indian Wars of the nineteenth century).[73] The director of the film was non-Indigenous (Kevin Michael Costner). Wente asserts, "Authorship of cinema is dictated by who the creators are, not who is on screen."[74] As a site for restoring kin and relationships, Jackson, Arnaquq-Baril, and Wente also punctuate that for a film to be Indigenous, the creators must be Indigenous. They did not discuss, however, how one's Indigeneity is affirmed. Wente makes a strong case for why *Indian Horse* (2017, adapted from the novel by Ojibwe writer Richard Wagamese by non-Indigenous creatives) is not an Indigenous film, though the story itself is very important.[75]

Jo Smith complicates the categorization of Indigenous filmmaking by acknowledging two unique cases of cross-century collaboration in which two non-Indigenous-directed ethnographic documentaries assisted two twenty-first-century Māori scholars to fulfill their distinct land-based responsibilities to their communities. Smith concludes, "As such, filmic content such as this may arise from colonial contexts, yet the use made of this material by contemporary Indigenous practitioners and activists, tests the parameters of what might constitute . . . 'Indigenous film-making.'"[76] Smith's inclusive and generous definition of Indigenous film has flexible contours that accommodate for collaborative filmmaking. An exhaustive examination of creative collaborations is beyond the scope of this work, but to add to Smith's example I want to highlight the film *Trouble in the Garden* (2018), directed by Roz Owen. Owen, a non-Indigenous creative, sought out the direction, input, and expertise of Raven Sinclair (Cree/Assiniboine/Saulteaux/Métis) from George Gordon First Nation. Sinclair also directly reworked the script to drown the centering of the white antagonists and to give voice and agency to the protagonist, suitably named Raven and played by Cara Gee (Ojibwe). Sinclair's collaboration was critical and earned her credit as the executive producer. She had authorial power and final approval of the script, and in this instance the film director worked closely with her. Without Sinclair's input and creative direction, this film would contain only a few Indigenous actors (one in the lead role; the rest are extras who play land protectors and other minor roles, with few speaking parts). There are numerous films and television shows that feature at least one, or even many, Indigenous actors, but without Indigenous agency as a creative behind the camera, the categorization of them as Indigenous is tenuous.

Indigenous films are visual stories made by creatives who are Indigenous. If one's Indigeneity is tenuous and there is a lack of reciprocal relationality and relationship to Indigenous land and family, whether through kinship, Clans, or citizenship, then can one claim to be Indigenous? Justice writes, "It's vital to remember that not all claims to Indigenous identity and community affiliation are legitimate; there's a long, sad, and sordid history of settlers 'playing Indian' to gain land, money, or fame, or for some personal purpose, often with profoundly negative material impacts on communities."[77] Visual storytelling that pronounces and prescribes Indigenous film and filmmaking as being honest and responsible to their kin and community puts forth the requirement to be an ethical filmmaker. Lying about one's Indigenous identity is fraud. These conversations have escalated on Turtle Island in the twenty-first century but are not new.[78] Indigenous visual stories include creative Indigenous aesthetics and are liberated through hane'tonomy. To put it bluntly, these two facets are more challenging, if not impossible, to integrate by non-Indigenous creatives. Indigenous identity or Indigeneity is unique to the individual who is Indigenous, and this surface-level discussion is not meant to be a generalization of the ongoing nuanced conversations.

In December 2020, the public was made aware of a scandal that had been simmering in Indigenous film circles in Canada (and certainly globally) for years prior. News broke that rocked the Indigenous film community: filmmaker Michelle Latimer had been fraudulently claiming she was Indigenous. These fraudulent claims propelled her career and cultural capital as one of the few "Indigenous" leaders in the film industry. The revelations of her Indigenous identity fraud came to light at the height and popularity of the television series *Trickster*, based on Haisla First Nation author Eden Robinson's novel; Latimer had gained Robinson's permission and trust by deliberately lying about her ostensible Indigenous identity and experiences. The show was not renewed for a second season, creating a domino effect, including suddenly ceasing the work that benefited and showcased outstanding Indigenous actors and crew. The Indigenous Screen Office released the following statement in response to the Latimer controversy:

> We understand that different nations and Indigenous people have different concepts and approaches to determining identity, and there is not one way to be Indigenous. Lineage, kinship, citizenship, and cultural knowledge are all ways to understand Indigenous identity. For the many who have lost their connections, learning what community they claim and who claims them is a necessary part of the journey, particularly before it comes to claiming resources and opportunities meant to repair the damage that has been done through colonial practices. . . . We recognize that great harm can be caused when space, resources and opportunities are taken by those with unconfirmed or contested connections to their Indigenous identity.[79]

Since the revelations became public, there have been several responses from Indigenous creatives, community members, journalists, and non-Indigenous allies about the harm caused. In a poignant reflection, Blackfoot/Sámi filmmaker Elle-Máijá Tailfeathers wrote, "She has gained the trust and love of many. As in any tight-knit community, when one person succeeds, we share that success as a community. She was a leader. She was someone emerging filmmakers could look to and say, 'If she can do it, then so can I.' Those young filmmakers are now contending with the reality that the most successful Indigenous filmmaker in Canada is a white settler with a distant Indigenous heritage."[80]

Additionally, Ginger Gosnell-Myers (Nisga'a and Kwakwak'awakw), a fellow for decolonization and urban Indigenous planning at Simon Fraser University's Morris J. Wosk Centre for Dialogue, shared her frustrations, which reflect the collective frustration of how harmful lying about one's Indigenous identity is: "Becoming Indigenous is not an opportunity to advance one's career. We see through Latimer's example how far one can take the possibility of maybe being Indigenous, and also how harmful it can turn. This is not a victimless offence. It is a continuation of white privilege and cultural genocide—quite simply, it's wrong."[81] Latimer and some of her supporters have claimed that Indigenous People who brought these claims were demonstrating lateral violence. It is not laterally violent to tell the truth and to call out Indigenous identity fraud when that fraud has perpetuated white privilege and cultural genocide. To be lateral, then people would have to be on the same playing field from the outset; this was not the reality in this case.

In 1980, Gretchen M. Bataille and Charles L. P. Silet published one of the first books on fake Indigenous People in film. Their book is called *The Pretend Indians: Images of Native Americans in the Movies*.[82] The term *pretendians*, fused from *pretend* plus *indians*, is one that has gained cultural, political, and social currency. Michelle Latimer's fraudulent claims of being Indigenous add to a growing list of pretendians who infiltrate spaces, claim voice and experiences, and take resources from Indigenous People. Anishinaabe writer Drew Hayden Taylor co-directed the 2022 documentary *The Pretendians*, which premiered for *The Passionate Eye* documentary TV series on the CBC News Network. In addition to the Latimer case, he explores other high-profile cases of pretendianism.

Jolene Rickard has a strong stance on those who occupy and claim creative spaces without doing the hard work of honoring one's responsibility to the Indigenous community one is accountable to. She wonders where we will be fifty years forward if individuals continue to fraudulently claim Indigenous identity: "claiming Indigenous subjecthood, but to know nothing of the history, our traditions, the practice, why there's a resurgence of our languages, why understanding languages, even if not a speaker, is important to understanding place."[83] Knowing Indigenous places underscores Indigenous identity: "Indigenous peoples are those who have creation stories, not colonization stories, about how we/they came to be in a particular place—indeed how we/they came to *be a place*."[84] While written about the U.S. political context, "Decolonization Is Not a Metaphor," an oft-cited essay by Eve Tuck (Unangax̂) and K. Wayne Yang, parallels the situation in Canada. They offer six "settler moves to innocence," or when "non-Indigenous peoples mak[e] moves to alleviate the impacts of colonization. The too-easy adoption of decolonizing discourse (making decolonization a metaphor) is just one part of that history."[85] Two of these moves address fraudulent claims of being Indigenous ("settler nativism" and the "settler adoption fantasies") and how these moves facilitate the illegal occupation of space and resources. "Settler nativism" is when "settlers locate or invent a long-lost ancestor who is rumored to have had 'Indian blood,' and they use this claim to mark themselves as blameless in the attempted eradications of Indigenous peoples."[86] They cite Vine Delora Jr.'s designation of this as the "Indian grandmother complex," which continues to have faux-cultural currency in the arts and in academia.[87] Tuck and Yang point out the ironic reversal of pretendian logics: "in the racialization of whiteness, blood quantum rules are reversed so that white people can stay white, yet claim descendance from an Indian grandmother."[88] Blood quantum is the practice of dividing one's identity by fractions. Imagine a circle: a full circle is representative of full bloodedness; cut the circle down the middle and there are two halves, or half-bloodedness, and so forth. Blood quantum is legislated by federally recognized Indigenous Nations to determine who is or is not a citizen, and some Nations do not allow a person to dual enroll, further fracturing one's Indigenous identity. It is racial politics that are self-destructive and genocidal. Justice says, "Blood rhetorics become part of the problem—reciprocal kinship becomes, if not a full solution, part of the return to wholeness."[89] Both blood quantum and the grandmother excuse converge, which resulted in the legislation of the Pocahontas Exception or the Pocahontas Clause on March 8, 1924, which "allowed thousands of white people to claim Indian ancestry, while actual Indigenous people were reclassified as 'colored' and disappeared off the public record."[90] The expulsion and reclassification are glaringly ironic, since 1924 is the same year that American Indians were granted U.S. citizenship on June 2.

The second move to innocence is called "settler adoption fantasies." Tuck and Yang offer the long history of adult adoption stories in the U.S. context. Individual family members are not able to enact sovereignty in matters of tribal citizenship. Family members who symbolically adopt individuals out of love and trust assume that love and trust to be returned. There are community members, Elders, kin, friends, and colleagues divided on both sides of the Indigenous identity line. Michelle Latimer, Carrie Bourassa, Joseph Boyden, Buffy Sainte-Marie, and Mary Ellen Turpel-Lafond have argued that because they were adopted (as adults!) into legitimate Indigenous families, they can co-opt and appropriate that Nation's Indigenous identity.[91] Indigenous families or individuals have and will continue symbolic adult adoptions, which make the adopted adult solely the adopted family's kin. This does not grant the welcomed new family member the right to claim Indigenous identity. When a fraudulent claim of one's identity is directly attached to the name of an Indigenous community without their knowledge and consent, that community has been violated and they are owed reparations.

Colonial, white supremacist government impositions on quantifying our Indigeneity should not be the metric by which we prove our own identity or embrace and welcome kin. Enacting and enforcing blood quantum laws is deeply problematic. When Indigenous Peoples are actively centering Indigenous communities to restore and advance relationality with hózhǫ́ (or in ways that are culturally applicable to their distinct Nations) and this is disrupted by deliberate acts of betrayal and lying, trust is difficult to restore. When our lived trauma and historical memory of intergenerational fissure are actively appropriated for individual advancement, it delays and stalls the healing from generations of colonial atrocities, systemic racism, and cultural genocide. Indigenous visual storytellers are creatives whose autonomy—hane'tonomy—and trust with community stories come with responsibilities. Visual storytelling addresses diverse topics and issues, which have included "the beautiful losers, belligerent drunks, failed activists, and born-again traditionalists who make up our community.... It [Indigenous film] will not turn away from complex issues like debates over identity.... To fly, Indian film must embrace the extraordinary complexities of Indian life, in the past and the present. It must face up to both the ugliness and beauty of our circumstances."[92] To work in the field of Indigenous film studies is to embrace "complex issues like debates over identity," which has been tackled by select Indigenous filmmakers (for example, Tracey Deer's *Club Native* from 2008) as critiques against their own communities, challenging their political and cultural sovereignty.

Futures of Restorying and Restoration: Indigenous Visual Storytelling

Visual storytelling and hane'tonomy are not relegated only to the big screen. In fact, 2021 and 2022 are paradigm shifting for Indigenous talent on the small screen. Visual storytelling opportunities became available because of the presence and agency of Indigenous showrunners.[93] Indigenous showrunners will be pivotal to ongoing creative work for visual storytelling. Karissa Valencia (Santa Ynez Chumash) is the Indigenous showrunner of *Spirit Rangers* (2022), a Netflix children's animated series.[94] Another is Sierra Nizhoni Teller Ornelas (Tábąąhá or Edgewater Clan, born for Naakai Diné'é or Mexican People, Tó 'aheedlíinii or Water Flowing Together Clan, and Naakai Diné'é or Mexican People), the cocreator, showrunner, and one of the writers of *Rutherford Falls*, which was touted as the first Native American comedy series on television but was not renewed for a third season.[95] Teller Ornelas shares that "the Navajo are a matrilineal tribe, so it's not weird for women to be in charge. And I had great templates."[96] Her matrilineality is evident through her Clans, and she has a powerful origin story. Teller Ornelas talks about her roots: "When my family survived the Navajo Long Walk—the Navajo equivalent of The Trail of Tears—at Bosque Redondo, the government gave everyone a census number and a name. . . . My great-great-grandfather said, 'I tell the stories of my people, I'm a storyteller.' . . . So, they named him Teller. Working in television is just the continuation of his art form."[97] Teller Ornelas can trace the art form of storytelling back to the Long Walk as well as the origins of her family's colonial-imposed last name. She inherited the art form, and her stories shone brightly in 2021 and 2022.

Rutherford Falls includes Indigenous creatives at all levels of production and highlights the preservation of two distinct histories through intersecting storylines. The fictionalized Minishonka Tribe and the traditional lands on which the fictional town Rutherford Falls now lays claim reflect historical and ongoing contemporary realities, showcased through Indigenous humor. Rematriating visual storytelling with humor and humanity is a long time coming. *Rutherford Falls* is just one of two television series that elevated Indigenous presence on television. *Reservation Dogs*, co-created by Sterlin Harjo (Seminole and Muskogee) and Academy Award–winner Taika Waititi (Māori, Te Whānau-ā-Apanui), debuted to great fanfare. The episodes are directed by various Indigenous creatives: Sydney Freeland (Diné), Blackhorse Lowe (Diné), Erica Tremblay (Seneca-Cayuga), Danis Goulet (Cree-Métis), and Tazbah Rose Chavez (Diné). The shows feature Indigenous actors (cast in lead roles), Indigenous script writers, Indigenous music, and Indigenous aesthetics that uplift Indigenous humor and overcome Indigenous pain.[98]

The seven filmmakers from the 1960s, Bowman's work, the staging of and hosting by Dinétah, and the presence of Diné actors and extras throughout each decade of cinematic history constitute a continuous Diné presence behind and in front of the camera.[99] The intergenerational Diné filmic output made space for creatives in the twenty-first century: the leaves and ears of the figurative corn stalk. Their presence will continue to cultivate stalks in the grand field of Indigenous visual storytelling. Two of the longest-working Diné creatives are Sydney Freeland and Blackhorse Lowe. In my visioning of this chapter as a field of corn, I see them as blossoming and pollinating to make pathways for others. Much like how ancient corn has survived trade routes, colonization, drought, invasive species, and pesticides, Indigenous film has evolved and yet stayed the same as it/they live(s) on. Ancient corn and Indigenous visual storytelling will continue beyond our current lives, and yes, on the Sixth World. Indigenous creatives have demonstrated that the roots of their craft are fertile and have proven fruitful, given the explosion of Indigenous creativity. This is restoring relations. Diné hane'tonomy exemplifies Indigenous film and is an example for other Indigenous Nations who are seeking their own unique space in the field.

The next chapter uses a Diné epistemic lens as analytic and focuses on *Drunktown's Finest* (2014), by Sydney Freeland, to demonstrate what I call "reel restoration." Her director credits cross multiple genres, and she has directed three features and multiple television shows. In 2023, a Netflix documentary called *Rez Ball* will be distributed as well as the highly anticipated Marvel show *Echo* (2023), starring Menominee and Mohican actor Alaqua Cox. To illustrate how Freeland cleverly incorporates hane'tonomy, look for her homage to Tony Hillerman in *Grey's Anatomy*, seasons 17 and 18. Freeland cast Navajo and Soboba actor Robert I. Mesa to play Dr. James (Jim) Chee, whose characterization as Navajo detective Jim Chee was made famous by Hillerman. Dr. Chee is the first (and only) Indigenous physician to appear in the series.

CHAPTER 3

Reel Restoration in *Drunktown's Finest*

> The Holy People lived here in the beginning. They built the first hooghan, made the first weapons, sang the first songs and made the first prayers. Diné language, ceremonies, history, and beliefs began here. This is where we began.
> —LUCI TAPAHONSO, *A RADIANT CURVE*

> They say this land isn't a place to live, it's a place to leave.... Then *why* do People stay?
> —NIZHONI SMILES, CHARACTER IN *DRUNKTOWN'S FINEST*

In this chapter's first epigraph, Diné poet and scholar Luci Tapahonso captures the dawn of the Diné as a radiant becoming, gifted by the Diyin Diné'é, or the Holy People.[1] Conversely, the lamentation of fictitious character Nizhoni Smiles illuminates a collective attitude about Dinétah. Land, both ancestral Navajo land and the contemporary Navajo Reservation, is the focus of their musings, brought into tense dialogue as a place at once loved and loathed, admired and admonished, a place of origin and a place to flee from. These tensions are at the heart of the contemporary Diné diaspora and the focus of the 2014 feature film *Drunktown's Finest*. Sydney Freeland (Diné) wrote and directed this award-winning film, and Robert Redford was the executive producer.

I frame my analysis of *Drunktown's Finest* with the Diné philosophy and epistemology of hózhǫ́.[2] Hózhǫ́ is best translated as to be in a state of wellness, balance, peace, and harmony, culminating in beauty. Tapahonso defines hózhǫ́ as follows: "As a Navajo person, I was taught that my efforts and energy should always be directed at maintaining a state of hózhǫ́—a state of balance with all things around me, living and non-breathing. Hózhǫ́ means that all things should be right and proper. It means maintaining good health, avoiding excess in all things, being thankful and prayerful, adhering to the old stories and songs, believing in oneself, and recognizing one's responsibility towards all aspects of the world we live in."[3]

In this film, Freeland illuminates how Diné identity, self-representation, and belonging are strained by exposing the intricacies and complexities of contemporary Navajo lives and places, which are at odds with hózhǫ́. I propose the concept of "reel restoration" because "reel" is polysemous: it is a metonym for film, and as a verb, "reel" is defined as "to stand or walk or run unsteadily" and "to be shaken mentally or physically."[4]

An abundance of scholarship examines representations of Indigenous People in film, and in tandem with my analysis anchored by hózhǫ́, I turn to Michelle H. Raheja's *Reservation Reelism* and Joanna Hearne's *Native Recognition* to seek restoration in *Drunktown's Finest*.[5] I argue that "reel restoration" conveys how Freeland's film defends the Diné from decades of aggressive, violent, and anti-Indigenous imagery, restoring Indigeneity, humanity, and ultimately hózhǫ́. Acknowledging the significance of hane', k'é (kinship and family), ceremony, and language and how they are anchored in Navajo land, the film addresses disharmony, sickness, alcoholism, and disconnection and seeks restoration through hózhǫ́.[6]

Freeland renders a visual counternarrative through hane'tonomy of her hometown, Gallup, New Mexico, featured in an episode of the ABC program *20/20* that aired in the late 1980s. It highlighted the alcohol epidemic and gave Gallup the derogatory nickname "Drunk Town, USA," violently eclipsing all other Gallup citizens.[7] Jake Skeets's poem "Drunktown" (2018) describes the namesake as *"Drunk is the punch. Town a gasp."*[8] Local non-Indigenous business owners and racists have historically seen Gallup as reeling with Indigenous alcoholism, chaos, sickness, and disconnect, or what Diné speakers call hóchxǫ́ (the opposite of hózhǫ́).

Drunktown's Finest contextualizes why the nickname is problematic; it is Freeland's attempt to "show how diverse the reservation is, where the three main characters came from. They each represent different communities."[9] Freeland was influenced by Alejandro González Iñárritu's 2000 feature film *Amores Perros*, in which three storylines intersect in Mexico City.[10] Similarly, *Drunktown's Finest* cross-cuts three storylines of Luther "Sick Boy" Maryboy (Jeremiah Bitsui), Nizhoni Smiles (MorningStar Angeline), and Felixia John (Carmen Moore) in the fictional border town of Dry Lake.[11] As representative of diverse Diné cultural and political identities, Sick Boy's, Nizhoni's, and Felixia's on-screen journeys unfold from their aversion to the Navajo Nation to embracing it, through hózhǫ́. Through contemporary depictions of Navajo People and places, Freeland adds to the growing field of Indigenous filmmakers telling their own stories, engaging in hane'tonomy, or what is recognized in the field as narrative, cinematic, or visual sovereignty, as discussed in the previous chapter.[12] Her work offers a corrective to Hollywood and mainstream media makers who film with forked lenses, as ABC's *20/20* did.

In *Drunktown's Finest*, the recognition, enactment, and embodying of Diné epistemologies are part of each character's journey on the "virtual reservation," a concept coined by Raheja. She explains that "the virtual reservation is as complex and paradoxical as its geographical counterpart. It is a site that displays Indigenous knowledges and practices in sharp relief against competing colonial discourses."[13] To come to a state of hózhǫ́ and restoration, the three lead characters must confront challenges to their unique Diné identities that pervade Diné homelands, such as racism, transphobia, sexism, toxic Indigenous masculinities, anti-Christian rhetoric, and socioeconomic and systemic discrimination.[14]

I commence my analysis by focusing first on the introductory rez / border town tour montage of *Drunktown's Finest*, in which Freeland employs a handheld camera, resulting in documentary-style realism.[15] The handheld technique is necessary in *Drunktown's Finest* because it exposes Gallup's finest, portraying an accurate sense of the diversity in Gallup, which was not captured by ABC's film crew. Freeland's eye captures what outsiders see (buildings, façades, signage, and art on walls) and goes beyond these to film actual Indigenous People as a way to foreground the fictional narrative's complexities. After analyzing the montage, I organize the chapter into three parts that demonstrate "reel restoration." Each character's arc and storyline intersect at (ceremonial) running, k'é (kinship grounded in matriarchy), and the hane' that teach of hózhǫ́.[16] The stories on the virtual reservation parallel those of many living Indigenous People, on actual reservations, as well as in border towns, urban areas, and rural communities.

In Chaos It Begins

Drunktown's Finest opens with a fast-motion, time-lapse establishing shot, cycling from darkness to early morning dawn to daylight. The mise-en-scène features a neighborhood from the north side of the town in the foreground, with a mountain in the far distance accompanied by the diegetic sound of a train whistle blowing. Nighttime traffic lights zoom on the distant highway as the clouds overhead usher in the sun. Diné teachings necessitate that human beings talk to the Holy People while offering tádídíín (corn pollen), at dawn, prior to the rising of the sun. These Diné practices begin with the Diné saying "kodóó hózhǫ́ dooleeł," translated to English as "it begins in beauty" or "in beauty it begins."[17] Instead of opening with traditional Diné protocol to greet the sun, *Drunktown's Finest* opens with Nizhoni's lament, reflected in the chapter's second epigraph, jiní: "They say this land isn't a place to live; it's a place to leave.... Then *why* do People stay?"[18] In English, the Navajo expression "jiní" means "they say" or "they said" and is normally attributed to the Holy People's teachings, or about teachings passed down orally, jiní. Kelley and Francis write, "Traditionalists themselves consider jiní to be the most stable holder of knowledge."[19] Tapahonso says jiní "refers to people who told the story at some time long ago."[20] The colonial tactic of weakening and disrupting Diné language has resulted in the deeply internalized erasure of the meaning of land, oral stories, and how land directly relates to Diné identity. Nizhoni's utterance of "they say" is subtle and is completely overshadowed by her bigger complaint about place, revealing that *how* we tell a story as well as what these stories carry have been co-opted by the colonial lie. One lie is that Diné Bikéyah is not livable, but in the film the place that Nizhoni is referring to is the fictional town called Dry Lake, based on the real, identifiable border

FIGURE 8 Opening scene of *Drunktown's Finest*. From *Drunktown's Finest* trailer.

town named Gallup, which is situated between two of the four Diné sacred mountains. The three main characters call Dry Lake home, yet they all want to escape.

In interviews, Freeland said that she wanted to explore contrasts "between beauty/ugly, contemporary/traditional, Western/non-Western. You have some people who leave the reservation and there are pros and cons to that, but it's the same for people who stay."[21] Teamed with cinematographer Peter Holland, Freeland offers such contrasts in the first two minutes of the film through a fascinating visual narrative montage by intercutting distinct scenes from everyday life in Gallup. The introductory sequence fluctuates between documentary, handheld footage, and fictional scenes from the feature film. Additionally, the two-minute montage keeps pace with the twang of a guitar, commencing the song "Beggar to a King," written by Jiles Perry Richardson Jr., "The Big Bopper." Freeland chose a version performed by the Wingate Valley Boys, a Diné country-western cover band that had reservation fame in the 1960s:

> I have [had] sunk as low as a man could go,
> the world has turned me down.
> Then you pick[ed] me up
> and you kiss[ed] me a sweet,
> and change[d] a beggar into a king.
> Yes, you took the rags from off of my back
> and you gave me love to keep me warm.
> Yes, you pick[ed] me up
> and you kiss[ed] me sweet,
> and change[d] a beggar into a king.[22]

The Big Bopper's original lyrics use past-tense verbs, whereas the Wingate Valley Boys altered the verbs to reflect the present tense, suggesting an ongoing search for hope and restoration. The lyrics anchor us to the reeling realities that the citizens of Dry Lake, or as Freeland reclaims, "Drunktown's Finest," face every day, as captured by handheld, traveling shots, taken from the passenger seat of Nizhoni's moving car. Throughout the montage, the camera quickly alternates contrasting shots that reflect varying degrees of difference in terms of setting, kinetics, patriotism, poverty, commerce, Indigenous cultural pride, and youth culture. As dawn gives way to daybreak and Nizhoni's anguish over "place" lingers, the film begins with a shot of the actual Highway 491 heading southbound, focusing on a close-up of a fictitious sign: "WELCOME to DRY LAKE NEW MEXICO. Population 20,000." There are two young boys riding their bikes on the side of the busy highway, alluding to the next generation heading into Dry Lake. The name "Dry Lake" is itself a contrast, or better, a paradox. Gallup was once called by its Navajo name, Na'nízhoozhí, which is best translated as "spanned across" or as "the place of the bridge" and refers to an old pedestrian bridge that spanned across a body of water that is now dried out.[23] Not only has the water that once gave life to the area lost its literal currency (it is dry), but water has also lost its cultural currency. Tó (water) plays a prominent role in traditional Diné literary and oral stories and still is valued and used in spiritual and cultural practices. In *Drunktown's Finest*, however, there is a glaring absence of the cultural recognition of tó. Despite the "dry" reservations that border Dry Lake, it is depicted as a place where the community is drowning in distinct sorrows, mostly caused by the abuse of "firewater," the beverage of choice that fuels the stories of the main characters.

After the welcome sign, the camera immediately cuts to hitchhikers walking on the side of the littered highway, heading into town or returning home from an all-nighter, perhaps. The timeless beauty of the red rocks of Navajo land contrasts with Dry Lake's once prominent, now dilapidated, motels that line the historic Route 66. The U.S. flag and New Mexico state flag wave side by side, a patriotic salute to the colonizers. The camera also rests on an oversized mural of the Navajo Code Talkers, featuring the late Samuel Billison and other Navajo warriors from the United States Marine Corps.

The introductory montage highlights several instances of public intoxication, poverty, and despair similar to those images featured in the *20/20* episode. In one shot, we see a man lying in a drunken slumber, next to a chain-link fence. In another shot, a security officer stands over a man lying on the sidewalk, struggling to stand. Freeland zooms in on the high number of jaywalking hitchhikers, drunk and sober, which accurately depicts everyday Gallup.[24] The camera captures hitchhikers walking in the foreground, while an abandoned cargo train sits on the tracks in the background from the railway line that once brought prosperity to Gallup through the Union Pacific Railroad. Diné historian Jennifer Nez Denetdale's review of the film states: "The three characters' trials foreshadow the state of border towns like Gallup that sit on indigenous [sic] lands of the Navajo and Zuni, places where systemic violence in the form of poverty, racism, discrimination and the exploitation of Native peoples, primarily Navajos, is ongoing."[25] Freeland's efforts at contrasting said systemic violence result in a dizzying array of images of impoverished yet moving people juxtaposed with images of static dwellings that constitute diverse neighborhoods in Dry Lake. Freeland contrasts the poverty of the street scenes to the wealth of prosperous neighborhoods, ranging from affluent, gated communities, featuring multilevel stucco homes with tile shingles, to middle-class single-family, ranch-style homes, to the more common trailer park accessible only via dirt road.

Gallup thrives on the exploitation of Indigenous artistry (by way of the euphemism: tourism). Freeland exposes this through drive-by images of pawnshops and trading posts, notorious for selling "Indian jewelry" and arts and crafts at inflated prices. She contrasts these images of façades and buildings with scenes of actual Indigenous artisans and their booths in front of what appears to be Earl's Family Restaurant. Located on the historic Route 66 in Gallup, Earl's Family Restaurant was opened five generations ago by a settler family. Today Earl (one of the great-grandsons, who is in his late sixties) can be seen talking with customers, and he continues to support Indigenous artisans through direct selling. At Earl's, Indigenous crafters set up booths outside the doors of the restaurant, and they can also go table to table inside the restaurant to sell their handcrafted wares directly to buyers who are dining. While pawn shops and traders charge inflated prices, Earl's Family Restaurant plays a pivotal role in Gallup tourism and offers sellers and buyers the opportunity to barter and build community as buyers wait for their meals, reflecting an intermingling of cultures that offers a dynamic to the town's reputation.

The perspective switches from kinetic cinematography to documentary-style, still photography. A skateboarder wearing dark shades, toque, and headphones smiles directly into the camera. Freeland pays homage to Indigenous skateboarder culture, a popular sport in Indian Country. Many Indigenous entrepreneurs, like Apacheskateboards.com, Wounded Knee Skateboards, 4wheelwarpony, and Native Threads (who sponsor professional Navajo skateboarder Bryant Chapo), design and produce skate decks and apparel that combine Indigeneity with skater culture, promoting wellness and providing a healthy outlet for Indigenous youth.[26] Freeland juxtaposes this smiling close-up with the scarred and tattooed back of a gang member. The tattoo spells "Native" across his shoulders. Indigenous gangs attract a staggering proportion of youth on and off the rez. This scene ends with a group shot of the gang members, donned in various hues of blue and plaid, complete with blue headbands knotted at the front, as they flash their gang sign, what appears to be the letters *V* and *W*, directly at the camera. They cradle an empty bottle of vodka, the focal point of this tightly framed mise-en-scène.

Transitioning back to the traveling shot, the nondiegetic gospel song still audible in the background, Freeland's gaze settles on the sign of the historic El Rancho Hotel, where Hollywood celebrities like John Wayne and Ronald Reagan stayed. Both are famed for their roles in Westerns as cowboys, as *indian* killers. She then contrasts the El Rancho Hotel, temporary home to Hollywood's white heroes, by cutting to a jail cell that houses brown inmates in various states of inebriation.[27] The juxtaposition of heroic cowboys and drunk *indians* clearly nods to the *20/20* episode that inspired Freeland's counternarrative.

Freeland contrasts the town of Dry Lake with the reservation in the next scene, in which a hitchhiker walks along a dirt road, wearing white heels, a denim miniskirt, a red top, a cropped sweater, and a jacket slung over her right shoulder. She hails a ride and jumps into a white pickup truck. There is a jump cut to the truck pulling off the side of the road. The dominant image is of a sign, featuring two large emblems of the Great Seal of the Navajo Nation, that says: "NOW LEAVING DRY LAKE. ENTERING NAVAJO RESERVATION." The cinematography shifts to capture a Navajo aesthetic in which landscape figures prominently: sheep and goats overrun a two-lane highway, which is a testament that twentieth-century governmental policy to reduce livestock on the Diné Nation is on the mend.[28] The natural topography of sage, Navajo tea, and piñon trees is sliced by dirt roads that lead to home sites. Finally, the introductory rez / border town tour montage ends by driving by Red Rock National Park, which is east of Gallup. We are back in town, on the historic Route 66 in front of a store covered in oversized murals that convey southwestern Indigenous motifs: a sandpainting, a silversmith, a basket weaver, a potter, a rug weaver, and pottery. A year after the film was released, Freeland was invited to the National Museum of the American Indian's Gustav Heye Center in New

York to screen *Drunktown's Finest*. She was quoted in the *Navajo Times* saying, "You have all the traditional art forms—painting, weaving, pottery, silversmithing—that are all forms of storytelling. Filmmaking combines all the other art forms into one. It's another form of storytelling."[29] Her concentrated focus on these iconic Diné storytelling methods was a commentary on the significance of visual storytelling, depicting her unique Diné-centered decoloniality as hane'tonomy.

The final shot in this sequence rests on a welcome sign that is framed by more artistic storywork featuring a Navajo wedding vase, a woven rug, a Navajo wedding basket, an ear of corn, and a squash-blossom necklace. The array of images of Diné material cultural items evokes stories from precontact narratives as well as nod to postcontact influences. The Diné art featured on the mural is in stark contrast to a lone man whose jeans are muddied at the knees, one of "Drunktown's Finest." He is not wearing a squash-blossom necklace, nor does he have any of the accoutrements that signal Navajo Indigeneity or a connection to our storied origins as he stands in front of the proud mural. The lone man is never credited, as this shot is part of the handheld, documentary-style intercuts. He is not an actor. His coincidental appearance in front of the grand mural is one of the many contrasts that Freeland sets up in the opening sequence. I read this particular scene as amplifying the wealth of Diné culture to outsiders, albeit commodified via a façade, an aesthetic mural. The unnamed Indigenous person holding up the wall represents thousands of unnamed Indigenous People who uplift the tourist industry and whose diversity gets reduced to a trope. Their lives and stories remain isolated and unknowable, and it is at this juncture that Freeland strategically concludes the rez / border town tour montage with the introduction of the fictional narrative, in which she brings into focus three diverse individuals whose lives and stories are universal and familiar, diverging from the trope.

Drunktown's Finest cross-cuts three storylines of the lives of Nizhoni Smiles (MorningStar Angeline), Luther "Sick Boy" Maryboy (Jeremiah Bitsui), and Felixia John (Carmen Moore). It is 4:38 a.m. in Dry Lake and all the characters' stories begin. Sick Boy is reeling. He is drunk and staggers from a store and is subsequently thrown in jail for assaulting a police officer. Nizhoni is sleepless. She suffers from insomnia and is frantically sketching a vivid nightmare that startled her from a restless sleep. Felixia is earning money. Sitting in the front seat of a parked vehicle with a john, she is sexually servicing and getting serviced.

Sick Boy is the archetype for men as macho thugs and wants to become a warrior (in the army) to get his family off the rez. Nizhoni represents the Christian, educated urban community; she is called "Bible Lady" by Leroy-Leroy (James Junes) and Copenhagen (Ernest Tsosie III) because she wants to be a missionary. Felixia is a transgender woman, whose daily struggle brings to light the cruel realities of being 2SLGBTQI+, yet she aspires to be an off-rez, international model. Through their overlapping stories, Freeland allegorizes them to illustrate states of being and striving to become hózhǫ́.

Running Away

For Diné, running before the Holy People and the sun wake up promotes wellness, instills perseverance, and builds physical and emotional strength and endurance; it is associated with ceremonies, particularly the Kinaaldá ceremony. Daily early dawn "running to catch the sun" is something that contemporary youth should continue to be taught beyond Kinaaldá ceremonial settings.[30] In this context, Freeland sets up the characters' individual conflicts. Sick Boy, Nizhoni, and Felixia have either witnessed or participated in the violence that pervades the Navajo Reservation: domestic violence, gang-related violence, racism, overt and covert homophobia and transphobia, jealousy and hostility perpetuated by alcohol and drug abuse, sexual and gambling addictions, and intolerance and fear. At the beginning of the film, they do not see the value in their land and home and seek ways to leave, to run away. They do not see their endurance as ceremonial, which is ironic given that *Drunktown's Finest* begins on the first day of a Kinaaldá ceremony.

The Kinaaldá is one part of the Hózhǫ́ǫ́jí (Blessing Way) ceremony, originating from the story of Asdzą́ą́ Nádleehé, or Changing Woman, the most revered Navajo deity.[31] Coupled with the fact that the stories explain that Asdzą́ą́ Nádleehé created the first four Clans (k'éí), this establishes her as the mother of all Diné. The Kinaaldá lasts four days and celebrates a female's change from girlhood to womanhood by way of her first menses. *Drunktown's Finest* begins on the first day of Max's (played by Magdalena

Begay) change. She is Sick Boy's younger sister, and he has custody of her. The Diné believe that the person undergoing the ceremony becomes Kinaaldá and embodies Changing Woman. *Drunktown's Finest* is framed by Max's Kinaaldá. The movie spans four days, and while Max is shedding her youth to womanhood by undergoing the physical demands of the Kinaaldá ceremony, which include predawn running toward the east and corn grinding, Sick Boy's, Nizhoni's, and Felixia's trials take precedence—their running is not ceremonial.[32]

Luther "Sick Boy" Maryboy is twenty-one years old and wants to join the military. While his birth name is loaded with Christian imagery, his chosen nickname, Sick Boy, which he is widely recognized by, is critical for reel restoration. It is no accident that Freeland gave this revealing appellation to Luther, for she expressed her interest in exploring contrasts in *Drunktown's Finest*. States of beauty contrast with states of ugliness. In Diné bizaad (Navajo language), the term *hóchxǫ́* means "ugliness, sickness or chaos," which is epitomized in Sick Boy's character.[33] When we meet him at 4:38 a.m., he stumbles out the doors of a twenty-four-hour 7-2-11 convenience store, flipping the employees a middle finger while cursing them. To reel is to behave violently and disorderly, which he continues to do after he exits the 7-2-11. As he is publicly urinating on the side of the store, a Navajo Nation police van pulls up. The officer, his hair tied in a traditional tsiiyéél (hair bun), asks if Sick Boy has been drinking. Sick Boy, clearly drunk, denies he has done anything, and while the officer attempts to cuff Sick Boy, he slaps the officer in the face. Continuing to violently resist arrest, Sick Boy is thrown in the van, landing him in jail for the remainder of the night. Sick Boy is a ringleader and regularly engages in such chaotic and disharmonious behavior with his thug friends Julius (Kiowa Gordon) and Ruckus (Naát'áaníí Nez Means).[34] As a soon-to-be father, however, he also knows he needs to straighten up, and to do so, he wants to join the army, which will take him away from the rez and from his circumstances. It is not until the end of the film that Sick Boy introduces himself as Luther to the medicine man, Harmon John (Richard Ray Whitman), who is conducting Max's Kinaaldá.[35]

Nizhoni is seventeen years old and has plans to attend Calvin College, a Christian liberal arts college in Michigan. Unlike Sick Boy and Felixia, Nizhoni was whisked away from a life on the rez during her infancy. Her birth parents died in an alcohol-related car accident, and she was adopted by white, middle-class parents, whose surname is Smiles.[36] Nizhoni has been primarily educated in Michigan, and her adoptive mother, Phoebe, taught her to fear and to avoid the reservation and her biological "alcoholic" family. It is erroneous to say she is running away from the rez. Nearing adulthood and on her way to college, Nizhoni is drawn to her biological family and secretly searches for them. When we meet her at 4:38 a.m., she has been jarred awake from a nightmare in which she saw wreckage from a car accident, red handprints, and flashing red lights. Her mind reeling, she sketches in her dream journal a white horse with red handprints all over it. This "painted pony" foreshadows the identity of her biological parents, whose names were Darlene and David "Buster" Pinto. A pinto is a spotted or painted horse, and during one scene involving her evening community service work, she chanced upon one. Just as her biological parents met their death in a car accident, so does a white horse that has been struck by a woman driving under the influence of drugs; in her attempt to save the horse, this drugged-up person leaves her bloodied handprints all over it, just as Nizhoni's dream prophesized.[37] The accident happened on the rez, not in Dry Lake, and confirmed what Phoebe held as truth: "I knew your family. I knew the world they came from and you know what, if I lived under the conditions they did, I probably would have drank myself to death too." Phoebe's sentiments echo Raheja's description of the public's understanding of the rez as a place of "dysfunction, and disappearance."[38] In the end, Nizhoni is not running from the rez but attracted to it; she is running from judgment of the rez and from Dry Lake's reputation.

At 4:39 a.m. we are introduced to Felixia. Her lustful eyes, prominent dimples, and full red lips, enhanced with intimate chiaroscuro lighting, fade to the background as her male customer casts his gaze onto her tumescence, which, though blurred, dominates the frame. Practically salivating, the john wants to suck Felixia, and she asserts that this will cost extra. She takes his money, and despite fumbling over loud children's toys that are in the front seat of the vehicle, he prevails and proceeds to pleasure Felixia. Felixia's age is not disclosed, but she procures a fake ID in order to drink and to enter the casino. Most importantly, the ID confirms her identity as a female so that she can model in the Women of the Navajo (WON) calendar, which will be her ticket out of Dry Lake, a place where homophobia results in violence, as evidenced by a recent assault that her gay friend Eugene (Wambli Eagleman) endured. When Felixia sees Eugene's big black eye, she is shocked and empathetic, and she remains adamant about competing for a spot in the calendar. Eugene is equally concerned for Felixia's safety, but her genuine concern for his mistreatment prompts him to exclaim, "Give 'em hell" at the WON calendar auditions. Encouraged, Felixia compares her fake ID alongside the original and observes: "Wow, I can't even tell which one is fake!" For Felixia to become an authenticated female, albeit from a fake government document, is to have a bit more protection against trans- and homophobic violence. Eugene and Felixia know what it is like to "be real" in a world that encourages violence. Felixia is still the target of hostility, loneliness, and even jealousy from other women who are threatened by Felixia's attractive exterior, and for these reasons, she seeks to run away from the rez.

The film opens with the protagonists' parallel storylines, introducing them as distinct from each other. The day that Sick Boy is discharged from jail, he spends the daylight hours getting high with his friends instead of running errands for his pregnant partner. In a chapter that I co-authored with Robert Alexander Innes, "Transforming Toxic Indigenous Masculinity: A Critical Indigenous Masculinities and Indigenous Film Studies Approach to *Drunktown's Finest*," we discuss how their chance encounter at the checkout culminates in a night of flirtatious partying that ends abruptly when Sick Boy discovers Felixia is a transwoman. His transphobia is in direct opposition to traditional Diné teachings, and we argue that the film addresses issues of toxic Indigenous masculinities while being framed by the very teachings that the protagonists resist. At the house party, Sick Boy and Felixia toast to "becoming adults and shit and getting the fuck out of here!" Running away is not a prominent motif of the majority of Diné-directed films, according to Randolph Lewis. He identifies the homecoming motif as common in the works of Blackhorse Lowe, Nanobah Becker, and Bennie Klain.[39] The homecoming motif is not new in Indigenous literary arts, as it is a trope found in works by select authors like N. Scott Momaday, Leslie Marmon Silko, and James Welch from the era often referred to as the "Native American Renaissance." For Lewis, homecoming in the Diné films was informed by the protagonists' search for the restoration of kinship relations through wellness, which constitutes hózhǫ́. Freeland's work departs from other Diné filmmakers at the intersection of land and homecoming.

Sick Boy, Nizhoni, and Felixia are strategically introduced before sunrise, a time traditionally reserved for Diné prayer and early dawn running as part of lifelong wellness and hózhǫ́. Their lives, reeling with chaos, disharmony, and violence, are in dire need of restoration. Their solutions are, at the outset, to run away from the rez, reflecting a collective consciousness of some contemporary Diné youth.

K'é (Kinship): Family and Matriarchy

> I understood that who I am is my mother, her mother, and my great-grandmother.
>
> —LUCI TAPAHONSO, *SÁANII DAHATAAŁ*

While homesick and feeling lonely atop the Eiffel Tower, Luci Tapahonso offered tádídíín (corn pollen) in prayer and recognized that her identity, strength, and harmony came from k'é, or matrilineal kinship, as celebrated in her 1993 book of poetry, *Sáanii Dahataal: The Women Are Singing*. Having left her homeland to pursue higher education and a career, like so many Indigenous youth are encouraged to do today, Tapahonso writes and sings of the criticality of land, kinship, and staying connected to communities. Sick Boy, Nizhoni, and Felixia seek hózhǫ́ (although they never once utter this) through running away, and in doing so, they overlook k'é, a traditionality that they have access to.

K'é, or kinship, is determined by the matrilineal Diné Clan system. Each person who identifies as Navajo has four Clans (k'éí), beginning with their mother's Clan (whose Clan derives from her mother's Clan). In *Navajo Sacred Places*, Kelley and Francis echo this sentiment: "Being a Navajo was (and still is) defined by one's ties to Navajo clans, named kinship groups whose members inherit membership from their mothers."[40] When addressing other Navajos, Elders, and leaders, it is common courtesy to introduce oneself in the Navajo language, adhering to Clan protocol: the Navajo person's mother's Clan is named, followed by the paternal mother's Clan, whom they are "born for," followed by the chei's (maternal father's) Clan, and ending with the paternal father's Clan (nálí). In addition to informing others where one comes from, observing Clans also secures relatives and staves off potential forbidden (incestuous) partnerships, which I explicate in the next chapter.

The matrifocal teachings that elevate Asdzą́ą́ Nádleehé as the model for all women to aspire to are related in the Navajo origin stories. These stories, originally oral, have been preserved in writing, ensuring a Diné continuum that privileges k'é teachings. Though accessible, the stories of Asdzą́ą́ Nádleehé's reverence are set in the background in this film, and modern-day matriarchs (i.e., Women of the Navajo) are looked up to instead. The Women of the Navajo (WON) is an actual calendar that was begun in 1992 by owner-manager Larry Thompson and was one of the first to feature Indigenous models for consumption.[41] Forty years prior to that, in 1952, the first Miss Navajo was crowned in a pageant that continues annually on the Navajo Nation. Navajo women (unmarried but over eighteen years old) compete for this revered title and are judged on their intimate knowledge of and fluency in Diné bizaad, Navajo culture, and Diné history. Contestants must further demonstrate their cultural and culinary expertise by sharing a Diné talent, preparing fry bread, and, uniquely, butchering a sheep for community consumption. Filmmaker Billy Luther (Diné, Hopi, and Laguna Pueblo) showcased the stories of contestants struggling as they vie for the title in the documentary *Miss Navajo* (2007). The Miss Navajo Pageant has never privileged Western definitions of beauty, yet it continues to motivate young Diné women to strive for this esteemed title, which elevates the victor as a Navajo Nation ambassador, modeled after Asdzą́ą́ Nádleehé. Freeland employs rivalry as a narrative arc for Felixia, highlighting the competitive nature of the selection process, which promotes Western standards of beauty. Each model selected poses with Navajo jewelry and fashion, signaling that the pageant is "culturally traditional."

Felixia is selected as a finalist for the WON calendar after impressing the judges with her Diné-language fluency. As finalists individually walk on to the stage, ostensibly with their introductory speeches fully memorized in English, Juror Roweena (Amber-Dawn Bear Robe) abruptly asks them: "Há't'ííshdóone'ę́?" (What are your Clans?).[42] The first two contenders do not understand Navajo, and they are immediately dismissed and disqualified. At her turn, Felixia—dressed in a body-positive, form-fitting black satin dress and sparkly stilettos—walks across the stage to the center and begins her self-introduction in Bilagáana bizaad (English) but is immediately interrupted by Roweena: "Há't'ííshdóone'ę́?" Without hesitation, Felixia replies:

"Shí éí Felixia John yinishyé." [My name is Felixia John.]
  [Her first Clan is inaudible.]
  "Tsi'naajinii báshíshchíín." [I'm born for the "Black Streaked Wood People" Clan.]
  "Mą'ii deeshgiizhnii da shicheii." [My maternal grandfather is from the "Jemez Clan." (Some also translate this as "Coyote Pass People" Clan.)]
  "Hónágháahnii da shinálí." [My paternal grandfather is from the "One Who Walks Around" Clan.]

Roweena praises Felixia for her Navajo-language fluency and adds, "Beautiful girls are a dime a dozen. But the women in this calendar must represent *us*." Felixia exposes her connection to Diné lifeways and kinship ties and tells the judges that her grandparents raised her and instilled Diné bizaad and teachings, what Hearne says are "representational acts of familial or genealogical recognition."[43] Though Felixia's mother and father are absent, she has her grandparents. Despite Felixia's cultural capital and familial support, she exposes how complex her relationship is to the community, as she prefers to forgo these gifts on the rez, for becoming an international fashion model. Because of her knowledge of k'éí, she is selected as one of the twelve models for the WON calendar, bringing into sharp focus just how valuable Navajo language and teachings are.

Freeland creates a juxtaposition of Western and Diné hermeneutics of beauty by making this issue of the WON calendar the first-ever swimsuit edition. Larry Thompson opposed this scanty depiction of his product and stated: "Women are taught not to be so flashy, just to be modest. I think some Navajo women still see this [calendar] as some sort of small violation of that.... Grandmas and aunties, they're the ones that look at it. You don't want to embarrass them at all."[44] Thompson and I corresponded by email on September 26, 2015, and he further attested that there will not be a WON swimsuit issue in real life. In the swimsuit photo-shoot scene, competing model Karah (Shauna Baker) puts crushed VirileGrow into an energy drink.[45] Under the guise of congeniality, Karah offers this drink to Felixia, who has been working all night. During Felixia's debut as a swimsuit model, this tainted energy drink gives her an onstage erection. Reeling, humiliated, and in tears, she runs off stage. Her dreams of becoming a model are shattered because of Karah's hóchx̨ǫ. Preempting real life, in which trans women are not allowed to compete for a spot in the calendar, Freeland exposes the transphobia that is prevalent. In 2016, activist Sharnell Paul claimed that she was discriminated against and disqualified for being featured in the real WON calendar because she is transgender, which Thompson denies.[46] Cultural knowledge and community connections are not necessarily valued for one to be recognized as an international model. Similarly, transphobia and external markers of beauty in the Western context are at odds with Diné matriarchal teachings and hózhǫ́.

Unlike Felixia, Sick Boy does not offer his kinship relations in the film. He does, however, speak some Navajo, which is illuminated when he gives Max, his little sister, a tip on how to remember the Navajo word for elephant. She is seated outside on the stairs, reviewing her Diné bizaad flashcards, when he comes home after a few hours locked up. He notices that Max is wearing a turquoise necklace and finds out that she has begun menstruating and that her Kinaaldá preparations are in place. As legal guardian of Max, Sick Boy carries the responsibility to convey matriarchal teachings based on the stories of Changing Woman, but he does not appear to have the tools and maturity to do so. Sick Boy has a severed relationship with their mother, Sheila (Rulan Tangen), who is the one that is truly sick. Sheila is an addict who lives in a motel with her abusive husband and young son. Her toxicity has been passed on to Sick Boy, as opposed to passing on Diné epistemologies that constitute matriarchal teachings and kinship responsibilities, or a life fulfilled with and by hózhǫ́. Sick Boy's pregnant partner, Angela (Elizabeth Frances), asks him to pick up Max's moccasins for the ceremony, which are at Sheila's house. Although he does not want to see his mom, Sick Boy agrees to pick up the moccasins and even offers to pick up dinner. However, he distracts himself and gets high with his friends and ends up partying with strangers instead. Sick Boy's initial encounter with Felixia happens in the check-out line at the grocery store, where they tease each other. The male gaze is in full effect as the shot pans from her heels upward to where his gaze rests: on her breasts. In the parking lot, he offers Felixia a ride to the party. Their body language and flirtatious banter reveal their mutual attraction as they merely exchange first names. The relevance of his knowledge of the Navajo kinship protocol is critical at this point in the film, because when there is a fleeting attraction between two Navajo People, it is common to jokingly ask, "What are your Clans?" in order to eliminate potential incestuous relations. At no point do they do this, which could have cued him to their familial connections. Because Sheila relinquished her maternal rights, Max is undergoing the Kinaaldá with guidance from Grandma Ruth (Toni Olver), who happens to be Felixia's grandmother as well as Nizhoni's.

Nizhoni is home from Michigan for the summer; while doing community service for her college scholarship, she actively seeks her maternal grandparents, Ruth and Harmon John. Because she was adopted, she has not been taught the value of k'é. In fact, Phoebe, the matrilineal figure in her life, legally (and secretly) severed Nizhoni's relationship to her maternal birth grandparents. Throughout Nizhoni's life, Phoebe tainted and fabricated what rez life is like, calling it "dangerous." Learning deception from Phoebe, Nizhoni secretly goes to the reservation, a place she has been taught to fear and loathe. She knocks on the door, and Grandma Ruth answers. Nizhoni asks if this is the home of Buster and Darlene Pinto's family, and Ruth realizes this is her long-lost granddaughter. She embraces Nizhoni, crying and calling her "shi yázhí, awéé!" (endearing Navajo kinship terms that best translate to "my little one, my baby"). After a long embrace, they sit surrounded by family photos and begin the process of healing and getting to know each other. Nizhoni was always led to believe that her maternal grandparents never tried to contact her as a child. Grandma Ruth tells Nizhoni that Phoebe hired attorneys and enforced an order of no contact. This is devastating, as Nizhoni realizes she was lied to. She was robbed of matriarchal teachings and the security of k'é. Though Nizhoni is reeling from this news, her k'é, her kinship ties and matriarchal connections, are now in the process of restoration and rematriation, marking her own healing and solidifying her Diné identity.

Tapahonso's poem conveys hózhǫ́ through matrilineality; she understands herself through her maternal genealogy, which goes all the way back to Asdzą́ą́ Nádleehé. Sick Boy respects these teachings, but because of the disharmony with his mother, k'é is temporarily disrupted. As Max's older brother, he is expected by cultural protocol to play an active role in her Kinaaldá. I was twelve years old, rough-housing in the front yard of my grams Sylvia's Shiprock home with a friend, when I started my period. My grandmother was so happy for me, as she ran around the home in excitement. I was confused, as I did not understand what there was to be excited about since I did not really know the significance of the Kinaaldá and k'é. I was thrilled she was happy for me until she mentioned she was about to call all the uncles and men in the family. I was immediately ashamed, embarrassed, and begged Grams not to tell anyone. I never did go through my own Kinaaldá, which I always regretted and corrected for my daughter when she became a woman. Even though we were living in Canada, far away from the four sacred mountains on the prairies, we had bags of whole dried corn, yucca, and all the Kinaaldá necessities on hand, as I had been preparing for my daughter's Kinaaldá for years. In 2018, with blessings from my New Mexico family and support from my Cree partner, our Cree, Métis, Saulteaux, Choctaw, Sac and Fox, Quapaw k'é, family and friends, we celebrated my daughter's transformation. Each morning, she ran toward the east, farther than the day before; she ground corn; and we all helped prepare and bake the alkaan (corn meal cake baked underground) as she became Kinaaldá with hózhǫ́. Like me, Felixia and Nizhoni also did not experience their own Kinaaldá ceremonies as they came into womanhood. Nizhoni was raised by non-Diné Christians, and as a trans woman, Felixia will never experience a first menses.[47] Felixia will come to understand her importance as nádleeh, "who were no more female than they were male," as retold in Navajo journey narratives.[48] Nádleeh also means "one who is constantly changing" or simply "changing," as in the deity Changing Woman, Asdzą́ą́ Nádleehé. Connected by the matriarch, Grandma Ruth, they all have the opportunity to restore their understanding and appreciation of k'é, which is one critical component to come to a state of hózhǫ́.

Restoring Hózhǫ́

In the Diné language, nizhóní conveys the English adjective "beautiful." The Diné word *hózhǫ́*, defined earlier as wellness, balance, peace, and harmony, conveys an idea of being in the state of beauty (but not as an adjective, like nizhóní). The words *nizhóní* and *hózhǫ́* share the stem *zhó*, which indicates various contexts of "beauty" and acts as verb, adjective, and noun. Nizhoni's name literally means "beautiful," and her friend Elmer (Kenneth Ruthardt) greets her with "Hello, Ms. Beautiful!," to which she dismissively replies, "That is so sweet!" Paul Zolbrod clarifies that notions of beauty and ugliness are "not taken as two entirely separate forces in Navajo thought. Rather, they are seen, so to speak, as opposite sides of the same coin."[49] In contemporary times, Nizhoni is a common girl's name, whereas it used to be unheard-of to name a child Hózhǫ́ due to the philosophical nature of the term. In the introduction, I offer the lengthy philosophical passage provided by Vincent Werito. His explanation of hózhǫ́ highlights how a simple denotative translation of hózhǫ́ is not adequate to convey the underlying Navajo epistemology and philosophy of "beauty." The essential components of hózhǫ́ philosophy are

> (1) having reverence and respect for nature, for myself, for others, and for the land and (2) nurturing my spiritual faith. . . . When the word "hózhǫ́" is used now to describe the beauty and peacefulness of a place or the good attributes of a person . . . it reminds me of when I was in a similar place or state of mind; . . . I now realize that while the essence of the meaning of hózhǫ́ could be interpreted as a fixed or constant idea to imply a state of peace and harmony, it can also be interpreted and understood as an ever-changing, evolving, and transformative idea, especially in how an individual applies and interprets its meaning to her or his life.[50]

The concept of hózhǫ́ entails holism, respect, and dynamism and cannot easily be placed on a binary, comparative plane to the adjective *nizhoni*. To synonymize these two words would be to oversimplify the philosophical understanding of becoming hózhǫ́.

While hózhǫ́ was formerly unheard-of as a first name, I read the medicine man's first name, Harmon, as a short-form of harmony, signifying hózhǫ́, due to the characteristics he embodies. Harmon is respectfully and dutifully preparing for Max's Kinaaldá, which he is also conducting. Over a period of four days, Sick Boy faces several challenges that impede his contributions to the ceremony. With Max's moccasins finally in hand, he delivers them to the site, where he meets Harmon and introduces himself as Luther.

Knowing Luther wants to flee Dry Lake to join the army, Harmon engages him in a discussion about warriorism. This recalls a previous scene (before Luther meets Harmon), in which he is with his friends Julius and Ruckus. Julius tries to recruit Sick Boy to assist in their upcoming Sudafed heist, in which they plan to steal a large shipment of Sudafed to make drugs: "The only way to get shit, is to go out and take it. But you can't be afraid. . . . You gotta be willing to put yourself in harm's way." Sick Boy chimes in: "Like a soldier!" and Julius belittles this: "No. Fuck soldiers, man. . . . Soldiers are for the army. Soldiers take orders. They do what someone else tells them to do. You and me, us, we're warriors!" Prior to colonization, Diné soldiers were known as warriors. In fact, according to traditional Navajo literary histories, our first mother gave birth to the warrior Hero Twins, Naayéé Neezgháni and Tó Bájísh Chíní, who saved the Bilá' ashdla', or humankind. But, because of Sick Boy's lack of matrilineal teachings and his state of hóchxǫ, he abuses drugs and alcohol, neglects and betrays his pregnant wife, and picks fights on a whim. His thug friends seek his leadership, and he advises them on how to "hypothetically" choose the right gun for their planned robbery, yet he does not have their respect, as they mock his dreams of joining the army and call him "Captain America." With this elementary understanding of warriorism, his badass gangbanging masquerades as warrior qualities.

Luther listens to Elder Harmon's teachings about the qualities that make up a true traditional Navajo warrior: how to fight, protect, and survive. But the most important teaching is when Harmon surprises Luther with this: "The mark of a true warrior is one who knows when to retreat." Luther sees retreating as losing. Losing is what Sick Boy excels at. During the final day of Kinaaldá preparation, the extended family is preparing the earth for the fire that will cook the alkaan (corn cake), and they need plenty of chopped wood that will burn overnight. After learning recently that Luther is ineligible to join the military, Angela refuses to speak to him, and Luther is frustrated. Furthermore, he admits that he does not know how to chop wood. His failure to become a warrior and to contribute to the ceremony marks a change toward restoration. Luther ultimately heeds Elder Harmon's advice and retreats. At dawn on the final day of Max's ceremony, the same day of the planned armed robbery, he does not meet up with Julius and Ruckus and chooses instead to join his little sister in the final run of her Kinaaldá. Luther sheds his appellation of Sick Boy in this act of hózhǫ.

Hózhǫ and nizhóní are further contrasted in Felixia's character. As a transgender woman, she seeks respect and recognition that she is externally beautiful (or nizhóní). Dinéjí Na'Nitin, teachings from the Diné journey oeuvre, reveal a positive attitude toward multiple genders that is at odds with the prevalent conservative reservation ideology, or as bell hooks so aptly observed:

> Cross-dressing, appearing in drag, transvestism, and transsexualism emerge in a context where the notion of subjectivity is challenged, where identity is

always perceived as capable of construction, invention, *change*. . . . Within white supremacist capitalist patriarchy the experience of men dressing as women, appearing in drag has always been regarded by the dominant heterosexist cultural gaze as a sign that one is symbolically crossing over from a realm of power into a realm of powerlessness.[51]

While Felixia may have internalized the negative, patriarchal gaze of powerlessness, she was raised by "pretty traditional" grandparents in a culture that honors matriarchy. Unfortunately, colonization and epistemicide maintain a firm grasp on Indigenous Peoples, ideologies, and teachings, and it becomes evident that she does not yet understand hózhǫ́ teachings that celebrate nádleeh. Sensing Felixia's tenuous ties to the community, Grandpa Harmon shares a story from Navajo emergence hane'. This episode retells the separation of the sexes and the role of nádleeh and restoration:

> Long time ago, all Navajo lived alongside the great river; the men, the women, and the nádleeh. One day they began to argue over who was more important than the other. The men said they were because they hunted. And the women said they were because they tended the crops. On and on they argued until finally, they decided maybe they were better off without each other. The men rafted across the great river, and they took the nádleeh with them. And for a while everything was fine. Then the men began to miss their wives and children, but they were too proud to go back. So they sent the nádleeh back to check on things. And the nádleeh returned with the message: that things weren't so well with the women and that they missed the men and that they had no one to hunt for them. It became apparent both sides needed each other; the men needed the women and women, in turn, needed the men. And they both needed the nádleeh. To this day we carry this lesson. This balance. And I know you, you [are] struggling with acceptance and this world can be cold and hard on our people. But you must always remember: wherever you go, whatever you choose to do, you always have home here. This place, for you.

Grandpa Harmon's iteration is inclusive, is loving, and embodies the principles of k'é and of hózhǫ́. Felixia has a plane ticket to New York, and Grandpa emphasizes that "this place" will always be home, where she is always welcome. It is also a reply to Nizhoni's question that opens the film and this chapter. Felixia is nádleeh living and navigating in a hateful society that does not respect and acknowledge this traditional identity that is embraced by her grandparents.[52] Chadwick Allen's *Blood Narrative* offers a nuanced interpretation: "The grandparent-grandchild bond and the scene of indigenous [sic] instruction—or their devastating absence—play significant roles. . . . The bond between grandparent and grandchild figures the relationship of contemporary indigeneity to the ancestors."[53] While her grandparents were grounded in their traditions and taught Felixia language, they were not oppressive with their teachings. Their bond embodied balance, or hózhǫ́, which was unlike the aggressive Christian conversion campaigns and colonization tactics that muted nádleeh stories and closeted those who were "out." This epistemicide continues to result in daily violence. In 2001, Navajo transgender teen Fred Martinez (sixteen) was bludgeoned to death by a transphobic racist. Martinez's story is featured in the documentary *Two-Spirits* by Lydia Nibley, bringing international attention to multigendered Indigenous identities and to the epidemic of bullying, an attention that Freeland also sought to advance. She admits to not knowing of nádleeh and their once prominence:

> The grandma and grandpa characters represent the more traditional aspects of Navajo culture. And one of those aspects includes the concept of 3rd and 4th genders. The mindset on the reservation tends to be more conservative, but because this is part of the culture, it made perfect sense that they would be accepting of Felixia. . . . Now here is the ironic part—I grew up on the reservation but had no idea about this aspect of Navajo culture. The first time I really heard about it was when I moved to San Francisco. I met a trans woman who, when learning that I was Navajo, was like "Wow, the reservation must be so loving and accepting of the trans people!" I didn't know what she was talking about at the time, but I was able to research and learn more about this. It ended up that I had to move to San Francisco to learn about my own culture. . . . I am a member of both the Native community and the LGBT community.[54]

Becoming hózhǫ́ necessitates recognizing and respecting traditional Diné stories that tell of the nádleeh. Wesley Thomas, a professor of Diné cultural studies, begins his essay "Navajo Cultural Constructions of Gender and Sexuality" by explaining how "multiple genders were part of the norm in the Navajo culture before the 1890s. From the 1890s until the 1930s dramatic changes took place in the lives of Navajos because of exposure to, and constant pressures from, Western culture—not the least of which was the imposition of Christianity."[55] This affirms Freeland's lack of knowledge about nádleeh, as these teachings have been suppressed for more than a century. Thomas is featured in the documentary *Two-Spirits*, as an expert on Navajo gender constructions. His voice-over narration explicates four traditionally acknowledged genders: (1) asdzą́ą́, the feminine woman; (2) hastiin, the masculine man; (3) the nádleeh, or male-bodied person with a feminine essence; and (4) the dilbaa', or female-bodied person with a masculine essence.[56] Denetdale attests that "contemporary gay and lesbian Navajos regard the creation stories as proof that Navajos recognized more than two genders and that third, and possibly fourth, genders were accepted and celebrated. They have embraced the *nádleehí* as evidence of acceptance in Navajo society and as a model for their own lives."[57]

Hastiin Harmon's story validates Felixia's place in Dry Lake's society; her family accepts her as nádleeh and she embraces this identity. She has been raised with grandparent teachings that embody hózhǫ́, and Asdzą́ą́ Nádłeehé, Changing Woman, is coincidentally manifesting in ceremony right outside Felixia's trailer in the family ceremonial hooghan. At the end of the film, and on the final day of Max's Kinaaldá, Felixia dyes her strawberry-blonde hair back to natural black and helps Grandma Ruth make bread, assuming the role of a matriarch and ensuring that the family is nourished, fed, and sustained. She also meets Nizhoni, who is her sister, according to traditional Navajo kinship relations because their mothers are sisters. The film erroneously calls them cousins, real cousins (as opposed to "Navajo cousins"). Luther's, Nizhoni's, and Felixia's stories converge at the end of *Drunktown's Finest*. Their k'é restored, their characters are healing from the reeling. Freeland's hane'tonomy offers nuance to the beautiful diversity that makes up Dry Lake.

The community of the factual town of Gallup did not sit idle while the label "Drunk Town, USA" was sullying its reputation. In 1990, a local, grassroots, nonprofit organization, Northwest New Mexico Fighting Back, Inc., was envisioned to "reduce the demand for alcohol and other drugs in San Juan, McKinley and Cibola Counties, through community organizing and mobilization, public awareness and technical assistance."[58] A resident of Gallup, EiRena Begay, says a growing community movement encourages living healthy, sustainable lives that include promoting Gallup as an "adventure destination" via newly built trails geared for hiking, cycling, and running. Begay admits that it is challenging to see Gallup in a positive light, especially given the prominence of a local antipanhandling campaign "aimed at dłaanis [a derogatory term for drunks], called 'Change in my Heart Not in my Pocket,'" which local Navajos interpreted as racist and more divisive.[59] While several businesses display signs with this slogan on it, which is meant to deter panhandlers from entering their shops to ask for handouts, liquor stores and bars welcome the dłaanis. Her frustration is heightened knowing that the local detox center is losing funding. Even so, support services continue to be available: "The once famous bar, 'The Round Up Saloon' has become the Hozhó [sic] Center. They offer counseling, AA meetings, and community classes like Zumba."[60] Despite the community-level action to alter Gallup's reputation, hóchx̨ǫ is prominent, like overt racism, sexism, trans- and homophobia, and poverty.

Denetdale critiques the Hollywood ending of *Drunktown's Finest* as unattainably redemptive and exposes other challenges to realizing hózhǫ́:

> In hopes of redeeming her hometown, Freeland ends her film with the trope of finding healing and redemption in tradition and culture. When Native peoples are traumatized, they need only channel tradition and healing will begin. The separation of "tradition" from the "politics" of challenging structures of domination and exploitation individualizes our responses to self-healing and keeps the undercurrents of a town like Gallup intact. Sometimes art is about making us feel good so we don't have to do anything about a problem that seems insurmountable.[61]

The happy ending does not expose the real-life "insurmountable" challenges that prevent the actualization of hózhǫ́. Elsewhere, I have responded to Denetdale's critique of the conclusion of the film: "As a result of over 40 years of cultural revitalization, a significant number of Indigenous people are looking to traditional ways to recover from their trauma."[62] This film's verisimilitude is reel restoration; characters depart from the wooden and dead *indian* representations of the past, and their diverse lives and experiences, though traumatic, are relatable.

In *Drunktown's Finest*, "channel[ing] tradition" for healing creates hope.[63] Freeland has brought international attention to Diné "undercurrents," creating awareness by using her platform as a trans woman and visual storyteller to begin to address these issues, which is foundational for restoration. The critical issues that Sick Boy, Nizhoni, and Felixia face cannot be solved in ceremonial time (four days), but the film elevates decolonial tools as a reminder that tradition did not succumb to epistemicide and this family's circle is, in fact, not completely broken. The film begins with Nizhoni's English-language plea, "*They say* this land isn't a place to live; it's a place to leave." My focus is to animate "they say" (jiní), as it is traditionally how Diné begin telling meaningful and didactic stories. The characters have been told "this land . . . [is] a place to leave" so frequently that it has become a new oral story, jiní. This internalized, colonial lie has been made traditional and they are actively contesting it: reversing the story, restoring our stories. Nizhoni has been lied to about her Diné family, Sick Boy has internalized the lie that leaving will resolve his toxic masculinity, and Felixia has embraced the lie that dyeing her hair blond and fleeing for the big city will invite acceptance.

Coming to a state of hózhǫ́, of harmonious, balanced, and beautiful living that entails acceptance and love for one's Diné identity and being, one's family and kinship relations, for land and home, necessitates recognizing and respecting the power of hane', of stories. The film ends at dawn on the fourth and final day of the Kinaaldá with Max—the best of all possibilities, as in *maximum*—emerging from the hooghan, symbolic of where "life began," jiní, as poeticized in the chapter's opening epigraph by Tapahonso. Max runs toward the East and is supported by family and commu-

FIGURE 9 Max running on day four of her Kinaaldá. From *Drunktown's Finest* trailer.

nity who run with her, depicting life. She is a matriarch in motion, having become Kinaaldá, in the image of Asdzą́ą́ Nádleehé, Changing Woman, signifying rebirth, reel restoration, and hózhǫ́ of a promising Diné future.

Freeland's hane'tonomy came from the stories of Diné journey narratives, in the world where men and women were separated. Some retell these events as happening in the Third World of the Hajíínéí; some say it's in the Fourth World of the Hajíínéí. In the next chapter, we ascend one world up and journey to the visual storytelling realm of Diné filmmaker Blackhorse Lowe, whose first feature film is aptly titled *5th World*. His hane'tonomy, humor, and deadly creative aesthetic as a director, producer, editor, and writer for television and film (short, feature, and documentary) speaks to his dedication to cinema. Lowe has been behind the camera since 2004 as cinematographer and director.

CHAPTER 4

Diné Diegesis

5th World

> As the floodwaters crashed together outside, the hole closed up and sealed tightly. The reed commenced to grow quickly, lifting the people above the rising water. The Holy People accompanied them. . . . This sky was solid and there was no opening in its surface, so Locust, who was good at making holes, began to scratch and dig. Eventually he broke through, and the people rejoiced. . . . One by one, the people climbed out of the giant reed into this, the Fifth World, the Glittering World.
>
> —IRVIN MORRIS, *FROM THE GLITTERING WORLD*

> When the people emerged and were birthed into the Glittering World, they came through the umbilical center of the earth mother, *Nahasdzáán*. She provides for all living things; she sustains life. We are her children, *biyázhí daniidlí*.
>
> —LAURA TOHE, "HWÉELDI BÉÉHÁNIIH"

Irvin Morris and Laura Tohe restory orality via Diné poetics and remind us that we are currently situated in the Glittering World, also known as the Fifth World. The Diné bahane' relate that Diné ascended from four worlds below this one, and I offer a truncated summary of those worlds in the introduction. The stories reassure us that we will always have a home despite a twenty-first-century Diné diaspora that sees Navajos living and thriving across the globe. Our stories and umbilical cords are anchored in Dinétah, connecting us to Nahasdzáán, our earth mother, whose cord we emerged from, according to Tohe.

In this chapter, I spotlight the Diné film *5th World* (2005), by Larry Blackhorse Lowe, hereafter referred to as Blackhorse Lowe, as that is how he is known professionally.[1] I argue that Lowe's visual storytelling conveys a Diné diegesis through sonic sovereignty and hane'tonomy. Lowe's movie is a fusion of imagery, sounds, silence, and contemporary worldviews that at once reflect, and are informed by, traditional oral stories—in Diné bizaad and English. The film's title, *5th World*, mirrors the Hajíínéí about traditional laws of the People of the Fifth World, particularly the importance of knowing the Diné laws of k'é, in which intimate partner love between Clan siblings is forbidden. Lowe's filmography includes directorial credits for four episodes of *Reservation Dogs*, the feature films *Fukry* (2019), *Chasing the Light* (2014), and *5th World* (2005), and the notable short films *Shimásání* (2009) and *Shush* (2004), among others.

I am inspired by Beth Piatote's and Dylan Robinson's theories of sonic sovereignty and hungry listening, which inform my development of an epistemic framework that I am calling a Diné diegesis. Inherent in the fact that this is a full-length feature film, the verisimilitude of place, setting, and staging contribute to the Diné-centric visual aesthetic. To fully understand the film requires multiple sensory registers and cultural cues, for which Piatote's and Robinson's work on sound is very helpful. The complex layering and overlapping of multilingual narration and oral stories in *5th World* have long been overlooked and ignored by mainstream filmgoers and critics. Early film reviews misunderstood Lowe's aesthetic as unoriginal and erratic. Randolph Lewis states, "Reflecting his self-taught cinephile aesthetic, his work feels like Eric Rohmer on the rez, with a mixture of odd camera angles, hypersaturated digital video, underground music and creative editing that reflects an obvious debt to Godard, Truffaut, and other French New Wave directors for whom he has expressed his fondness."[2] Additionally, Joanna Hearne and Zach Schlachter note Lowe's "nonlinear and fragmentary" audio and visual narrative.[3] While these are not overly harsh critiques, I go beyond and offer a Fourth Cinema reading of the film from a Diné episteme.

Barry Barclay envisioned a category of Fourth Cinema, in which "the old principles have been reworked to give vitality and richness to the way we conceive, develop, manufacture and present our films. It seems likely to me that some Indigenous film artists will be interested in shaping films that sit with confidence within the First, Second, and Third cinema framework."[4] Lowe's first feature film, *5th World*, responds to this dream. He privileges and reworks the "old principles" of ancient Diné stories and masterfully fuses them with a contemporary flare and aesthetic without disrespecting the roots of orality. He gives vitality to the setting of the old stories in Diné Bikéyah or Navajo land, which connects Diné directly to our celestial ancestors:

> Because the Holy People are so much a part of Navajo stories, and because they are associated with particular places, landscapes are strongly associated with these stories. Indeed, especially when Navajos passed down their chronicles mainly by word-of-mouth, the landscape provides a material anchor for those stories and thereby stores them. The landscape is a physical link between people of the present and their past. The landscapes and the stories that go with them depend on each other. In a sense, the landscape is part of the "text"—usually you can't grasp all the connotations of a story without knowing how the places in the story line up with each other, with other storied places, or with locations of other human events and natural process like the movements of celestial bodies.[5]

Despite Lowe's own explicit mention of his influences and background information that he has shared in interviews, there has not been a firm grasp of all the connotations that permeate *5th World*. The film reviews and scholarly critique of *5th World* focus on the film's editing fractures and nonlinearity, which are not necessarily negative critiques; they could signal respect for visual and narrative sovereignty, but they don't ever actually say that. They also do not connect the fissures and nonlinearity as a visual narrative storytelling technique, grounded in Diné autonomy—hane'tonomy—and land subjectivity. Métis filmmaker and video activist Marjorie Beaucage shared that she experimented with sound in her early work. She wanted Elders' voices to maintain their autonomy and did not insert subtitles or voice-over narration on top of the original voices: "the vibrations of sound are there in the voices and are needed."[6] These experimental sound techniques honor aural and visual autonomy, which is similar to Lowe's style.

On April 8, 2014, Beth Piatote (Nez Perce) gave a public lecture titled "Sonic Sovereignty in D'Arcy McNickle's *The Surrounded*" at Mount Royal University. Piatote's analysis of *The Surrounded* focuses on two narrative devices, particularly "the employment of sound, including ambient noise, drumming, and the hoofbeats of horses, in articulating alternative relationships to Salish communities and homelands that extend beyond the reservation and the surveillance scope of the law."[7] She calls this "'sonic sovereignty,' or the production of sound that reinscribes the boundaries of Native homelands, affirms indigenous [sic] autonomy, and contests the mappings of settler colonial administration."[8] I borrow from Piatote's nuanced reading of *The Surrounded* and assert that sonic sovereignty is at play in Lowe's editorial layering of voices on top of voices, of stories on top of stories, and of quick jump cuts across images.

In *Hungry Listening*, Dylan Robinson (xmélmexw) advocates for the practices of "resurgent and sovereign listening."[9] His study is primarily about musical performance, which is outside the confines of my work.[10] I adopt Robinson's work because performance, whether musical, visual, or filmic, benefits from his theory making. His book's title is from the Halq'eméylem language and "names settler colonial forms of perception."[11] Along with his critical self-reflective ear, Robinson advances the notion that we (most of us) "listen through whiteness" as it is "a 'civilizing' sensory paradigm that has been imposed on Indigenous people."[12] His proposal of reversal (in analyzing classical music performances) is relevant as an analytic to visual storytelling. What might it look like if Indigenous creative work is theorized using what he calls "Indigenous logics" and to "listen otherwise"?[13] His answer to this question is to enlist a decolonial theory of praxis that he calls resonant theory. He writes, "The act of listening should attend to the relationship between listener and the listened-to," whereby sound has equal "life, agency, and subjectivity . . . within Indigenous frameworks of perception."[14] It is here that my interpretative close listening and earwitnessing of the overlapping intergenerational, multilingual dialogues, silences, and other sounds of *5th World* are given life and subjectivity.

In appropriating and synthesizing diegetic sound from a Western theoretical framework and overlapping this with Piatote's and Robinson's anti-colonial positioning, combined with my conception of hane'tonomy, I show how *5th World* enunciates and articulates Diné diegesis through episodes from the Diné journey narratives. The stories, I propose, take on the imagery of the whorl of a weaving spindle, or the whorl of our fingertips from Diné teachings, and expand outward in a sun-wise direction, sometimes being told again at different moments of the film for repetition and for recentering. This is a cyclic, spiral whirling, storytelling method.

Diegesis in cinematography is distinguished between the overall framing of each shot as well as the sound, according to Annette Kuhn and Guy Westwell:

The diegetic world can include not only what is visible on the screen, but also offscreen elements that are presumed to exist in the world that the film depicts—as long as these are part of the main story. The term diegetic sound is in common use in the description and analysis of films, referencing any voice, music, or sound effect presented as having its source within the film's fictional world. This is in contradistinction from nondiegetic or extradiegetic sound—sound (such as background music [underscoring] or voice over) that is represented as coming from a source outside the story world.[15]

When I discuss "the fictional world of the film," I mean diegesis. When I am talking about sound or the absence of sound, I follow common film analysis conventions of referring to diegetic sound or nondiegetic sound, depending on where the sound is (or is not) in the fictional world of the film. Diegetic sound "originates from a source within the world created by the film, such as on-screen and off-screen sounds heard by characters (as opposed to nondiegetic sound)."[16] Nondiegetic sound "originates from a source outside a film's world and thus is not heard by the characters, such as musical scores and voice-overs."[17] Diegesis has a long, ancient history that precedes moving images. David Bordwell traces diegesis from Plato's theory of narrative to contemporary film theory:

> In book 3 of the *Republic,* Plato distinguishes two principal sorts of storytelling. There is simple or pure narrative (*haplē diēgēsis*), in which "the poet himself is the speaker and does not even attempt to suggest to us that anyone but himself is speaking." A lyric poem would be an example. In contrast stands imitative narrative (mimēsis), of which drama is the chief instance. Here the poet speaks though his characters, "as if he were someone else." In 1953, the term diegesis was revived by Etienne Souriau to describe the "recounted story" of a film, and it has since achieved wide usage in literary theory. "Diegesis" has come to be the accepted term for the fictional world of the story.[18]

Bordwell updates his definition of diegesis in *Meaning Making: Inference and Rhetoric in the Interpretation of Cinema* (1989) to include what the audience sees and how that relates to diegetic sound. He recognizes that the "spectator builds up some version of the *diegesis*, or the spatio-temporal world, and creates an ongoing story (fabula) occurring within it."[19] According to Chris Baldick, diegesis is also a theoretical construct in the field of narratology (the study of narratives and narration): "The diegetic level of a narrative is that of the main story, whereas the 'higher' level at which the story is told is extradiegetic (i.e. standing outside the sphere of the main story). An embedded tale-within-the-tale constitutes a lower level known as hypodiegetic."[20] Diegesis in oratory (speech) is the narration and narrative, originating from the ancient Greek, διήγησις.

Lowe's *5th World* is at once hane' and διήγησις, a telling and relating.[21] It is the oration of two stories: one of uninhibited, young love interwoven with a mature love story that exudes endearing commitment. These two love stories also align with Baldick's "embedded tale-within-the-tale." Additionally, there is a very short cautionary story, inserted between these two primary love stories. It is disguised as a mini-short film with its own title card, "John's Tale of Injun Woe" (which I discuss later in this chapter). Beyond the narrative, Kuhn and Westwell's definition of filmic diegesis adds another whorl, another layer of meaning to our metaphorical fingertip imagery. Finally, turning to Bordwell's updated definition, as a viewer and listener, I have interpreted and "buil[t] up" an ongoing "fabula" of the film that applauds and obfuscates the plot (seemingly a simple love story and road movie, whereby the protagonists begin in one geographic location and end up in another). The nondiegetic sound as voice-over, coupled with on-screen images and diegetic sound, constitutes a Diné diegesis that complicates the deceptive linearity of the fabula, revealing multiple layers or whorls.

The fictional world of *5th World* contains four storied fragments: (1) k'éí (Clanship) and k'é (kinship and relationality), (2) Diné Bikéyah, (3) disharmony or hóchx̨ó, and (4) silent cinematic hane'tonomy. The teachings and stories cannot be contained in a linear fashion. They overlap, whirling and forming a whorl, while also maintaining hane'tonomy.

K'éí and K'é

The origin of k'éí is one of the longer vignettes from the Diné bahane' and there are at least three versions of the origin of the Clans that have been published.[22] Diné literary scholar and author Irvin Morris alludes to the development of Diné Clans: "knowing your clan also ties you directly into the *Diné* creation story, because all the clans are descended from the four original clans that were created by Changing Woman from her body."[23] In her book *Navajo History* (1971), Ethelou Yazzie relates Diné cosmology about how the first four original Clans were from the celestial soma of Asdzą́ą́ Nádleehé. From the skin of her breast she created the Kiiyaa'áanii (Towering House People; also spelled Kinyaa'áanii); from the skin off her back, she brought to life the Honáháanii (One Walks Around, also spelled Honágháahnii); the Tódich'íi'nii (Bitter Water People) were made by taking skin from under her right arm; and the Hashtł'isgnii (Mud Clan, also spelled Hashtł'ishnii) were created from the skin under her other arm.[24] Yazzie further says that select animals were assigned to each of the four original Clans as "guardians."[25] The Kiiyaa'áanii (Towering House) were given Shash (bear), Honáháanii (One Walks Around) were assigned Nashdóí (mountain lion), Tódich'íi'nii's (Bitter Water's) guardian was Tłiish Tsoh (bull snake), and the Hashtł'ishnii (Mud) were given Dahsání (porcupine).[26] As an epic, the entirety of the Diné journey narratives takes time to recite and listen to, and not likely in one sitting.[27]

5th World opens with the sound of language and voice, or saad in Diné bizaad. We initially only hear the soothing, mellifluous voice of Auntie narrating the story of when she fell in love as a young woman. In this scene, we listen in as she asks her husband, Uncle, a question and he answers respectfully. We don't see any living People during this opening scene, but we hear the beginning of the Elders' love story, narrated primarily in Diné bizaad. At times during their oration, they mix in Bilagáana bizaad (English) words, as they share memories, their laughter, their kindness, and their love for each other. Their love story is epic. Throughout the film, we hear several parts of their love story re-created in the fictional world of *5th World* as vignettes. Like the epic story of Diné journey narratives, theirs is not recited in one sitting, and by the end of the film, we are left feeling that their great love continues, but we won't hear it. Lowe's cinematic techniques necessitate multiple, simultaneous sensory registers that privilege sonic sovereignty: we *hear* voice-over, multilingual narration, nondiegetic music, and uncomfortable silence but we *see* still images, montages, jump cuts, long shots, and title cards.

When the voices of Auntie and Uncle (played by Lowe's real-life parents, Carmelita B. and Larry A. Lowe) commence the film, we see their story unfold as a series of still images (black and white, sepia toned, and faded), intermixed with aging polaroid, some torn. The photos appear to be presented on screen in a somewhat organized chronology as Auntie explains how they smiled at each other and stole glances across the college campus, their subsequent courtship, their traditional Navajo wedding ceremony, their babies, and other life events. One early photo of Auntie is even signed "Lita" (for Carmelita) in cursive, revealing that these are not stock images. Ultimately, we understand in the first three-minute vignette that family is central.

There are eight separate vignettes that the Elders narrate asynchronously. Their oral storyline takes precedence over the visual images at times. As much of the narration is in the Navajo language, affirming Diné autonomy and agency, the subtitles distract from the background shots, challenging the notion that visual images are what makes a film. Sometimes, the narration directly contradicts the visual story occurring on screen at the same time. Lowe's editing is deliberate. For example, in one vignette, we hear Auntie and Uncle sharing how their own relationship evolved ever-so-slowly, while we see the live-action sequence of two young adults, Aria (played by LivA'ndrea Knoki) and Andrei (played by Sheldon Silentwalker), frolicking, snuggling, kissing, and not taking their relationship slow. While we can conclude that the underlying teaching is that we are witnessing the young adults disobey, or ignore, or refuse to listen to the Elders, which is disrespectful, that does not reflect the realities of how twenty-first-century youth are balancing their own autonomy with cultural dynamism.

Traditional Diné protocol necessitates a formal Clan introduction to establish kinship relations and to ward off potential taboo relations (as outlined in chapter 3). While we are witnessing the young adults' love affair blossom, we do not know their names until thirty minutes into the film. It is deliberate that the protagonists are not named until the midpoint of *5th World*. As Aria and Andrei are hitchhiking, Andrei's aunt and uncle see them on the side of the road and pick them up. As they get into the truck, Andrei introduces Aria to his aunt. This is not a careless forgetting on the part of Lowe but rather a tactical and climactic storytelling tool (hane'tonomy) that is only made clear in the final third of the movie.

In March 2009, Lowe and Seminole/Muscogee Creek filmmaker Sterlin Harjo sat down with Joanna Hearne and Zach Schlachter for an exclusive interview, which took place at the University of Missouri's KBIA radio station. Their conversation was published in 2013 as "'Pockets Full of Stories,'" featured in Marubbio and Buffalohead's *Native Americans on Film*. When Hearne asked Lowe how he came up with the idea for *5th World*, he explained, "I'd come off a relationship. [And I thought,] 'Well, I haven't seen a good love story in a while.' I really wanted something soft and naturalistic that kind of just flowed—about love.... That became a forty-five-page screenplay."[28] In this same interview, Lowe reveals the advent of his dad's voice-over narrative as a critical storytelling technique for the film. In Lowe's family, his father is a storyteller and relished capturing the attention of Lowe's mother. Her favorite story to retell is about how they met and fell in love. To talk about Diné love is to privilege your parents and their parents and matrilineal Clans that establish relationality. Love includes respecting and being responsible to your family, from close members to extended family. Intimate, partner love is interwoven, as lovers become family and establish relationality.

5th World replicates the story-within-a story or hypodiegetic technique but with a deliberate Diné diegesis that adds a third story as a short film in the middle of it. All these stories share the common thread of relationality and knowing k'éí laws, giving the overall film a Diné aesthetic and verisimilitude. These three distinct stories of love and lust operate as vignettes, and as such they are told cyclically, culminating in a modern-day film-length epic. The love stories of the twenty-first-century Bilá' ashdla' (Five-Fingered Ones) are that of Auntie and Uncle, Aria and Andrei, and cousin-brother John (played by Corey Allison) and Ateed Nizhoni (played by Sahar Khadjenoury). The Diné cultural allusions and insider knowledge are spliced with saad (a storied and creative soundscape), unique shot editing, extradiegetic techniques, and long shots of the landscape. These are techniques that when combined convey a form of Diné epistemology and exhibit what I have termed hane'tonomy. Raheja's analysis of Zacharias Kunuck's *Atanarjuat* (2001) is particularly relevant to the style and aesthetics of *5th World*. She writes, "The filmmakers ... take the non-[Diné] audience hostage."[29] I have substituted "non-Diné" where her original sentence says "non-Inuit" as the films share a cyclic storytelling structure intercut by "fractured" images and dwell on long takes of the Diné landscape. Critic Randolph Lewis says that Lowe's film demystifies Navajo landscape: "by following the essential logic of indigenous [*sic*] mediamaking (that cultural self-representation has no substitute), the new Navajo cinema rejects what outsiders have imposed on Native soil and replaces it with projects whose roots are deep in the Navajo Nation."[30] Understanding Diné kinship relations (k'é) and place-based Clans (k'éí) is essential to understanding the concepts of home and love in *5th World*.

Diné Bikéyah

Lowe grew up on Dinétah on the Diné reservation, in Nenahnezad, New Mexico, which is fourteen miles from Farmington to the east and twenty-two miles from Shiprock to the west.

> I'm originally from northwest New Mexico, this small town called Farmington, and there's a highway that goes from Flagstaff through Kayenta and into Farmington. So I would always go along that way on the weekends either for ceremonies or just to go visit family when I had some off time, and I was always really taken away by the landscape through there—Monument Valley, Elephant's Feet, all these really cool landscapes—and a lot of it really tied into the creation stories, how we believe our holy people came out of all these different experiences, but also a lot of tragedies and all these other things back in the day. And also at the time I was really heavily into Terrence Malick—*Badlands* and *Days of Heaven* and *[The] Thin Red Line*, which was just landscape and very naturalistic—and Andrei Tarkovsky, with these really long, beautiful shots of people in the landscape. *The landscape told you the story as opposed to the people, or there was a combination of both*.[31]

The "Elephant's Feet" invoked by Lowe are depicted in the traditional stories as Arrow Boy and Arrow Girl, according to Adair Klopfenstein, the director of Native American Studies for the Tuba City Unified School District.[32] Their formation on Dine Bikéyah invites critical interpretations that may not be experiential but are philosophical. This lengthy quote is Lowe's response to Hearne when asked how he chose the specific locations for *5th World*. Since listeners and viewers unfamiliar with Navajo land might not know where Nenahnezad is, Lowe declared that he was from the border town of Farmington. He was "influenced by First Cinema and home community."[33] Not leaving any doubts, Lowe clearly states that landscape was a character, a storyteller, within the fictional world of the film. Lowe divided the scenes (I count twenty-five transitions) with long takes of either the sky or the earth (Mother Earth and Father Sky). Some of these dividing transition shots feature the sky as either red from a sunset or blue and cloudy, and some of the land scenes are close-ups featuring the flora of the southwest desert, or of images of our iconic red rocks. When Hearne asked Lowe about specific and "most important locations," he acknowledged the story of the Tsé Nináhálééh (Monster Birds) as a prime reason why he chose to feature Tsé Bit'a'í at the end of *5th World*:

> I think once you get into the New Mexico portion toward the end, there's Shiprock. In terms of the mythology or the belief the Navajo people have in those certain locales, holy people originated from that area and there are all those stories about monster birds and the hero twins that went and saved the Navajo people from enslavement by other beings or animals. I tried to at least pay reference [*sic*] to it in some way. That, and it just looked pretty, too.[34]

The most important shooting location, in terms of meaning and optics, is Tsé Bit'a'í. Lowe says the English name of the Winged Rock, Shiprock, and alludes to the stories of creation, yet he does not overshare in person, nor does his script even mention the stories explicitly. Given that he answers with brevity, Hearne and Schlachter summarize *5th World* as "about families in transition, about generations moving between languages and between big cities and rural reservations.... Both films [including Harjo's *Four Sheets to the Wind*] are love songs to particular places, and powerfully foreground parental storytelling to frame young protagonists' relationships to homelands in specifically familial terms."[35] Succumbing to Robinson's observation that we are trained to "listen through whiteness," Hearne and Schlachter's summary only scratches the surface.

Lowe has said *5th World* is a road movie, albeit with Diné hitchhikers. As young college students in Phoenix, they plan their trip home, which takes them across the Navajo Nation, where the land is cast prominently. Cheyenne and Arapaho director Chris Eyre claims that land and landscape play a pivotal character role in all his films, due to the stories that the land holds.[36] At the beginning of *5th World*, they are looking over the "Road Map of the Navajo and Hopi Nations," planning their hitchhiking venture:

beginning in Flagstaff, to Tuba (Tuba City), K-Town (Kayenta), and ending up in Shiprock. For the first thirty minutes of the film, their adventures occur while hitchhiking. One prominent scene is as Andrei and Aria are walking along the highway, with the grandeur of Navajo land all around them. He asks her what her favorite movie is and she says John Ford's *Grapes of Wrath*, which impresses him since he doesn't know "many Injun broads who know about films and shit." She agrees: "That's true. I am pretty special." While they are getting to know one another, Lowe punctuates their flirtatious banter with the visual narrative of the landscape and of the iconic red rocks on the Navajo Nation. The nondiegetic voices of the Elders are audible in the background. We hear Andrei ask what they did on their first date. Auntie and Uncle both remember that they went to the movies! At the exact moment they share this memory (through off-screen diegetic sound), in which we *hear* their reminiscence, we *see* the picturesque red rock formations that made Navajo land famous in Hollywood Westerns, particularly those directed by John Ford. These aural and visual cues were Lowe's way to "pay reference [sic] to all the movies that were shot in that area—*2001, The Searchers, Grapes of Wrath*. The whole movie is cinephiles referencing other movies and other pop references and music and everything else."[37] Aria and Andrei make up a game where they take turns listing John Ford movies that were filmed in Monument Valley, and they include a shout-out to Metallica, who filmed their music video "I Dis-

FIGURE 10 Aria and Andrei resting near Elephant's Feet, Tonalea, Arizona. From *5th World* trailer.

appear" there.[38] They disagree on whether or not this one counts in their game of movies that were filmed in Monument Valley.[39]

Diné Bikéyah is not just made up of gorgeous and breathtaking landscapes that gift us piñon trees, Navajo tea, yucca, flowers, and other medicinal and nutritional food/plants. There are also the other-than-humans that share their homes with Diné, and Lowe captures horses and flocks of grazing sheep, which are a Diné staple that continues to provide sustenance and wool. While landscape shots dominate the hitchhiking scenes, the young couple's journey home also shows them at rest. In one shot, the duo sit near two sandstone pillars known around the Navajo Nation as Elephant's Feet, but it is actually Tonalea, Arizona, just east of the trading post between Tuba City and Kayenta. In this scene, Andrei and Aria share family stories of their experiences at peyote meetings and from their youth. Peyote meetings are brought up again, toward the end of the film, when Andrei sings peyote songs, claiming he is the "Johnny Cash of peyote meetings, baby!" Andrei and Aria's long, hitchhiking journey turned truck ride is expressed through hane'tonomy and sonic sovereignty. They exchange intimate conversations about a shared pan-religious ceremonial event that is widely practiced and adopted. As Diné, they demonstrate Diné humor, and they express their knowledge of cinema with a Diné flair. These instances reflect Piatote's observation that "sound in this context [these contexts] produces an alternative site for contesting dominance and asserting indigenous [sic] claims."[40]

Disharmony or Hóchxǫ́

In the previous chapter, I attribute hóchxǫ́ to "alcoholism, chaos, sickness, and disconnect." In *5th World*, and in the epic stories of the Glittering or Fifth World, hóchxǫ́ encompasses more attributes that align with Michelle Kahn-John and Mary Koithan's definition: "Hózhó becomes disrupted as a result of irresponsible thoughts, speech, or behavior, resulting in disharmony, or Hóchxó, which is manifested as chaos, ignorance, evil, sadness, grief, disharmony, imbalance—all that is contra to Hózhó."[41] From the world our celestial ancestors ascended from, the one we live in today offers challenges amid hóchxǫ́, and "our stories tell us that by the time that our ancestor people had reached the [Glittering] World, they were ready for some order in their lives."[42] To achieve harmony and order, we strive for hózhǫ́, which is grappled with and depicted in contemporary Indigenous creative works.

There are three situations in *5th World* that I correlate with hóchxǫ́, particularly irresponsible and disrespectful (disharmonious) speech, behaviors, and ignorance. The situations are (1) young adults sans Elders, (2) cousin-brother John, and (3) Andrei's postsex behavior. I argue that Lowe's cinematic hane'tonomy reflects a unique Diné-centric diegesis.

Sans Elders

Throughout *5th World*, we witness and listen to intergenerational humor. It is striking that out of earshot of the Elders (Auntie and Uncle), the conversations that the young adults engage in are misogynistic, racist (anti-Black and anti-Mexican), transphobic, homophobic, and self-hating (hateful toward other "Navs," short for Navajos), which is in stark contrast to the Elders' light-hearted, inoffensive, and humble humor that reflect respect and hózhǫ́.

Early in the film, Aria and Andrei hitch a ride from Navajo comedy duo James Junes and Ernie (Ernest) David Tsosie III, who star as themselves. During the car ride, they joke around about how Navajo women don't have asses, which turns into a more hateful rant about interracial relationships—from Aria's perspective—where Diné women who "mix" are betraying their roots, so she frowns upon them. Her vocalized disgust is jarring, and Ernie attempts to tame the topic by bringing up how complex falling in love is for "Navs" because Clans get in the way. Aria, seated between James and Ernie in the front, looks confused during this matter-of-fact comment that is otherwise common knowledge among culturally informed Diné. These realistic situations are a filmic commentary about the prevalent and ignorant mindset that has pervaded Diné communities and families, fracturing inclusive, loving, and reciprocal k'é and k'éí teachings found in hane'. Diné women are revered and through our Kinaaldá ceremonies are taught to emulate Asdzą́ą́ Nádleehé (Changing Woman) and her teachings, which are in stark contrast to Aria's hateful and racist oration (though she is not the only character to spew hóchxǫ́-laden speech). When the young adults parrot divisive and unenlightened utterances, they reflect ideological whiteness that is in desperate need of restoration.

Cousin-Brother John's Scenes

Mainstream films typically have a three-act structure, whereby the second act is called the "rising action" or the "confrontation." Lowe's narrative structure as hane'tonomy is unique, and I connect this rising action and confrontation to the concept of hóchxǫ́. Just past the midpoint, there is a short film-within-the-film preceded by a hypertoxic masculine discussion between Andrei and John. Shortly after Auntie and Uncle butcher a sheep for a feast, which is filmed through a Diné lens of cultural sensitivity, Andrei and John are seated underneath a tree, joking around and out of earshot of Elders and Diné women. The topic is about the complexities of contemporary Diné love, rooted in k'é and k'éí. John spews, in a surfer-rez accent: "For me, for me man . . . girls come and go." Andrei interjects: "Like Ferraris?" John continues, "Man, I'm just takin' her for a test drive! I don't know. Chicks are too crazy, man; especially around here. Man, you get with one girl, you get another one; you find out that [she's] either your sister, your aunt, cousin, your grandma! Shits all fucked-up over here!" Andrei laughs along, while John hems and haws, which foreshadows shame, regret, and disdain for Diné laws that govern k'éí.

This situational scene is necessary for context of the overall film's primary teaching but unusual in that it interrupts the entire feature-length movie, as its own movie complete with a silent-era title card and introductory actor credits. Following John's rant, we see the following on the screen: "John's Tale of Injun Woe," which is an obvious reversal of Mark Twain's "Injun Joe." This mini-short film is an example of Diné diegesis. Lowe's technique privileges facial close-ups and extreme close-ups of John and the character listed in the credits as "Ateed Nizhoni" (where at'ééd means "girl") to suggest intimacy. Lowe also employs flickering, fluorescent lighting, grainy cinestyle, and awkward camera angles in this scene to evoke confusion and chaos, or hóchxǫ́. While John's voice-over nondiegetic narration to Andrei is in the present time, on-screen metadiegetic memories and flashbacks are the visual complements of this mini-short film. There is no diegetic sound in the mini-short film. The only thing we hear is John's voice-over narration-turned-confession. We see John's lust-driven encounter with Ateed Nizhoni escalate in the backseat of her car. We hear John regretfully lament his intimate timing: "Dumbass me, [I] asked her what her Clans are!" John is painfully embarrassed and guilt-ridden by almost engaging in forbidden sex (as outlined by k'éí), and shouts to Andrei, "She's my sister, man!" Ateed Nizhoni turns out to be "Injun John's" sister by Clan. Interestingly, John says he did not have the heart to tell her why he stopped kissing her and why he immediately fled the scene with his pants down. John's complex character—at once misogynistic, toxic, and culturally grounded in Diné systems that he woefully honors and respects—acts as another way to teach while it foreshadows the tragic and heartbreaking denouement of the film.

After the conclusion of the embedded short film, *5th World* cuts to the next morning. Aria and Andrei are preparing to leave Auntie's and Uncle's. Their brief visit was welcome, but their destination is Shiprock. Auntie disapproves of hitchhiking, so the Elders loan them their "dirty" truck. This alludes to the Christian ideals that passionate and impromptu sex before marriage is dirty. To balance the dirty exterior of the truck, the inside cabin becomes a space of dirtiness after Andrei and Aria consummate their relationship there later that day.

Andrei, Postsex

Time has passed in the fictional world of the film since Aria and Andrei are introduced. Lowe says, "These two characters . . . get to know more about themselves and the landscape."[43] Their intimate conversations while hitchhiking, the advice given to them through the voices of gods (Auntie and Uncle's love story, which is the overarching oral narrative), and the numerous family-based scenes have solidified their love. They stop on the side of the road to profess their love and spontaneously have sex. Afterward, both in bliss, they joke about their hunger (for more sex) and stop at a roadside café, where Andrei and Aria joke about slipping into "total mutton ecstasy" while bleating like sheep.

Their postsex happiness is intercut with a flashback. In Diné bizaad, we hear Uncle tell Andrei and Aria: "We planned. Every step, we planned. We didn't rush into it. . . . At every step we had a ceremony." This cautionary council fell on deaf ears; the film suddenly flashes forward to the present, with Andrei and Aria sated, driving, and bleating. Suddenly, Aria asks Andrei what he and his cousin-brother "*Jo-oo-ohn*" were talking about underneath the tree.[44] It is at this point where the critical discussion of k'éí finally occurs between the two young lovers. Andrei tries to avoid the question and says their conversation was "something about Clans; nothing too important. [*long pause*] What were your Clans anyways?" Aria answers, "I thought we already went through this." He nervously asks her to humor him and share her Clans again. In Diné bizaad, she says she is Red Running Through the Water, born for Coyote Pass People. To which he incredulously asks, "No; seriously, what are your Clans?" She repeats, in an incomplete Navajo sentence, "Táchii'nii dóó Mą'ii deeshgiizhnii." This is the immediate turning point in the film. He continues driving, visibly agitated, and his facial expressions reveal hóchxǫ́—confusion, anger, disbelief, and grief—which was a direct result of their actions.

Lowe's creative eye and editing do two things: he abruptly but convincingly ends this scene and integrates the next scene with a series of artistic jump cuts that depict Andrei's inner turmoil of disgust, regret, and guilt. Lowe implements various shots of a distressed Andrei (who is finally named, via full-screen-sized title cards that say, word by word, shot by shot: "This. Is. Where. Andrei. Screams. . . . FUCK!") The accompanying noise (sound) in this fast-paced, heart-pumping montage is cringeworthy. A screeching sound evolves into the vocal scream-singing by the lead singer of a house-party band, whose vocals are the exact ones that Andrei is said to be screaming: "Fuuuuuuuck!" This entire postsex, house-party scene is overdubbed by nondiegetic sound. There is no diegetic communication or house-party noises—we only hear loud music, which creates disorder. We see Andrei withdraw from Aria, by ignoring, avoiding, and betraying her. We see his bad treatment of her, but we don't hear anything. The conversations are reflected only as subtitles, which is how Lowe unveils that Aria is Red Running Through the Water, like Andrei and John. Conniving "Injun John" plots an alternate union between Andrei and the lead singer, Melaw. According to John's subtitles, Melaw is not Nav, so there is no way the two could be related by Clan. Andrei's postsex conversation with Aria depicts the consequences of not heeding Elder and storied advice to take things slow. Sonic sovereignty here is consequential. Young adults still have much to listen to and learn from through the teachings of the Diné philosophy of Sa'ąh Naagháí Bik'eh Hózhǫ́ǫ́n before they advance to adulthood. Denetdale outlines the interdependence of the philosophy's applicability to situations like those we witnessed in *5th World*: "for the Navajos, the continuing significance of clan relationships, a sense of community with the land, and the importance of pastoralism are connected through a philosophy that stresses the continual search for *hózhó*, the path to harmony and Old Age."[45]

Mistakes and errors are inevitable, as even the ancient teachers from cosmology erred. Some teachings, however, should be adhered to, like respecting and honoring Clanship protocols. In *Navajo Stories of the Long Walk Period*, Hosteen Tso Begay writes: "When the clan system is forgotten, this will be the end—just like walking off a cliff."[46] Has Andrei forgotten one of the most important teachings? Might he be on the edge of this metaphorical cliff? Throughout the film, we come to understand that Andrei is grounded in Diné bizaad, as he converses with his Auntie and Uncle, promises to return to fulfill his kinship obligations to help with the planting and harvest, and lives Diné culture. That he directly ignored the first step of Diné 101 when forming new relationships—establish k'éí—is reflective of the consequences from Fourth World hane' of Diné journey narratives where forbidden sexual unions resulted in "monsters," or Naayéé. The Naayéé evoke hóchxǫ́, which is manifested in Andrei and his postsex behavior.

Silent Cinematic Hane'tonomy

After Andrei and Aria discover their incestuous actions, as they are siblings by Clan, they are simply stunned and ashamed (but for different reasons). Andrei knew better; Aria is depicted as innocently unaware and her shame can be read as confusion. Lowe translates these affectual moments as silence. Scholars and film critics have viewed, listened, and critiqued his cinematic choices through whiteness, dismissing the silence and long shots of land as inexperienced and artsy.[47] Though there is very little spoken dialogue, Lowe overlays the visual narrative with the nondiegetic sound of a lo-fi soundtrack by Corey Allison (who stars as cousin-brother John) and the unnamed house band. In the closing scene of *5th World*, Auntie's and Uncle's most important words overdub fond flashbacks of Aria's and Andrei's trek from Phoenix. Auntie and Uncle share, off-screen, that their Elders offered them sage advice at their traditional Navajo wedding. Auntie and Uncle regret that they did not listen to all their teachings, as now some have died. The teachings about Diné-centered love are valuable and were not originally told to instill rigidity and fear. The knowledges of the Protector Twins at the site of Shiprock Peak, the hane' of Clan origins and relations, and the teachings about consequences promote Diné sovereignty and cultural laws and values. Larry W. Emerson eloquently evokes Asdzą́ą́ Nádleehé, reminding us that "our kinship system is born of Changing Woman, who knows no harm and knows only love, compassion, and care. Why not assert and privilege Diné-centered sovereign action in this manner?"[48] Diné-centered sovereign action promotes hózhǫ́ and is reflected in the characters of Auntie and Uncle. Though we do not *see* them doing much, we *hear* their epic love story in disjointed vignettes; this is Diné diegesis. The teachings and privileging of Diné bizaad over visual imagery are evocative of Sa'ąh Naagháí Bik'eh Hózhǫ́ǫ́n. While wrapping up their epic love story (which is ongoing), Uncle jests in the Navajo language that, on his Navajo traditional wedding day to Auntie, he (too) did not really listen to Elders and their important teachings: "all I want[ed] to do was make love!"

The film could have ended here, with these jokingly wise and honest words (in Diné bizaad and subtitled by Lowe). However, *5th World* pauses on a long shot of the landscape, cut in half by a highway. Andrei is driving Aria home; she lives under the protection of Tsé Bit'a'í's towering wing. Lowe insists on conveying uncomfortable silence, as all we hear is the truck's wheels whirring down the highway. Andrei finally breaks the silence and asks Aria which road he needs to turn on to deliver her home. We hear the turn signal and other sounds coming from inside the deathly still interior. He pulls to the side of the road and we see Tsé Bit'a'í, dwarfed by the long shot of the surrounding landscape, as it appears far off in the distance. The awkward silence lasts a few beats; the time is filled by a series of long takes of their heartbroken expressions until Aria finally gets out of the truck. Without words and teary-eyed, he drives away abruptly, leaving Aria on the side of the road, with Shiprock peak directly behind her.

Tsé Bit'a'í now becomes the focal point, as several long takes of the monolith are loosely framed from various angles and distances and only the sound of the wind is audible. The Diné diegesis concludes with an image of Aria dressed in her traditional Navajo clothing, with her hair in a tsiiyééł (Diné-style hair bun), as she is looking in a mirror. While she gazes at her image, reflective of Asdzą́ą́ Nádleehé (Changing Woman), a photo montage from her chaotic and short-lived love with Andrei appears in rapid succession. While not explicitly evident, one can conclude that she is donned in her traditional, ceremonial attire, perhaps readying for

FIGURE 11 Aria in traditional clothing. From *5th World* trailer.

her own special wedding day. At the beginning of *5th World*, Aria narrates a prophetic dream to Andrei: "And here I was . . . all by myself. The whole thing was just a big tease." I understand Aria's muteness as very symbolic from the moment she shared her Navajo-language Clans to answering his question of which road to turn off at. She ultimately answers with "the Fourth One" (meaning she lives on the fourth road, coming up).

The film is called *5th World*, which is a direct co-option of a vignette of the larger literary body of Navajo journey stories. The Fifth World, or the Glittering World, is where we are today, and it is the refuge from the chaos and disharmony of the Fourth World. Aria's utterance of "the Fourth One" could be a cautionary reminder. It could also, literally, just be that she lives four roads up. But if we test the allusion to the Fourth World as shared in the journey narratives, we recall that this is the world that describes how mountains and rock formations unique to the Diné landscape were made. In the Fourth World we are taught cautionary stories of gambling and impatience. We also learn about the powerful creation of the celestial beings: the sun, the moon, and the stars. Other moments in the Fourth World include the introduction of death, disharmony, and disorder, which were brought into our contemporary realities. The climb up into the Fifth World puts humans on the stage where the effects of the actions from the Fourth World play out: specifically, during the separation of the sexes in the Fourth World (where women are blamed for the lusty manufacture of monsters) by reportedly, jiní, having sex with cacti, and "fashioned stones, wood, and feathers."[49] These monsters, discussed previously, were subsequently slain by the Hero Twins at specific sites on the contemporary Navajo Nation. One of these sites was Tsé Bit'a'í, or Shiprock Peak, which Lowe dwells on as long takes at the end of *5th World*. Lowe has stated, "It's important that our stories are shown everywhere. . . . Film is an immediate delivery device of ideas and culture. It reflects who we are at this moment—our emotions, our languages, our way of living in this world."[50] By enlisting and insisting in silent cinematic hane'tonomy for the final scenes of *5th World*, Lowe's editorial genius forces us to think carefully about what that silence is saying and doing. This took me back to the teachings from the Fourth World of the journey epic, because of Aria's emulation of Changing Woman at the end. Aria is confident and does not dwell on the many betrayals, yet she has learned from her big tease, Andrei. The closing extreme close-up of Andrei's face reveals desperation and regret. He must shed his own monsters to come to wellness and harmony, and fortunately, he has the strong kinship network to do this. The denouement of *5th World* demonstrates how the Tsé Bit'a'í stories can be incorporated into visual storytelling for contemporary Navajos as the site of creation, destruction, forgiveness, rebirth, harmony, and restoration.

Facing monsters, whether one's own or literary ones, is central to the stories in the next chapter. The purpose of monsters, destroyers, and predators is to dissuade People from coming to a state of hózhǫ́. From the fifth world of Dinétah stories, the next chapter makes a literary journey to Denendeh. This chapter was inspired by my work with Dene students, Elders, and community members and our mutual curiosity to unearth more about Diné and Dene relationality through storytelling, firmly grounded in respecting traditional Dene laws. Dene literary arts is rich, expansive, and flourishing, and this is just one small step forward.

CHAPTER 5

Denendeh Storytelling

Kinship Restor(i)ed

> Our system, before the white man came, it was a storytelling system. This telling, the Elders have that, and . . . will tell the parents "Teach your baby when your baby starts to talk. Teach him about *Yamoria* law, how to be good citizens. How you can love each other and work together. Good, no violence, no fighting, love each other that way you will do good."
>
> —GEORGE BLONDIN, "I STILL AM IN LOVE WITH THE LAND. I AM STILL IN LOVE WITH MY HISTORY"

In the Navajo language, the concept for story and narrative is hane'. In the Dene languages of Dënesųłıné, it is honi, and in Tłıchǫ it is hondi.[1] Honi/hondi/hane' are cognates, and I argue that they affirm Diné and Dene relationality, demonstrating restoration of the "storytelling system" that privileges the teaching of Dene laws, or Yamoria law, according to the late Dene Elder, writer, politician, and land protector George Blondin from the Northwest Territories. The tenets of Dene laws are essentially to share, help, love, be respectful to Elders, not be lazy, be polite, encourage youth to behave, pass on teachings, and be happy. They reflect the Diné philosophical tenets of hózhǫ́ and saad. Luci Tapahonso foretold of saad: "[It] is not separate from the memory of the land, the wind or the night sky. It is the essence of what we were taught: that as long as we recognize our responsibilities to each other and the world, we will go on."[2] Viewing ancient and contemporary Dene storytelling through a Diné lens reveals literary linkages of kinship love, accountability and reciprocity, resilience, and survivance. The teachings of Nihimá (our mother, kéyah), the elements, and celestial beings instill goodness, harmony, cooperation, balance, peace, and wellness (or hózhǫ́ and Dene laws), which all but ensure thriving Dene and Diné futures.

This chapter is organized into four sections, grounded in traditional Dene laws. Rather than an exhaustive study of Denendeh storytelling, it is selective and exploratory, where story (honi/hondi/hane') is the nexus of kinship and restoration (of land, languages, families, and Dene laws). The first section, "The Dene of Denendeh," is a broad historical and geographic overview. The second section is "Dene Oratory," in which I clarify how the literary criticism on restorying influences my thinking. Oratory is the foundation of restorying and of restoration; I introduce the Dene cultural hero as told through honi/hondi. I expand on orature in the third section, "Contemporary Dene Storytelling," including an analysis of literature and a foray into beadwork as story. The concluding section, "Dene Yati and Dene Language Restoration," introduces two language initiatives. Dene poets and artists long for language fluency, which they grapple with in their creative works. The exploratory work reflected in this chapter barely scratches the surface of the wealth of Dene storytelling as restorative.[3]

The Dene of Denendeh

This book has been a storied journey from Dinétah ("Land of the People") to Denendeh ("Land of the People"). Dinétah is in the southwestern United States, locating Diné governance and Peoplehood within the sacred mountains, Tsisnaajiní (also Sisnaajiní), Tsoodził, Dookʼoʼoosłííd, and Dibé Ntsaa, Dził Náʼooditii, and Chʼoolʼíʼí.[4] The vast geographic homelands of Dene communities are in Denendeh, or north of the Medicine Line in what is currently Canada. My point of reference starts at the middle of the provincial border of Alberta and the Northwest Territories to illustrate some Dene communities from Denendeh based on the four cardinal directions.[5] To the east are the Sayisi Dene (northern Manitoba); to the south are the Tsaatine (Beaver) and the Tsuut'ina (Sarcee). To the west are the eastern Gwich'in, the Kaska Dena; the far western Dene are the Tsek'ehne (Sekani), Dakelh (Carrier), and Tsilhqot'in (Chilcotin). To the north is the northern Dene Nation, composed of the Dehcho (formerly the Mackenzie Dene) and including the Łíídlįį Kų́ę́ (South Slavey); there are also the Tłı̨chǫ (Dogrib), Dënesųłiné (Chipewyan), Wıìlıìdeh

(Yellowknives), Sahtú Dene (North Slavey or Hare), and Mountain Dene.[6] Each community speaks a version of Dene, illustrating the diversity of living Dene languages, though endangered.[7] The languages specific to this chapter are Dënesųłiné (Chipewyan) and Tłįchǫ Yatiì (Dogrib). The dialect of Wıìlıìdeh Yatı (spoken by Yellowknives) is from Tłįchǫ Yatiì. I use the word *Dene* to generalize when appropriate.

Despite similarities among a few key words across our languages, Diné and Dene are culturally, historically, politically, and geographically different Indigenous Nations of People. As one anonymous peer reviewer of this book noted, our "differences are part of being a relative." In chapter 1, I shared a Tsé Bit'a'í origin story that connects the Diné and the Dene, affirming our relationality. My original objective was to uncover honi/hondi/hane' that would demonstrate and solidify how stories transgress time, distance, and communities and to link the Diné and the Dene. However, I have come to realize that there does not have to be other stories directly evoking Tsé Bit'a'í. For instance, when two people meet each other for the first time and discover they are related, there is usually an immediate recognition of relationality, despite not having known each other previously. They continue to be relatives, as they had been prior to meeting. This is demonstrative of kinship. As in the lone Tsuut'ina-told Tsé Bit'a'í origin story, people who have met and are related do not need to meet more distant relatives to affirm their kinship. Tłįchǫ Dene storyteller Richard Van Camp is a creative northern cousin (a kinship term of endearment). "Cousin" is both literal and inclusive, but it also sets people apart as different. Van Camp observes, "Through our stories and traditions and languages, we are reclaiming ourselves, coming together, gathering, and gaining strength through our love and connection—remembering and recalling our stories and passing them on for medicine and strength and love and healing."[8] The inclusive sentiment of reclamation, gathering, and storying reflects Dene law as well as the Diné philosophy of striving for hózhǫ́. Through stories (oral, traditional, restoried, and beaded), I bring our cousins together across the thousands of miles that currently divide us, by uniting over non-Tsé Bit'a'í honi/hondi/hane' as a model to restore relations. Restoried stories, or restorying, is the active recovery (restoration) of literary absence, according to Daniel Heath Justice (Cherokee):

Denendeh Storytelling

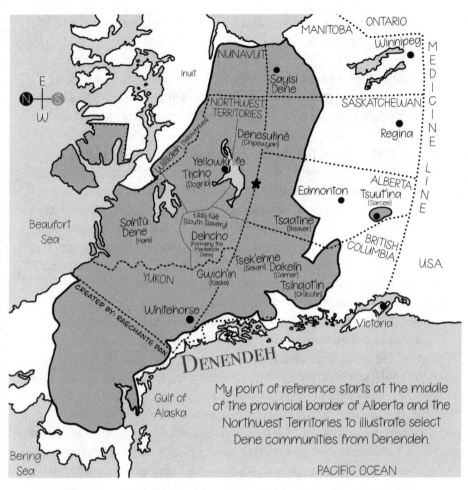

MAP 3 Denendeh. Created by Raechante Dan.

As a writer and scholar for whom story is the central axis of understanding, the absences and the hard-fought returnings of some of our stories—who we are, where we come from, how we came into relationship with one another—have carried some of the deepest grief and the most transformative joy in my life. Some people are fortunate to have access to these things from cradle to grave, but not all of us have that luck. For many, our lives are a process of restoring—re-storying—the bonds that connect us and our families to those who came before and to those who come after, while grappling as honestly and fiercely as possible with the consequences of the ruptures in those relations.[9]

The stories I introduce are primarily those that are restoried, "the hard-fought returnings" that affirm Dene being and origins; storytellers return to their origin stories, recognizing kinship to ancestral orators.[10] I turn to the ancestral orators of Dene writers to demonstrate Diné and Dene kinscapes. Métis scholar Brenda Macdougall advances a theory about Métis kinscapes based on the work of historian Sami Lakomäki (who coined the term *kinscape*). She writes, "Metis society revolved around . . . relational constellations defining a cultural landscape that, in turn, permitted a people to maintain political and economic cohesiveness despite being dispersed across large geographic expanses."[11] Diné and Dene literary arts reflect and revitalize living languages, oral stories, and laws of the land for the People that are tantamount to the "relational constellations . . . across large geographic expanses," which constitute the notion of kinscapes that Macdougall adopts.[12] The Diné and Dene kinscapes transgress state-implemented borders and uphold Diné and Dene relationality "with, across, and beyond the physical bounds of political, geographic, and cultural borders."[13] It is through Indigenous literatures' "focus on the art of relationships—with ourselves, our living relatives, our ancestors, and the land" that we enact restorying and restoration to achieve hózhǫ́.[14]

My interest in transborder Dene kinscapes and oral stories was ignited when I was embraced as a relative north of the Medicine Line by Dene students, and moreover when I learned the Tsuut'ina (a Dene community) version of Tsé Bit'a'í's origin, which I interrogate in chapter 1. My maternal family hails from the reservation community called Shiprock, distinguished by the landmark Tsé Bit'a'í, or "Winged Rock." Tsé Bit'a'í has been restoried in the Diné journey narratives as well as by the Eagletail family from Tsuut'ina. Oral stories that honor her existence are well known in Dinétah, as is the incomplete variant that the landmark resembles the fossilized wing of an ancient avian. Stories affirm relationality, and curiosity about Diné and Dene kinship and our geographic separation has culminated in renewed interest to unearth answers, whether literal or metaphorical. Justice writes, "Metaphors alone can't encompass what it is to be human, nor can lived experience. For that, we need stories."[15] Upon hearing the Tsuut'ina story, I was encouraged to integrate the work of Dene storytellers and to shift my initial focus from a strictly Diné one to include oral, literary, and visual honi/hondi from our Dene relatives in Denendeh. While compilations, anthologies, and entire courses are built around Dene literary arts, I reference only select storytellers.

Dene Oratory

Georges Erasmus is a Tłı̨chǫ orator from Behchokǫ̀.[16] He served as the former president of the Indian Brotherhood of the Northwest Territories (1976–83), which changed its name to the Dene Nation in 1978. He was also elected National Chief of the Assembly of First Nations, a role he served from 1985 to 1991. Erasmus's work propelled Dene (and Indigenous issues at large) into the public spotlight, earning him recognition and inclusion as a member of the Order of Canada. Of traditional Dene laws, he says,

> Long before Europeans decided to look for resources and riches outside of their own boundaries, the Dene nation existed. We had our own way of life, we had our own laws by which we governed ourselves, by which we lived together—laws for educating young people, laws for respecting old people, laws respecting our land. We had our own ways of worship and our own economic system. We had a complete way of life. We ourselves decided what was best for us and for our land.[17]

This quote is evocative of Erasmus's lifelong work to protect the land, to point out how Denendeh natural resources were extracted, and to emphasize political and cultural sovereignty (self-governance) through Dene laws. His oratory remains important and the laws guide People on how to live in mutual respect and harmony. The nine laws (Dǫne Nàowo) as expressed in Tłı̨chǫ Yatıì are

1. Ayìi naxits'ǫ sìi ełeghàahdi: Share what you have.
2. Ełeèts'ahdì: Help each other.
3. Ats'ǫ Ełeghǫnets'etǫ: Love each other as much as possible.
4. Goʔ ǫhdaà hoti wenaet'ı̨xè asìi hazhǫ, naximǫ whela sìi wenaet'į̀: Be respectful of Elders and everything around you.

5. Too whahte eyits'ǫ dzę̀ę̀ eghàlaahdè: Sleep at night and work during the day.
6. Dǫ nezı̨ ahłı̨ eyits'ǫ dǫne ch'aa gahde-le: Be polite and don't argue with anyone.
7. T'ekaà eyits'ǫ dǫzhìa wenaet'ı̨k'èk' èhogeʔa ha: Young girls and boys should behave respectfully.
8. Nàowo wek'ers'ezhǫ wet'à dǫne hoghàgets'ehtǫ ha: Pass on the teachings.
9. Ats'ǫ naxìnàà nezı̨ naxìxè gòeʔà: Be happy at all times.[18]

Sharing, helping, loving, being respectful to Elders, sleeping at night and working during the day, being polite and peaceful (which models for youth how to behave), passing on Elders' teachings, and being happy are principles that encourage communal wellness, balance, harmony, peace, or hózhǫ́. Like hózhǫ́, Dene laws are not the "destination" but the journey.

Erasmus was in a political position to advocate for sovereignty. In his role as a politician and leader, some of the Dene laws were more challenging to achieve (like "don't argue with anyone"). To remind all citizens of Dene autonomy, as grounded in precontact teachings, he clearly articulated Dene narrative autonomy, hane'tonomy, as cultural and ecological wealth that surpasses colonial notions of extractive wealth.

In addition to emphasizing precontact Dene autonomy, the chapter's opening oratorical epigraph highlights the Dene laws as Yamoria laws by invoking a cultural hero and storied Dene lawmaker. Yamoria is the Dene Sahtú name that means "he who travels," "walks around the world," or "the great traveler" and is also commonly known as Yamozha.[19] Yamozha is also spelled Yomǫ̀ǫ̀zha. Other names are "Atachuukaii for the Gwich'in, Yamoria for the North Slavey, Zhamba Deja for the South Slavey, Hachoghe for the Chipewyan and Yamozha for the Tłı̨cho, and Yellowknives Dene."[20] Dene communities determine the name of the cultural hero, and the essence of their stories is the same. Yamoria/Yamozha existed to make laws for the People: he "usher[ed] out an age of darkness, and [brought] in an age of freedom for the Dene."[21] Yamoria/Yamozha "was perhaps the most powerful medicine person throughout history. He was able to fly anywhere with the spirits. He was able to go from place to place very quickly. He could talk to any animal or bird, with no problem. He could make himself into an animal if he wanted to."[22] He "came to change the lives of the Dene and encourage them to care for each other and establish equality."[23] Some stories say the cultural hero had a sibling named Sazea, Yamória, or Yamoga.[24] Yamozha/Yamória "stories conveyed [Dene] traditional law to the people; and thus functioned as a legal institution."[25] Yamoria's/Yamozha's storied presence was also as cultural hero who could shape-shift and a Dene Protector who used his powers to kill giant animal monsters that threatened the Dene—this echoes the Diné Hero siblings: Naayéé Neezgháni, the Protector, and Tó Bájísh Chíní, the Peacemaker, who also overcame adversity caused by metaphorical giants.

It is significant that Yamoria/Yamozha has a brother—as several Indigenous stories highlight the kinship roles and responsibilities between elder and younger siblings. The Dene siblings separate in adulthood and eventually rekindle their kinship and reunite for a short time:

> The end of the two brothers is as mysterious as their beginnings. Some stories say Yamoria continued down the Mackenzie River and floated out into the Arctic Ocean. [Fred] Sangris, [Yellowknives Dene Elder,] says both brothers, old and grey, reunited in Lac De Gras, about 300 kilometres northeast of Yellowknife. There they argued about who had better medicine power, and fought an epic battle, making the earth roar and shake. This fight created many of the lakes that dot the landscape north of Great Slave Lake, as the brothers dragged each other across the territory.[26]

While contrary to a few of the Dene laws (arguing, disrespecting, and overall disharmony), the story of the feuding brothers explains topography. That the Dene stories do not offer insight about the separation of the siblings and of Yamoria's/Yamozha's globetrotting allows for a few possibilities. In chapter 1, I shared a Tsuut'ina story of the separation of feuding brothers that ultimately landed one brother and his family in Dinétah, while the other brother stayed in Denendeh. Ultimately, the fragments of oral stories, when combined, make up a saga that is ripe for further study. Yamoria/Yamozha could travel far, and because of his medicine power he could shape-shift. Language and stories traveled with him, which suggests that he shared them with others during his travels. It is also not out of the question that Yamoria/Yamozha spread his seed, creating kinship relations and restorying to adapt to diverse geographic environments and landscapes. In "How Stories Connect Us," Van Camp says *Gather* prompted him to think about "how the universe has scattered us across this beautiful planet of ours, but it's stories that unite us."[27] The scattering respects cultural diversity yet embraces selective cultural adoption. Honi/hondi/hane' have power; they are dynamic, alive, and didactic.

As a cultural hero, Yamoria/Yamozha offers a way to explain the spectacular through the affiliated stories, which is like other Indigenous epics that involve shape-shifters or cultural transformers. Indigenous studies scholar Robert Alexander Innes argues in his book *Elder Brother and the Law of the People* that "the values embedded in these spiritual stories are more important than their historical accuracy. . . . These stories did and continue to exist in oral and written form."[28] Likewise, Diné historian Jennifer Nez Denetdale emphasizes the relationship of oral history to Navajo cultural sovereignty, "for the teachings of our ancestors are reaffirmed in the retelling of stories."[29] Innes's observation is that the point of traditional stories is not their believability but rather to remember that they "continue to guide Aboriginal peoples' interactions. [Stories] can assist scholars to understand these interactions and to demonstrate cultural persistence, revitalization, and resistance to colonization."[30] Contemporary scholars continue to advance the interdependence of oral history and laws of the People, traditional governance, and decolonization. Restorying and restoring traditional honi/hondi/hane', respected as laws of the People, are decolonial acts and have been creating meaning for as long as humans could communicate with one another, across geographic kinscapes, and with hózhǫ́.

Contemporary Dene Storytelling

In 1999, "I Still Am in Love with the Land. I Am Still in Love with My History," the published account of George Blondin, urged parents to uphold the Dene "storytelling system," which privileges orature. As if a literal response, twenty-one years later, Yellowknives Dene author Katłįà (who has also published under the name Catherine Lafferty) reimagined oral traditions, hondi, in her debut novel, *Land-Water-Sky: Ndè -Ti-Yat'a* (2020). Several characters' names are in the Dene language (Wıı̀lıı̀deh Yatı̀ dialect) and honor land-based terminology, reflecting the book's title. "Land" is storied as Àma; "water" can be interpreted by two characters, Dahtı̀ (which means fresh morning dew) and Deèyeh (meaning "calm water"); and "sky" is depicted by Yat'a (the celestial mother to Dahtì). In a refreshing restorying of the lone cultural hero trope, Katłı̨à's novel further emphasizes kinship through Sizèh, the Elder. Although an Elder for the bulk of the book, Sizèh is introduced early on as the youngest brother of a pack; his father is the antagonist. Together, these characters work together to end disharmony and darkness, portrayed by a cultural destroyer, Nąąhgą. As a literary epic, *Land-Water-Sky* braids the characters and implicit Dene laws throughout six Dene episodic vignettes, beginning in time immemorial and concluding in the year 2030.[31]

The novel's Dene-language title, *Ndè-Ti-Yat'a*, consists of three words in the dialect of Wıı̀lıı̀deh Yatı̀, which is one of two Dene languages spoken by Yellowknives Dene; the other is Dënesųłıné. There are many cognate words in Wıı̀lıı̀deh Yatı̀ and Diné bizaad (the Navajo language) that speak to shared experiences with the land and kinship. Using Diné or Dene words to convey nuances of meaning is narrative autonomy, or hane'tonomy, as I have introduced earlier in the book to talk about visual storytelling autonomy. *Ndè-Ti-Yat'a* warrants unpacking: ndè means land, ti means water, and yat'a means sky. Two of these are cognate words in Diné bizaad: the Navajo word for water is tó, and sky is yá. Our respective words for "land" are very different (ndè and kéyah), much like our geographic surroundings.[32] Denendeh is replete with water—lakes, rivers, swamps, and tundra—which expands my lived experience amid the four sacred mountains of Dinétah where water is sparse. Dinétah or Diné Bikéyah beauty comes from red rocks, sandstone, desert landscapes, and small mountain ranges with piñon and juniper trees.

The novel opens with a story called "Àma" and is set in the Northwestern Hemisphere in "time immemorial." I interpret Àma as Mother Earth (Nahasdzáán) personified. Àma is an analogy for the land (ndè). 'Ałk'idą́ą́' jiní, the hondi begins by introducing a striking stranger, a handsome man whose vision magic manipulates a woman into a powerless trance. Under his evil powers, she is unable to consent, to think, or to act independently. He coerces her to lead him to her home community, where he terrorizes her parents and the Elders: "He wants the people to know who he is, that he is alive and dangerous just as the stories told. He wants them to know that he has and will always rule the land."[33] The stranger abducts Àma to live as his wife and takes her to his home, where he rapes her. She births a pack of children who are described as having thick, rough skin and untamed hair that grows on their feet and hands, which they also walk on. Katłįà restories the ancient Tłįchǫ story of creation, which explains their English name of Dogrib to comment on the rape of Mother Earth, the rape of women, domestic violence, and maternal abandonment as contemporary kinship ruptures that can be restored. In time, Àma wakes from the power he has over her and realizes that "his figure has a striking resemblance to a wild manlike animal, like the stories that she was warned about as a child."[34] Àma's role as life giver ends after she bears "his pack." They ultimately fight with their children present; he gashes Àma behind the knee and she "charges at him with her blade in a sudden protective maternal fury . . . driv[ing] the dagger into his flesh, piercing his paw so savagely that she rips his middle claw off."[35] He is permanently disfigured and his once boastful attitude that "no man on Earth . . . can stop him" foreshadows the rest of the novel's trajectory.[36] Tragically, her self-survival means she must leave her children, for which she is deeply remorseful. Throughout the ages, Àma, their mother, searches for them and "speaks out loud to them, hoping they can hear her in their hearts."[37]

Some of Katłįà's life experiences inspired the characterization of Deèyeh, introduced in medias res, in the year 2000. Deèyeh is an archaeology student who traveled home to the fictional Háyorîla Nation to learn more about Dene identity, teachings, and familial relations. She was fostered outside the community and was raised without love, stories, and teachings. Upon her return, Deèyeh befriends Elders, the local Chief, and his wife, Goli. After an initial feast, the Chief takes on the role of storyteller, teaching Deèyeh "the stories of the Háyorila people, including the legend of the rock that stood at the top of the island, so aptly called Nàejì Rock."[38] This scene reflects Dene laws in multiple ways: they shared food and demonstrated love, respect, and happiness, while passing on teachings. Nàejì Island is an homage to Katłįà's grandmother's birthplace, Nishi Island, which is near Behchokǫ̀ in the Northwest Territories. Katłįà says, "Nàejì means healing in my language, and for me that is what the island is, a place of healing."[39] The Chief continues, "The sacred rock was placed on the highest point of the island. We believe it to be the place where the great legendary warrior kept watch protecting the island from the beasts that roamed the Earth."[40] The Chief's hondi focuses on Nàejì Rock and the land, Dene decedents, community, a "legendary warrior," and monstrous antagonists. Dahtì is the legendary warrior, the Protector, whose parents are Mòzhįą (his father and a mortal) and Yat'a, an "outsider... a gift from the Sky Spirits... brought down to Earth to live as one with humans... created so she could share her gifts and keep the stories and legends of the spirit world alive."[41] The protection of Nàejì Island is in tandem with the capture, judgment, and eternal sentencing of Nąąhgą and requires the cross-century coordination and connection of Dene relations as Protectors. The character icons and their actions are familiar tropes across oral stories from diverse Indigenous Nations, making this epic a restorying.

Yamoria/Yamozha stories classify him as well traveled—across vast lands and temporalities. Well-traveled heroes like Àma, Dahtì, and Sizèh are often in search of destroyers or antagonists who are equally cosmopolitan. Katłįà restories a figure who "had travelled to distant lands and seen all that the world had to offer. But it was the North that welcomed him with a cold ruthlessness that suited him best."[42] Nąąhgą is a character braided throughout the novel; Katłįà defines him as "a bushman shapeshifter."[43] In *The People of Denendeh,* June Helm compiles oral stories from interviews and ethnographic reports on the Nąąhgą (which she asserts is from Wìilìideh Yatì). She writes, "Northern Athapaskans usually have references in English to 'bushmen,' 'bad Indians,' or ... 'spies'"; she lists at least six different variants of Nąąhgą.[44] The stories Helm shares about the Nąąhgą describe them as summer roamers who hibernate like bears in winter underground lairs and who travel in packs in search of women and children, which parallels Àma's storyline. As Nąąhgą is a shape-shifting traveler (which is characteristic for cultural heroes), it is important to distinguish him as a destroyer.[45]

Nąąhgą is both antagonist and storyteller, as he narrates the final story of the novel. He appears throughout the cycle of stories as the mysterious destroyer/animal figure that preys in the shadows or in human form as a handsome, albeit greedy, stranger, Louie Sloan—Louie in chapter 3 and Sloan in chapter 5. In the early chapters as Nąąhgą, he rapes Àma, murders Yat'a, and lusts over controlling the land. Later, as Louie, he is a bully and a drug kingpin. His cronies fear him; he spends generously, donning "custom made cufflinks [that] matched a large silver metal claw that he wore on his missing middle finger."[46] As Sloan, he is a deadbeat moocher, glaringly illustrating what happens when Dene law 5 is not adhered to. Sloan is a charmer; coupled with his chiseled good looks (and missing finger), he entrances and traumatizes Lafì (which means girl) for more than six years, until 2007. In both chapters, Louie and Sloan appear to transform, are destroyers, are opulent spenders, are violent, have insatiable appetites for good meat, and throw fits when not satisfied. These are classic windigo/wendigo/wetiko/wheetago behaviors.[47] Louie *and* Sloan, or Louie Sloan, is dreaded, greedy, selfish, and monstrous.

Stories about the dangers of strange men abound in oral traditions; these speak to the horrific truth that many survivors of the missing and murdered face. Readers of the novel, which spans centuries and storylines, are witness to rematriation through restorying and restoring imbalance and kinship ruptures. Àma and Lafi ultimately free themselves from a shape-shifting predator's four-fingered grasp. Even in death, Yat'a "had the power to control the heavens"; as such, her presence as thunder, lightning, and rain aids in bringing peace, harmony, and balance.[48]

Deèyeh's chapter braids ancient characters, cultural heroes, contemporary Elders, and nonhuman kin to reveal kinship ties that she was deprived of. Deèyeh is aligned with matriarchal kin, Àma, as they have parallel experiences that occur centuries apart. For instance, Deèyeh also gets attacked and bitten by Tłi (dog), "on the meaty part of her leg behind her knee," and is miraculously healed by the waters that surround the island.[49] Through these storied characters, she experiences the healing and destructive powers of the land, water, and sky. Deèyeh's chapter is one of discovery, as she literally unearths archaeological evidence that proves the fictional Dene community's cultural and legal inheritance to the land. She also discovers, for the first time, community, kinship, and love, which unearth stories and teachings that reflect Dene culture. One early scene introduces Deèyeh to Dene hand games, where "most of the men were wearing fantastic handmade caribou hide vests adorned with fine beadwork. The women were wearing ankle high crow boots decorated in beautiful beaded flowers."[50] The Métis, self-proclaimed "Flower Beadwork People," are said to have "acted as agents of change in the decorative arts of Dene clothing fashions."[51] Other examples of Dene clothing fashions that Deèyeh might have seen are mittens, tunics, and babies in fully beaded moss bags. As one who beads, I am attracted to the cultural bannock crumbs in honi/hondi/hane' when authors reference beaded vests, moccasins, and jewelry, as this chapter does.

As Deèyeh is interning as an archaeology student, she might have studied that archaeologists have unearthed precontact beads made from stones, shells, hollow bark, and quills, some of which date back four thousand years.[52] Beadwork created from postcontact materials celebrates Indigenous existence and continuance, and in addition to the beaded florals that Deèyeh admired, beadworkers' designs are influenced by Indigenous surroundings, including animals, berries, waters, and skies (cosmos, planets, and the universe).[53] Beadwork "can be used as a mnemonic device... [and] acts as a vehicle of knowledge transfer."[54] Traditional stories carry knowledge; they are not limited to the oral or alphabetic but are also beaded. Beadwork nourishes, sustains, and connects Peoples and communities. Because Deèyeh is a returning community member, Katłįà realistically portrays a young woman who might not catch rich cultural cues but who can appreciate the aesthetic power of beadwork.

Deèyeh's story is the longest in the story cycle; the shortest is the final hondi, called "Ną̀ą̀hgą." It takes place in the future, in 2030 CE. Ną̀ą̀hgą is the narrator and characterizes himself as "nothing more than the purest form of evil."[55] He confirms and affirms the ancient hondi of his presence and destruction as well as comments on the effects of colonization and land dispossession, which resulted in houselessness, climate change, societal collapse, and capitalism. In the end, Ną̀ą̀hgą is tricked by his son, described initially as "the youngest, the runt of the litter, who bears a distinctive silver streak on top of his head," and later described as a knowledgeable Elder intimately familiar with Nàejì Island named Sizèh, a man with a "silver streaked head."[56] Sizèh captures Ną̀ą̀hgą and brings him to the island, where Àma enacts revenge. We learn that centuries-old Dahtì (the son of Yat'a), twenty-something Deèyeh, and Lafì work together with Àma to entrap—but not kill—Ną̀ą̀hgą. To kill him would be to enact neocolonial epistemicide, which is at odds with Dene laws, hózhǫ́, and restorative kinship justice. Matriarchs play a pivotal role in humankind's survival. Over the centuries, from time immemorial and into the future, the kinship bonds that unite Àma, Yat'a, and Deèyeh (or Land, Sky, and Water) demonstrate restoried matriarchal justice. To restory cultural heroes as multigenerational and personified as land, water, and sky privileges dynamic Dene knowledge.

Katłįà acknowledges Dene knowledge-holder John B. Zoe for his assistance and for granting her permission to retell the stories. Zoe says, "There always needs to be new tellers, because times change... but it still resonates even today. Especially this time of year (autumn) when people would have these feelings or sightings or something has shifted in front of them, it brings them back to the beginning of time stories."[57] Restorying "beginning of time stories" that are in new mediums and genres is an acknowledgment of Dene laws and literary autonomy, or hane'tonomy. *Land-Water-Sky:* Ndè -Ti-Yat'a validates how "our literatures connect us to one another, build imaginative possibilities for and between our varied forms of community, show us possibilities we didn't know existed, or return us to knowledge we had forgotten or put to the side."[58] Along with John B. Zoe, Tłįchǫ Dene literary and visual storyteller Richard Van Camp mentored Katłįà. Van Camp is a copious writer who has given the world imaginative possibilities through his ever-growing body of literature.

Dene laws are in tandem with stories of cultural heroes who are great travelers and powerful transformers. In many of Van Camp's stories, children, young adults, and Elders are the heroes. He believes he is the only Tłįchǫ Dene to publish in all the following genres: "a novel, a comic book, a graphic novel, and a collection of short stories. . . . [His 1996 novel] *The Lesser Blessed* is now a feature film with First Generation Films."[59] He has published two graphic novels in the series *The Spirit of Denendeh*, and his pandemic-released book of stories, *Gather: Richard Van Camp on the Joy of Storytelling* (2021), includes orature from Elders across the land. His unabashed joy and love for his home, for his community, and for storytelling are infectious.[60]

Van Camp's story "The Fleshing" is about a battle between a (cultural) hero and a destroyer. The destroyer is Wheetago but is also a stand-in for the tar sands. The selfless hero is sixteen-year-old Bear, who is tasked with protecting and saving a house full of terrorized hostages from Dean, who is actively shape-shifting into the cannibal Wheetago. Bear accepts his responsibility and does not question it: "whatever Dean was, he would taste the bite of Tlicho power!"[61] He was willing to die for his friends and relatives, "let it be defending my community. . . . I had the power of my ancestors and I had Sensei's training."[62] Like those in harm's way of the Wheetago, so is the land, which was foreshadowed in the nightmares that Bear has been enduring; he concludes both have to be stopped. The land is the source of stories and life. "The Fleshing" has an unresolved ending, making evident that some critical issues in Indigenous communities will not be resolved quickly or justly. Not all battles can be won. The tar sands (Wheetago) are linked as the cause of cancer in humans and animals; they have poisoned fresh water and related aquatic life and are actively killing the Earth. Van Camp illustrates the Dene laws of sharing, helping, loving, respecting, and being happy and joyful while facing monstrous odds. Healing and restoration are suspended, giving way to a beautiful moment of young love and encouragement.

Van Camp's adoption of futuristic heroic presence and young love in "The Fleshing" complements the two cultural heroes of oratory introduced by Blondin (Yamoria/Yamozha) and restoried by Katłà (the personified land, waters, and sky). Their roles define Dene laws, which intersect with kinship and land restor(i)ed, demonstrating coming to hózhǫ́. Van Camp asserts that stories are medicine. Dene poet and photographer Tenille K. Campbell goes one word further and proclaims they are *nedí nezų* ("good medicine" in Dënesųłiné), which is the title of her second book of poetry.[63] The stunning cover art of Campbell's book of poems showcases contemporary Dene beadwork, and to behold it is good medicine. Campbell commissioned Tlingit (Na-Dene speakers)/Nuxalk artist Heather Dickson to bead a custom piece for the cover, which harmonizes and incorporates story, land, and relationality that are evocative of Campbell's home. Dickson and Campbell "imagine wild roses, picking blueberries and cranberries, and the tiny wildflowers that grow abundant."[64] Dickson chose colors that reflect the Denendeh landscape and honor Turtle Island kinship connections: "I made sure to include her grandma's patterns of blue and purple florals in the middle of the piece, as well as my grandmother's floral beading pattern of the three little petal flowers, using both to represent the matriarchs in our lives. In the middle of the wild rose is abalone, representing the ocean and the time when Tenille lived in Vancouver, and there are turquoise beads representing connections to the Diné and her travels south."[65]

Kindling kinscapes through beadwork is a powerful way to nurture Indigenous existence, while spotlighting deadly creativity. Existing and creating, however, are at direct odds with colonial ideals that legislated death.[66] Gregory Schofield (Red River Métis) explains, "I teach my students how Indigenous women used beadwork as a way to resist colonial violence, as a way of maintaining and preserving identity—but also as a way of telling stories. It's beadwork as a form of resistance."[67] Resistance is a journey toward restoration. To bead is to restory because "maintaining and preserving identity" can be challenging when said identities have been prescribed by colonialism. To restory such predefinitions is resistance. Transcending borders through beadwork was realized through a beaded map project, which united beadworkers from across Turtle Island.[68] They beaded cartographic kinscapes of the colonial-named provinces and states. The restoried beadwork project connected Indigenous Peoples, much like ancient and oral stories do. Beadworkers actively engaged beadwork methods, materials, and aesthetics and land-based stories to re-create and restore place. Beadwork remapped Turtle Island, demonstrating resistance and reclamation.

"Beading a story is like weaving," according to the poetry of Elizabeth Woody (Confederate Tribes of Warm Springs, born for Tódich'íi'nii). Woody was Oregon's first Indigenous Poet Laureate in 2016 and has a prolific career as a writer and educator. Her poem "Rosette" connotes a circular beading technique as a storytelling device that is meditative and healing. The beaded rosettes were originally named so because the result was a "small rose" or a round flower; a rosette is now understood to be a circular medallion.

> Beading a story
> is like weaving,
> a spiral, space making itself in the light
> and colors pick up
> what one loves on the needle
> like a song.
> Over and over,
> the repetition is solace.
> A vibrant note in the thread
> moves through this fabric.[69]

Beads are what one loves; each bead is a story building block, a vibrant note from the body of Diné knowledge. Woody conjures the technique of weaving, which is another way to depict visual stories. As a Diné reader, I was drawn to thinking about how one would weave a rosette on a Diné loom, which is upright. Woody also evokes the spiral, or the whorl, which can be an allusion to the whorl of a spindle or to one's fingertips (as discussed in chapter 4). Woody's poetic cadence not only brings the act of beadwork to life; she also restories from oratory, which is a continuum, restoration, and survivance. A nod to a common, if not beloved and repetitive, technique used by beadworkers, "Rosette" has infinite story possibilities.

While the Dene are lauded for their flower beadwork, the Diné are typically applauded for silversmithing, weaving, and basket making. The Diné indeed bead.[70] One way I connect through restorying and honoring kinship is by doing beadwork. I grew up in a family of beadworkers, and most of us continue to bead; I have been beading for almost thirty years. Ellen K. Moore published the only scholarly account of Diné beadwork, titled *Navajo Beadwork: Architecture of Light*, in 2003. She observed a plethora of styles, techniques, and colors storied through beadwork, which she says constitute "the newest of Navajo cultural expressive systems."[71] In Moore's study, she observes that "Navajo beadworkers' design choices are eclectic, utilizing personal visions and adaptive responses to changing spiritual and economic opportunities. Although they share the concerns and impulses of artists everywhere, they are more often than not also grounded in Navajo culture."[72] Diné journey narratives reflect the existence and implementation of beads made from white shell, turquoise, abalone, and jet (listed in order to reflect the storied Diné colors and directions). The regalia, moccasins, earrings, necklaces, medallions, and hair pieces I have created restory facets from Diné culture. One comment I often get is that I must be very patient to bead. Beadworking puts me at peace, and I don't sell my beadwork. I gift it, and as such every piece has meaning.

Coming to a state of hózhǫ́ (harmony, peace, wellness, beauty) involves acknowledging traditional stories, which encourages ignoring the invisible boundary of the Medicine Line. Accounts of movement and travel demonstrate the survival of kinscapes and kinship (k'é). Honoring lands, waters, and skies (from blue skies to northern lights) is part of our kinship responsibilities.[73] Unlike the land, the skies are not divided by colonial borders. Despite not being able to experience the northern lights, the Diné in the Southwest maintain a significant connection to the sky, as outlined in the journey narratives. Indigenous Peoples in the North are privileged to bear witness to the beauties that the night sky offers, which Diné are deprived of. I have beaded hane' of the night sky. In recognition and honor of my Cree older sister, Dr. Louise Bernice Halfe, as Canada's Parliamentary Poet Laureate, 2021–23, I beaded her a crescent-shaped gorget, which acknowledges my Tsalagi side and contains colors and imagery of the northern lights, reflecting Halfe's Cree name: Sky Dancer. The Cree and Dene believe that the northern lights signify ancestors, dancing in the sky, "revered for the northern lights who return every winter and fall to mesmerize us with their nightly dance."[74] Dr. Halfe's lyrical poems exude love, humor, pain, and resilience, transcending cultures. In turn, I interwove size 13 glass-cut beads with Cree, Diné, and Tsalagi stories to reflect the active, living, spoken, written, and creative word through a beaded gorget.

Dene Yati and Dene Language Restoration

Dene-language advocate Willis Janvier from La Loche, Saskatchewan, began uploading videos on his daughter's birthday, November 18, 2020, which initiated a permanent podcast called *Dene Yati* to promote Dënesųłıné. Yatié means "word, speech, prayer, language, advice," so, Janvier says that Dene Yati means the "Dene-Speaking Podcast."[75] He posts regularly to his YouTube station or on Facebook Live. His shows are also accessible through Apple podcasts. Janvier invites guests from all over the Dene Nation as well as from the Diné Nation to appear on his show.[76] He has asked the Diné guests if they know any stories of how Dene and Diné are related, and ultimately how our People separated. To date, only one of the four Navajo guests have provided a story (hane').

On March 3, 2021, TJ (Terry James) Warren, a citizen of the Diné Nation, appeared on the *Dene Yati* podcast. Warren began, as is custom per Diné protocol, by naming his four Clans. He is Tł'ógí dine'é, born for Bit'ahnii; his chei is Tł'ááshchí'í, and his fourth Clan is Kin łichíí'nii. Janvier said that the Dene no longer have a Clan system like the Diné. Throughout the episode, they compared stories, taboos, cultural practices, and of course words that are cognates from our respective languages: some nouns and numbers. The Dene word for horse (łįcho) sounds like the Diné word for dog (łééchąą'í), whereas the Diné word for horse (łįį) sounds like the Dene word for dog (łį). Another language similarity regards kinship terms for close relatives, like "younger sister," which is a cognate in Dënesųłıné and Diné bizaad. Warren explained that the Diné bizaad expression for "the other Diné People in existence" is Diné náhódlóonii. When asked if he knew a story about Dene/Diné separation, Warren said he has heard fragments of many conflicting stories, which he distinguished as either general or spiritual stories. He also shared that Diné Elders cautioned for a reunification because there are unnamed cultural reasons for separation. Warren's family's story—making very clear that he does not speak on behalf of all Diné—is of the pipe, which echoes the Tsuut'ina story of the pipe, retold in chapter 1. Warren locates this "Ice Age" story as part of the Hajíínéí, the Diné stories of emergence. 'Ałk'idą́ą́' jiní, there was a group of People that were traveling by foot together across the ice.[77] It is said (jiní) that the ice cracked and broke in half. As the two halves started to separate, relatives were trapped on two distinct drifts, separating. To try to save them from separating, one relative reached out with a pipe. The other side of kin relatives grabbed on to the long end, but the pipe ended up breaking in half. With the separation of the pipe came the separation of our People. Some ended up in the Southwest of what is now the United States, while others remained in the North. This echoes the Tsuut'ina story from chapter 1, which explains that the bowl of the pipe ended up with the Diné, while long pipes with stems are used by the Dene in Denendeh.

The Hajíínéí are expansive and epic, and it is through the various worlds that Warren distinguished a restorying. While I have not been able to locate a story that resembles this among the journey oeuvre, I am grateful for his family's extensive knowledge and for his public sharing of this on the *Dene Yati* podcast. Warren ended with the following comment: "What we see today is the reunification of Diné histories, stories, and relationships, and we need to support one another to be able to revive a lot of things in our communities." To revive is to restore. Getting past the taboos of coming together through language and sharing stories can accomplish the rekindling of our kinship. In fact, Warren explained that the Diné-language etymology of the word for "Diné" is testament to the current-day geographic location of Diné in the Southwest. Diné is generally accepted to mean "the People," but Warren said if you break down the word *Diné*, "Di" means "up above" and "né" means "those below." The Diné, then, are those that are geographically right in the middle of Turtle Island (whereby the Dene are "up above," in the far north, and "those below" are in current-day Mexico, or down south from Diné). While Warren shared the Elder's caution about bringing the Diné and Dene back together, the Dene have actively been organizing such rendezvous.

In July 2005, the first "Dene Gathering" was held on the Tsuut'ina Nation. The weekly southwest U.S. newspaper the *Navajo Hopi Observer* reported, "The Tsuu T'ina [sic] language belongs in the Athabaskan language family. . . . The Dene are the first people to settle in what is now the Northwest Territories."[78] Unfortunately, official Diné representation at the Dene Gathering did not materialize; however, fourteen years later, in 2019, the Tsuut'ina Nation organized and hosted an "international Dene reunification" event where "Dene people from as far away as Siberia and Mexico as well as the United States and Canada" were in attendance.[79] The Tsuut'ina Gunaha Institute was established in 2008 "to preserve and revitalize a strategy to improve the overall health of the Tsuut'ina Language. [It] has also played an essential role in uniting various Dene Nations across Turtle Island to safeguard our identity as Dene People."[80] Led by Dene-language advocate Elder Bruce Starlight, the organization aims to showcase Dene cultural heritage, language preservation, and Dene networking through sharing food, songs, and stories. Restoring k'é (relationships) and language preservation is work that Starlight has dedicated his life to.

In 2018, I was co-director of the Office of Academic Indigenization (OAI) at my former institution, Mount Royal University (MRU), and was approached by Victoria Wanihadie from the Tsattine or Dane-zaa, also known as the Beaver People, in northwestern Alberta for a potential partnership on Dene-language revitalization. Victoria had been advocating for Beaver/Dene-language preservation and wanted to apply for federal funding through the Department of Canadian Heritage, which sponsored an "Aboriginal Languages Initiative," a component of the Aboriginal Peoples' Program, but a requirement was to have institutional support.[81] MRU agreed to partner and to oversee the grant writing and administrative bureaucracy for this unique Dene-language initiative, which we called "Preservation and Revitalization of the Tsattine (Beaver) Language and Beaver Ways in Northwestern Alberta." OAI co-director Liam Haggarty and I hired master grant-writer Sabina Trimble; through collective collaboration, the application was successful, and we were funded $74,244. For the life of the project and while Liam was on sabbatical, the interim co-director, Kit Dobson, and I advocated for MRU to reciprocate by providing in-kind services that included classroom space, technology help, and parking to support language teachers, learners, and community members for the Dene-language revitalization initiative.

Starlight is one of only twenty-nine remaining speakers of Tsuut'ina; he and Victoria developed and led a unique language revitalization project that brought Dene speakers and learners together. Starlight would teach Dene classes at no cost to student learners, as this was covered by the grant. During the fall term, he taught the language classes at the Alberta University of the Arts (formerly ACAD), and during the winter semester, he taught at MRU. These classes were live streamed to the Horse Lake First Nation in northern Alberta. Starlight would also commute every other week to Grande Prairie to teach in person to those who live streamed. Horse Lake used to be called Horse Lake Beaver Band, but Beaver was dropped. On their website they proclaim: "We are all First Nations; it should not matter if you are Beaver, Blackfoot, or Cree. We are all First Nations and we all live here."[82] This motto is inclusive and evocative of respecting kinship relations, across Nations. The project lasted a full academic year; at the end of each term, we feasted with the language experts, the Elders, the students, and the communities of Tsuut'ina and Horse Lake. Neighboring Dene communities (as far as two hours away!) also partook in the feasting and ceremonies that concluded the language classes. At the end of the fall term, Starlight gifted me with a Tsuut'ina name, "Four Holy Mountains Woman," in recognition of the Diné four sacred mountains, located in what is now Colorado, New Mexico, and Arizona. I am honored with a meaningful name in the Tsuut'ina Dene language, bestowed upon me by a kinship relative.

Contemporary Dene storytellers long for the restoration of language. Lisa Boivin from Deninu K'ue First Nation (near Fort Resolution) in the Northwest Territories; Tunchai Redvers, also from Deninu K'ue First Nation; and Tenille K. Campbell from English River First Nation in northern Saskatchewan actively revive words in their poetics as restoration. Boivin is an image-based writer and artist. As a Sixties Scoop survivor, she began painting to work through her disorientation and healing transformation, which began with learning the Dene language, meeting her relations, and building community. The first Dene word she learned was įdzíaze, which means "little heart," or strawberry. She also learned that "little hearts" are women's medicine, which informs her understanding of how to be a Dene woman. Learning how to be Dene—of any gender or fluidly—is a recurrent goal for poet and two-spirit social justice warrior Tunchai Redvers. They weave their experiences with spoken word and lament that they never met their maternal grandparents, reflecting kinship rupture. Redvers demonstrates resilience and survivance by integrating Dënesųłıné language and the "language of the land," which is reflected in their works, notably the Dene-language-titled poem "dëne súłiné."[83] Tenille K. Campbell's multilingual books of poetry *#IndianLovePoems* (2017) and *nedí nezų: good medicine poems* (2021) mostly focus on Indigenous erotica and sexy storytelling, but her humor and gift of wordplay also capture her love of her cultures, languages, and homelands. Métis scholar Aubrey Hanson captures this best: "Campbell knows how to put Native tongues to good use!"[84] In podcast 32 of *Roadside Attractions*, Campbell states that it is important for her to use Dene, Cree, and English because the languages naturally intermingle in everyday utterances as dual/multilingual expressions one can hear in her home community. She wanted "language to reflect the experiences of the women and the people up *North*."[85]

Through the lenses of Dene laws and hózhǫ́, this chapter introduced the restoration of honi/hondi/hane' (traditional stories) to demonstrate kinscapes, relationality, and literary reciprocity of the Dene and Diné. Cultural heroes, Hero Twins or siblings, or traditional lawmakers are Peacekeepers and Protectors who typically have to defeat giants, giant animals, or some sort of insatiable beast (sometimes their own kin) that feasts off humankind. While many are gendered as male throughout the orature and by orators, finding peace, balance, and wellness would privilege another lens, which Katłįà imagines. Matriarchs are depicted as collaborative, empowered, and supernaturally powerful. Through their victories, Indigenous lands, languages, laws, and lifeways are born and restor(i)ed— reflecting Dene law and teachings through Indigenous literary essence to achieve hózhǫ́. The beauty, the hózhǫ́, and the diversity of the lands of Dinétah and Denendeh are mirrored in the stories by Diné and Dene authors. Their survivance and resolve to be good relatives are modeled for Indigenous youth, the future. The stories transcend geographies and temporalities to convey ruptures and restoration of kin and identity, two-spirited and trans presence, body positivity, love, sensuality, language, and homelands for vibrant tomorrows. Restor(i)ed narratives entertain, teach, and connect the People. Literary arts can convey truths that privilege Indigenous knowledges and perspectives that challenge colonization and subvert abstract and harmful notions of Indigeneity. The stories and storytellers in this chapter reflect only a few stars in the brilliant constellation of Dene literary arts. As an avid promoter of Indigenous visual media, I would have liked to discuss Dene filmmakers such as the phenom Marie

Clements (Sahtú Dene and Métis), whose work includes plays, radio, a musical documentary, and a mind-blowing full-length feature, *Bones of Crows* (2022). She is an aesthetic storytelling genius and just one of many Dene creatives in film and television.

This book has been a literary journey that makes a temporal and geographical "jump." Like the Dene and Diné cultural heroes who can journey thousands of miles without much exertion, I began in Dinétah and end up in Denendeh (although with much more exertion than the cultural heroes!). Ever striving to achieve goodness (hózhǫ́ and adherence to Dene laws) implies that the end results (the destination) trump the journey to get there. The lands, waters, and skies journey daily between Dinétah and Denendeh and are restorative, which the honi/hondi/hane' demonstrated.

Conclusion

Náásgóó nizhónígo bee oonish dooleeł . . .

"In Beauty It Continues." By coming to a conclusion, I am merely saying that I have said what I can, in the space that is here. I now offer *Restoring Relations Through Stories: From Dinétah to Denendeh* for dialogue and critique, as I have only scratched the surface. Diné scholar of linguistics and my high school mom (she knows the insider joke) Melvatha R. Chee says that "Náásgóó nizhónígo bee oonish dooleeł . . ." conveys that this work in this field is for "anyone who wants to apply it to their work or expand on it." I offer these concluding thoughts in goodness.

I have argued for the recognition of hane' in oral, literary, and visual formats (spoken, published, directed, and beaded) to demonstrate hózhǫ́—coming to harmony, wellness, balance, peace, and beauty (restoration)—in the preceding chapters:

1. Restoring Tsé Bit'a'í's dislocation by knowing and respecting Diné bahane';
2. Restoring representations of *indians* in film by privileging self-representation and narrative autonomy, or hane'tonomy;
3. Restoring the reputation of a border town and Diné identities;
4. Restoring disharmony by acknowledging stories of kinship;
5. Restoring and restorying kinship through stories.

I began in chapter 1 by honoring my maternal family's hometown landmark, Tsé Bit'a'í, because she has been reduced to an empty image.

Conclusion

Without advocating for the stories that Grams and my dad shared with me, I would have been complicit in her storied erasure. Storied erasure references the non-Indigenous appropriations of Tsé Bit'a'í. When Diné are in conversation with harmful imagery (whether static or filmic), brilliance and beauty are restored. In January 2022, I received Diné pop artist Ryan Singer's calendar. His inspiration and creativity come from his love of *Star Wars*, which he fuses with Diné iconographic and cultural imagery that can be seen on Dinétah. Noteworthy is that two months of his calendar feature the Winged Rock, Tsé Bit'a'í. January 2022 features Tsé Bit'a'í sharing the land with AT-AT walkers (tall four-legged, all-terrain tactical armored units) and the sky with A-wing fighter jets. March 2022 features a malnourished green ruping (reptavian) atop Tsé Bit'a'í, which is how some restory and imagine what the ancient evil avian, Tsé Nináhálééh, could have looked like. Singer's art meshes constructs of storytelling time harmoniously by bringing life to two distinct stories that are to be understood as having already happened. Singer usurps *Star Wars* images alongside Diné everyday images to fascinating effect. *Star Wars Episode IV: A New Hope* has been dubbed in Diné bizaad as *Sǫ'tah Anaa': Siih Náhásdlįį'*, revealing a collective Diné fandom for all things *Star Wars*. The movie's famous opening crawl commences in a very familiar Navajo way: "A long time ago, in a galaxy far, far away" translates well to Alk'idáá' jiní, "It happened a long time ago, they say." While seemingly a nod to a future, Singer's art honors stories of old, and does so on the land (on Dinétah). Future research could synthesize and analyze other landmarks on Dinétah, including extending critical insights to artists like Ryan Singer.

In chapter 2, I added to the ongoing discourse of Indigenous film criticism and emphasized the need to promote the work of Indigenous filmmakers. Additionally, I argued that there is an established field of Diné film and television making. In 1975, Ethelou Yazzie delivered a speech, "Navajo Wisdom and Traditions," in which she advocated a position on media's effect on Diné traditional stories: "now, as television and radio penetrate into the most remote corners and the highest mountain settlements of the Navajo Nation, and have their impact on us all, it is important to record the stories before the advent of electronic media, and its insidious effect, transforms them once again."[1] Yazzie did not specify what version or variant of Diné stories should be recorded. This position assumes that recording stories retains a true copy of an original, but the vibrancy and narrative autonomy, or hane'tonomy, demonstrate otherwise. Transformational stories—from oral to print to visual—do not have "insidious effects" but rather enlarge Diné knowledges and support decolonization efforts. While Yazzie's work remains foundational as one of the few print sources on Diné literary history by a Diné knowledge holder, there are ways to harmonize storied variations with electronic discourses. Further studies could examine other forms of visual and aural media, including new social media platforms (socials), podcasts, video games, digital books, speeches, all film genres, performances, music and YouTube videos, and advertising.

Chapters 3 and 4 analyzed Diné-directed films to argue that restorations of Diné knowledges and teachings are embedded in the traditional stories from the Hajíínéí. Freeland's *Drunktown's Finest* includes stories about the separation of the sexes and the critical importance of nádleeh, and Lowe's chapter ascends one world "up" to the *5th World*. Lowe's unique and editorial creativity demonstrates visual narrative autonomy, hane'tonomy. Due to lack of space, I did not look at stories that go beyond the Glittering World. Visionary stories are, however, not a gap in Diné storytelling. Stories of Sixth World presence have been imagined in Nanobah Becker's *6th World* and Rex Lee Jim's poetry, such as in "Na'azheeh/Hunting," in which he envisions

> K'ad łą́ą́,
> > dah náá'diit'áhígíí bii' doo
> > áadi sǫ' łichíí' bidáádidoogáál
> Now all is ready
> > For the next shuttle flight
> > The red star will keep it from returning.[2]

With the proliferation of Indigenous film (and television), specifically Diné filmmaking, there are endless research opportunities. In-depth studies using Indigenous-specific analytics are the future of critical Indigenous media studies.

Chapter 5 introduced Dene literary arts. Journey narratives are the core of Diné literary history and oral stories. The journeyers were storied as cultural histories and lawmakers that kept the peace and protected the People. To find literary links to our northern cousins, the Dene, I turned to some of their honi/hondi. I began with oratory, then moved to contemporary Dene literature that restoried the stories of old. I veered off the beaten path to share stories of contemporary orators (if you will) who are fighting for language retention through creative initiatives. Throughout, the chapter was guided by Dene laws and hózhǫ́. Kinship was a running thread, as was protecting Denendeh, which echoed through my analysis. Land has become victimized as opposed to vocalized.

In 1978, Keith H. Basso recorded his conversation with then Chairman of the White Mountain Apache Tribe, Ronnie Lupe, who lamented, "Our children are losing the land.... They don't know the stories about what happened at these places. That's why some get into trouble."[3] Finding stimulating ways to encourage learning from the land and to resonate with Indigenous youth is a challenge that all generations face. The creatives and writers I explored have generated works that are helping close these intergenerational gaps. Learning from the land and prioritizing Indigenous stories are not always realistic or feasible for many who are struggling to live sustainable livelihoods. One commonality that the Dene in the far north and the Diné in the southwestern United States share has to do with resource extraction and uranium mining. On the Diné Nation, uranium mining officially ended in 1968, leaving more than 1,500 abandoned mines and their toxins on Diné Bikéyah. Perry Charley, a Diné scientist and representative on the Diné Uranium Radiation Commission, declared that hundreds of former miners died from exposure to uranium.[4] Restoring our relationship to the land is therefore vital and will translate to restoring relationality, but how is this done when stories and the storytellers are in constant tension?[5] In both vast lands, our recent relatives turned to and depended on capitalist blue-collar careers that took precedence over the stories the land holds, but not for lack of caring.

My late stepfather, an honorable, gentle, hardworking, and kind man named Ron Sandoval, worked as a dragline operator for forty-four years. Straight out of high school from the age of nineteen until his untimely passing ten days prior to his sixty-fourth birthday and just two weeks from retirement, Ron labored so that his family could have a decent living. With his modest salary, Ron provided for his children and extended family without hesitation. Far from affluent, we never lacked a comfortable living space, clothing, or food, and he prioritized enrolling his kids and his grandchildren into music programs and sports (which kept me out of trouble). While many scholars and environmentalists are quick to criticize the role of coal mining and resource extraction, it is not as black and white to many Diné families who owe their survival and livelihoods to this industry, when other careers were simply unattainable:

> Strip mining for coal is a large-scale and irreversible disruption of customary landscapes. It also pays royalties to the Navajo Nation government and employs many Navajos at union scale, making them among the best-paid in Navajoland. This dragline, poised on a former Navajo homesite, is in view (and earshot) of domestic prayer offering places of remaining residents nearby. Better integration of cultural resource inventories and post-mine land use planning, especially earlier in the mine plan than is now the case and with the guidance of the families who theoretically can return to their land after reclamation, could perhaps lessen devastation of sacred places and customary land-use patterns.[6]

In *Navajo Sacred Places*, Kelley and Francis include a photo of a dragline in the background and of the sacred site in the foreground but do not specify the exact location. Regardless, their critique is clear: protect the land and you protect the stories. While I agree with this to a large extent, I struggle with imagining what an alternative livelihood would have been, had it not been for my stepfather's dedication to his family, made possible through his lifelong job as a coal mine dragline operator. My late father, Lew Watchman, while not a dragline operator, was also employed on and off by the local mines as a welder. His maintenance of the draglines was necessary for the continuum and safety of others. In the far north, I came across stories by Dene authors who have a vexed relationship with mining, primarily of uranium. Tenille K. Campbell captures the tension beautifully: "This conflict is about how we show our love. Some of us will fight for the environment because we love the land and some of us will fight for our right to have this job because we love our family."[7] The Navajo Nation also has a long history with uranium mines and their effects (high rates of cancer as well as several abandoned mines to clean up). Further research could privilege the work of Diné and Dene scientists whose focus on environmental and ecological restoration is grounded by hózhǫ́ and Dene laws. Other areas of future work entail studying the connections that the

Diné and Dene share with damage to the Earth and how these manifest in our stories (oral, literary, and visual).

Hózhǫ́ nahásdłíí means "In Beauty, it is Finished" or "It is Fulfilled in Beauty."[8] Hózhǫ́ nahásdłíí is the formal way Diné prayers conclude and is repeated four times, while changing positions to honor each direction, starting in the east, then turning clockwise to the south, then to the west, and finishing off the last utterance of Hózhǫ́ nahásdłíí facing north. Concluding this book with Hózhǫ́ nahásdłíí is not meant to replicate or perform sodizin, a prayer, but I am using it literally: In Beauty, it is Finished.

NOTES

Preface

1. I do not italicize words in Diné bizaad. The only exception is if the word appears in a direct quote or is used as a definition. Also, because Diné bizaad was originally spoken and not written, there is some variance in spelling in primary and secondary sources. I try to maintain consistency in my own text, but differences in spelling in Diné bizaad exist. My rationale for not italicizing words in Indigenous languages comes from the following: "Decolonization recognizes the inherent value of all languages and recommends that authors, when using words from a language that is not English, refrain from italicizing these words as it only serves to set them apart as exotic, deviant or as part of a particular colonizing anthropological project." "Author Guidelines," *Decolonization: Indigeneity, Education & Society*, accessed July 10, 2023, https://jps.library.utoronto.ca/index.php/des/about/submissions.
2. The meaning of báshíshchíín is standardly translated as "born for," indicating one's second Clan: their father's mother's Clan. A person is understood to be "born for" their father. Larry W. Emerson teaches that báshíshchíín actually means "being in service to my father's People." Emerson, interview, *Reel Indian Pictures*.
3. In recognition of my Cherokee relatives, I diverted from Diné bizaad to the Cherokee language, identifying that we are Bird Clan.
4. Throughout, I capitalize Clan: "As a lowercase term . . . it conveys loose, informal organization instead of structure, history, and purpose. As an uppercase term, *Clan* describes governance structures, such as the Clan System of the Haudenosaunee, which involves eight Clans that transcend, and so integrate, the individual nations of the Haudenosaunee Confederacy. . . . Many other Indigenous Nations also have Clan Systems, which are an important part of traditional governance, and social and spiritual organization." Younging, *Elements of Indigenous Style*, 54.
5. I prefer Diné over Navajo, since *Navajo* is likely a distortion of Naabaahii (warrior), given to us by non-Diné. Though the legal name of our Nation (Navajo Nation) and still in predominant use, I limit my usage of it.
6. Yazzie, "Navajo Wisdom and Traditions," 1.

7. L. Emerson, "Diné Sovereign Action," 167.
8. Unless a direct quote or part of a formal name, like Indian Territory, I spell *indian* lowercased and italicized, as argued by Anishinaabe theorist Gerald Vizenor. He writes: "Native names and identities are inscrutable constructions; the ironic suit of discoveries, histories, memories, and many clusters of stories. Native identities and the sense of self are the tricky traces of solace and heard stories.... The *indians* are the simulations, the derivative nouns and adjectives of dominance, and not the same set as natives, the *indigène*, or an indigenous [*sic*] native, in the sense of a native presence on the continent.... The *indians* are that uncertain thing of discoveries, and the absence of natives, some*thing* otherwise in the simulations of the other culture. Natives are elusive creations; the *indigène*, that real sense of presence, memories, and coincidence is borne in native stories.... Native stories must tease out of the truisms of cultural exclusions and the trumperies of simulations" (Vizenor, *Fugitive Poses*, 69–70).
9. Though problematic, *Indigenous* is the term I use as a general umbrella to signify the People from Turtle Island and some Island communities. *Indigenous* is currently the most inclusive term, but it is not without its problems as a homogenizing one that erases distinctions among sovereign Indigenous Peoples. Therefore, I privilege Nation-specific terms, in their languages first, for example Diné, Dene, Nadene, etcetera. I also use corresponding English terms: for example, Navajo, if respectfully appropriate. Finally, when talking about Indigenous Peoples, I capitalize People.
10. Beavers, "The Bell Route."
11. See "Land Acknowledgements: A Guide," Student Success Centre, McMaster University, 2018, accessed July 10, 2023, https://healthsci.mcmaster.ca/docs/libraries provider59/resources/mcmaster-university-land-acknowledgment-guide.pdf?sfvr sn=7318d517_2.
12. Navajo origin stories tell of four sacred mountains, originally created by the Diyin Diné'é, to demarcate traditional territory. Navajo survivors returned to this territory, surrounded by the mountains, after their internment at Hwéeldi (Fort Sumner) from 1864 to 1868. The east mountain is Tsisnaajiní (also Sisnaajiní or Mount Blanca) in San Luis Valley, Colorado. The south mountain is Tsoodził (Mount Taylor), northeast of Grants, New Mexico. The west mountain is Dook'o'oosłííd (San Francisco Peaks), near Flagstaff, Arizona. The north mountain is Dibé Ntsaa (Mount Hesperus of the La Plata Mountains) in southwestern Colorado. Additionally, there are two inner sacred mountains, Dził Ná'ooditii (Huerfano Mountain) and Ch'ool'í'í (Gobernador Knob). Different spellings of the mountains exist.
13. Santos, *Epistemologies of the South*, 92. Santos writes, "Dominant epistemologies have resulted in ... the massive destruction of ways of knowing that did not fit the dominant epistemological canon. This destruction I call epistemicide" (*Epistemologies of the South*, 238). Furthermore, epistemicide is "the other side of genocide" (Santos, Nunes, and Meneses, "Opening up the Canon," xix).

14. I repeat this in chapter 5: The Dene Nation are composed of the Deh-cho (formerly known as the Mackenzie Dene) and include the Tłįchǫ (Dogrib), Denesuline (Chipewyan), South and North Slavey, Mountain, Sahtu-Dene (Bearlake), and Hare in the North. Other Dene Peoples include the eastern Gwich'in, and the Tsaatine (or Beaver) and the Tsuut'ina (Sarcee) in the west. There are also far western Dene known as the Sekani, Carrier, and Chilcotin.
15. I borrow and extend Brenda Macdougall's theorizing of kinscapes, which I detail in chapter 5. See Macdougall, "How We Know Who We Are."
16. Neskahi, "Allen Neskahi, Sr."
17. A hooghan is a traditional and ceremonial dwelling.
18. Gerald Vizenor explains: "The theories of survivance are elusive, obscure, and imprecise by definition, translation, comparison, and catchword histories, but survivance is invariably true and just in native practice and company." He continues, "The character of survivance creates a sense of native presence over absence, nihility, and victimry. Native survivance is an active sense of presence over absence, deracination, and oblivion; survivance is the continuance of stories, not a mere reaction, however pertinent" (*Survivance*, 1). A year later, he refined this definition to include the word *resistance*: "The nature of survivance creates a sense of narrative resistance to absence, literary tragedy, nihility, and victimry" (Vizenor, *Native Liberty*, 1).
19. Wyllie, "NEH Grants Back Pubmedia."

Introduction

1. This is the official title of the prestigious position. The Navajo Nation is our official name, though I prefer to write Diné Nation. I use both interchangeably.
2. L. Emerson, "Diné Culture," 66.
3. Emerson, "Diné Culture," 62.
4. Yazzie, "Navajo Wisdom and Traditions," 2.
5. Werito, "Understanding Hózhǫ́," 27–29.
6. Klara Bonsack Kelley and Harris Francis interviewed Elders (methods) to gather stories for *Navajo Sacred Places* (1994), adhering to proper protocols. In chapter 1, I share two different hane' (stories) of Shiprock by Reginald Nabahe. Regarding protocol, Nabahe told them: "Shicheii [polite term of address, man-to-man], if you really want to hear stories, we should get a sweathouse ready, then you must bring the wood for the next two to four days. Then we'll spend the next four days in the sweathouse telling one another these stories like this." Kelley and Francis, *Navajo Sacred Places*, 68. Nabahe's teachings prefaced twenty-first-century pedagogies and methods that are continually being refined to accommodate Indigenous learners in various environments.
7. Additionally, my thinking has been informed by C. Allen, *Blood Narrative*; Basso, *Wisdom Sits in Places*; Casey, *The Fate of Place*; Chamberlin, *If This Is Your Land*; V. Deloria, *Red Earth, White Lies*, Denetdale, *Reclaiming Diné History*; Dreese, *Ecocriticism*; L. Emerson, "Diné Culture" and "Diné Sovereign Action"; Farmer,

On Zion's Mount; Glotfelty and Fromm, *The Ecocriticism Reader*; Goeman, *Mark My Words*; Kelley and Francis, *A Diné History of Navajoland* and *Navajo Sacred Places*; King, *The Earth Memory Compass*; Kovach, *Indigenous Methodologies*; Lee, "Decolonizing the Navajo Nation," *Diné Perspectives*, and *Navajo Sovereignty*; Momaday, *The Man Made of Words* and *The Names*; Nabokov, *Where the Lightning Strikes*; Ortiz, *Speaking for the Generations*; Silko, "Landscape" and *Yellow Woman*; Tapahonso, *Blue Horses Rush In, A Radiant Curve*, and *Sáanii Dahataał*; Tohe, *Enemy Slayer* and "Hwéeldi Bééhániih"; Yazzie, *Navajo History* and "Navajo Wisdom and Traditions"; and Zolbrod, *Diné bahane'*. I outline Indigenous film scholars in chapter 2.

8. Kovach, *Indigenous Methodologies*, 84.
9. Kovach, *Indigenous Methodologies*, 25.
10. V. Deloria, *Red Earth, White Lies*, 36.
11. Diné College, "Diné College Principles."
12. Quoted in Lee, *Diné Perspectives*, 7.
13. Belin et al., *The Diné Reader*, 12.
14. The Navajo translation of coyote stories comes from Dempsey, "Ti' Dine Bizaad be yadeillti."
15. Bedonie et al., *Álchíní Bá Hane'*, 5, 6, 103, 104. I retain the spelling of each genre as it was originally published.
16. Justice, *Why Indigenous Literatures Matter*, 22–23.
17. Kovach writes: "Within Indigenous epistemologies, there are two general forms of stories. There are stories that hold mythical elements, such as creation and teaching stories, and there are personal narratives of place, happenings, and experiences" (*Indigenous Methodologies*, 95). I interrogate both types of narratives as well as visual storytelling—or film, television, and beadwork.
18. Tapahonso, "Singing in Navajo," 39 (my emphasis).
19. See Belin et al., *The Diné Reader*, for Jim's bilingual poems on saad (language/voice), 135–39.
20. Tapahonso, "Singing in Navajo," 39.
21. Innes, "Elder Brother," 135.
22. Kovach, *Indigenous Methodologies*, 108.
23. Kovach, *Indigenous Methodologies*, 97, 100, 103.
24. Justice, *Why Indigenous Literatures Matter*, 34; Daniel Heath Justice, Imagine Otherwise, accessed March 3, 2023, https://danielheathjustice.com.
25. Howe and Kirwan, *Famine Pots*, xix.
26. Van Camp, *Gather*, 22.
27. Justice, *Why Indigenous Literatures Matter*, 34.
28. Eugene B. Joe, personal interview, August 30, 2016.
29. Landry, "Shiprock Historical Society."
30. Kelley and Francis, *A Diné History of Navajoland* (2020), addresses stories as ceremonial, which departs from my analysis.
31. Fast, "The Land," 188n6.

32. Tohe, *Enemy Slayer*.
33. Naxos.com features the entire audio of the oratorio. See Grey, Tohe, and Christie, *Enemy Slayer*. See Anderson, "Enemy Slayer," for a preview of the making of the oratorio.
34. Tohe, "Cardinal Point 3. West / Fall / Adulthood. Scene 3," in *Enemy Slayer*, 5.
35. Denetdale, "Nation to Nation," 0:10–0:38. Denetale uses "Water Running Together," while some from the Tó 'aheedlíinii clan say "Water Flowing Together."
36. Denetdale, *Reclaiming Diné History*, 204n6.
37. Denetdale, *Reclaiming Diné History*, 11.
38. Denetdale, "Chronology," 365.
39. Tohe, "Hwéeldi Bééhániih," 79.
40. Tohe, "Hwéeldi Bééhániih," 82.
41. Tapahonso, *Sáanii Dahataał*, 7.
42. Tapahonso, *Sáanii Dahataał*, 10.
43. In May 2022, a permanent exhibit opened at the Bosque Redondo Memorial / Fort Sumner Historic Site: "Bosque Redondo: A Place of Suffering . . . A Place of Survival."
44. Correll, Watson, and Bruge, "Navajo Bibliography with Subject Index," 20.
45. Younging, *Elements of Indigenous Style*, 57.
46. Variations in spelling are likely due to typographical restrictions and do not change the meaning of the expression. The header "'ałk'idą́ą́' jiní" and its definition are from Luci Tapahonso's preface from *Blue Horses Rush In*, xiii. Earlier, Tapahonso published this expression as "alk'ídaa' jini." She wrote: "The mental and emotional participation of the audience is as crucial as the telling of the stories and the singing of the songs" (Tapahonso, "Singing in Navajo," 39). Tohe spells it "ałkidą́ą́' adajiní" in "Within Dinétah the People's Spirit Remains Strong"; Morris spells it "alk'idą́ą́' jiní" in *From the Glittering World*; and Skeets spells it "ałk'idą́ą́" in "The Other House."
47. Tohe, "Within Dinétah," 126.
48. Wally Brown, a Navajo historian, says that there is no word for "creation" in the Navajo language. Our stories begin "with the organizing of life." He also says the concept of "emergence" is not quite correct. He encourages viewers to think of the Hajíínéí (usually translated as emergence) as "the organization of Mother Earth" and to consult multiple sources for better understanding. See "Native American (Diné) Story of the Beginning," Navajo Traditional Teachings, January 12, 2021, YouTube video, 10:01, https://youtu.be/Gu9d3QGPLfU.
49. Some Navajo authors have published accounts about the Hajíínéí that reflect differences in details and contradict the sources I reference. Ethelou Yazzie writes that there were only Four Worlds, and it's the Fourth World that we are currently in (*Navajo History*). Emery Lester only describes the emergence up through the Fourth World and alludes to a Fifth but does not write about it ("The Emergence Story"). Aside from the differences in how many worlds are reflected in the oral stories, the overall plot and teachings remain in alignment.

50. Morris, *From the Glittering World*, 3.
51. Skeets, "The Other House."
52. Sam, "Jake Skeets Interview."
53. Yazzie writes, "While [the Holy People] are very powerful, they are not all-knowing, not all-powerful, and not all-good. They make mistakes and have human emotions. They can be invoked, supplicated, propitiated, and coerced to help the people of the tribe, or to cease doing damage. The Holy People also serve as ideals of behavior for the Navajo people to follow or emulate" ("Navajo Wisdom and Traditions," 5–6). Kelley and Francis define the Holy People as Navajo deities "whose outer form are landscape features, animals, plants, the atmosphere, and celestial bodies" (*Navajo Sacred Places*, 1).
54. Farina King's succinct summary of the Hajíínéí includes this critical information: "They went through the different worlds, represented respectively by the colors black, yellow, blue, and white, before settling in this world, the Glittering World. These colors correspond with those of the sacred mountains and directions in reverse order" (*The Earth Memory Compass*, 48).
55. Morris, *From the Glittering World*, 6.
56. Some variants say the People brought soil from previous worlds, which the current mountains are made from.
57. Morris, *From the Glittering World*, 7: "In four days a pair of twins were born to them, and these first children were *Nádleeh*, those who have the spirit of both male and female."
58. Lester says that Coyote stole from water buffalo's baby—named Tééhoołtsódii—as opposed to stealing from Water Monster's ("The Emergence Story").
59. This summary of the Hajíínéí is a great abridgement of Morris's retelling. I exclude several details, names, numbers, colors, and events, highlighting only key details that make up the epic. There are several versions that conflict with Morris's, and I chose his, as it is the title of his fictionalized autobiography and aligns with many previously published versions of the Diné organizational stories of life.
60. Kelley and Francis, *A Diné History of Navajoland*, 3.
61. Salabye and Manolescu, "Universal Center."
62. Frisbie, *Food Sovereignty*, 187.
63. Goeman, *Mark My Words*, 19.
64. Tohe, "Hwéeldi Bééhániih," 81.
65. In one hane', the Hero Twins were looking down through a sky hole with their father, Jóhonaa'éí. Their disorientation, when not within the confines of the four sacred mountains, is evident as they were scanning the Diné landscape from above. Naayéé Neezghání said: "I do not recognize the land. Everything looks so strange from up here. How different it looks. How remote from what I have grown accustomed to seeing on the ground." Zolbrod, *Diné bahane'*, 214; see also 397n53.
66. Morris, *From the Glittering World*, 41.
67. Clifford, "Dzil."
68. Denetdale, *Reclaiming Diné History*, 162.

69. Laguna Pueblo writer Leslie Marmon Silko also grew up in the Land of Enchantment, surrounded by the stillness of nature, desert and rock scenery, and refreshing spring water. She writes that the "landscape sits in the center of Pueblo belief and identity.... This sense of identity was intimately linked with the surrounding terrain, to the landscape that has often played a significant role in a story" (*Yellow Woman*, 43).
70. From the back cover of Basso's *Wisdom Sits in Places*.
71. Basso, *Wisdom Sits in Places*, 121.
72. Basso, *Wisdom Sits in Places*, 121.
73. Momaday, *The Man Made of Words*, 115; Momaday, *The Names*, 129.
74. Zolbrod, *Diné bahane'*, 364n7. Zolbrod's *Diné bahane'* is taught widely across Navajo land as a legitimate account of the journey narratives from Navajo literary history. Originally from Pittsburgh, Zolbrod is a respected educator, having taught on the Navajo Nation for more than twenty years. *Diné bahane'* was Zolbrod's early attempt to bring Navajo poetics to the mainstream, which inaugurated unexpected archival and ethnographic research about variations of the journey narratives. Zolbrod conducted meticulous research, consulting many printed resources, including the late nineteenth-century ethnographer (and surgeon) Washington Matthews's collection of Navajo ceremonies, stories, and songs, *Navajo Legends*. Matthews recognized the constellation of Diné literary arts and credited the multitude of intergenerational storiers whose iterations could not have intersected, yet they converged at the same end point. Unfortunately, Matthews was unable to translate Navajo stories concisely, prompting Zolbrod to try, resulting in *Diné bahane'*.
75. Casey's comprehensive, chronological study aims to "thrust the very idea of place, so deeply dormant in modern Western thinking, once more into the daylight of philosophical discourse" (*The Fate of Place*, xi). He observes the shunning of place and landscape with regard to colonialism and imperialism. Casey's neologisms of deplacialization, placeblindedness, and anti-places helped me think about the intersections and divergences between Western philosophy and Indigenous place-based work (*The Fate of Place*, xii).
76. Innes, "Elder Brother," 135.
77. Daybreak Warrior, a Navajo-language YouTuber, says there is no one word for "love" in Diné bizaad, though there are multiple ways to express endearment for others. The phrases share the same stem of "ayóó." Nizhoni, Sick Boy, and Felixia come to a recognition of "Ayóó'ádajó' nínígíí Béédahaniih" ("Remembering the Loved Ones"). "Navajo Word for Love," Navajo Code Talkers, December 6, 2017, https://navajocodetalkers.org/navajo-word-for-love/; Daybreak Warrior, "Navajo Word of the Day: I Love You," February 14, 2012, YouTube video, 1:18, https://youtu.be/47-LRscTKNc.

Chapter 1

1. Vizenor, *Native Liberty*, 10.
2. Vincent Werito adopts this saying in "Understanding Hózhǫ́ to Achieve Critical Consciousness," 25.

3. Denetdale, *Reclaiming Diné History*, 10.
4. Joe, "Shiprock Historical Society," n.p., but remarks are made on the fifth page of the magazine.
5. To understand a People's worldview and laws is to understand the land on which they live. Basso was told to "learn the names of all these places" (*Wisdom Sits in Places*, 42). Places are known by the visual description of a feature (or features) of their physical manifestation. He contends that a place's "name is like a picture" (46). Tsé Bit'a'í translates to "Winged Rock," "Rock with Wings," or "Wings of Rock" because that is what it resembles. A place's name is elevated by "spatial anchors" (101).
6. Momaday, *The Names*, 60. Many erroneous accounts about the English name of Tsé Bit'a'í reflect that the monolith looks like a ship's mast—for example, "'Legend of Shiprock,'" a fabricated story circulated in 1929 by Margaret Camp.
7. Griffin, "Handicraft Museum," 13.
8. Linford, *Navajo Places*, 264.
9. Kovach, *Indigenous Methodologies*, 61.
10. Erasmus, "We the Dene," 178.
11. In addition to family/community stories, the Tsé Bit'a'í' hane' (stories) are collected from select published accounts by Diné authors and scholars. They are part of an epic; entire stories are therefore truncated. Bééshłigai, "The Separation of Males and Females"; Cook, "The Creation of the Navajo People"; L. Emerson, "Diné Sovereign Action"; Kelley and Francis, *A Diné History of Navajoland*; Lapahie, "Shiprock Legend"; Lee, "Decolonizing the Navajo Nation"; Lester, "The Emergence Story"; Martinez, "Bringing the Sacred Mountains to the Fifth World" and "Changing Woman from Birth to Puberty"; Morris, *From the Glittering World*; Rustywire, *Navajo Spaceships*; Tapahonso, *Sáanii Dahataał*; Yazzie, *Navajo History* and "Navajo Wisdom and Traditions."
12. Kovach, *Indigenous Methodologies*, 37.
13. "Shiprock: Volcanic Sentinel in Northwestern New Mexico," New Mexico Nomad, January 31, 2021, https://newmexiconomad.com/shiprock.
14. Silko affirms, "As offspring of the Mother Earth, the ancient Pueblo people could not conceive of themselves without a specific landscape. Location, or 'place,' nearly always plays a central role in the Pueblo oral narratives. Indeed, stories are most frequently recalled as people are passing by a specific geographical feature of the exact place where a story takes place. The precise date of the incident often is less important than the place or location of the happening.... The places where the stories occur are precisely located, and prominent geographical details recalled, even if the landscape is well-known to listeners" ("Landscape," 269).
15. Basso, *Wisdom Sits in Places*, 31.
16. Tapahonso, "Singing in Navajo," 39.
17. This is uncredited because it is common Diné knowledge in the Shiprock area.
18. Wilcox, "7 Names for Calgary."
19. Eagletail, "Indigenous Language Lesson."

20. The article anticipated a decline in Diné speakers reported by the 2020 census. Denetclaw, "Data Shows Huge Reduction in Diné Speakers." Due to the worldwide pandemic, the 2020 census taking was repeatedly delayed and when finally implemented, only a fraction of Peoples were counted. Fonseca and Schneider, "Native Americans Fret."
21. Starlight, "Starlight Speaks Tsuut'ina."
22. Hal Eagletail is a Tsuut'ina cultural knowledge keeper and educator, local southern Alberta cultural consultant, and highly respected international powwow Master of Ceremonies (MC).
23. Nabokov, *Where the Lightning Strikes*, 91.
24. Metcalfe et al., "Isotopic Evidence," 528.
25. Brown, "800-Year-Old Moccasin."
26. Metcalfe et al., "Isotopic Evidence," 542.
27. Metcalfe et al., "Isotopic Evidence," 528.
28. His scathing critique of oral stories continues: "In story and song they memorialized the landscapes which supernatural heroes or trickster spirits had transformed into their present shapes, or special places where they left traces behind them. They noted how odd-looking rocks or other landscape features bore resemblance to characters in their stories, and they considered this more than coincidence" (Nabokov, *Where the Lightning Strikes*, xi).
29. Chamberlin, *If This Is Your Land*, 21.
30. Morris, *From the Glittering World*, 40.
31. Their flood allusions, and an earlier one published by Ethelou Yazzie, reflect "it is his [Mą'ii's, or Coyote's] interference with the Water Monster's Baby that causes the flood that forced the People to flee through the reed into . . . the present World as we know it" (Yazzie, "Navajo Wisdom and Traditions," 19). Morris's hane' tells of these events happening in the Fourth World and Yazzie's version says these events happen in the Third World. What is important is the premise: Mą'ii's mischief of stealing Water Monster's baby resulted in a great flood that forced everyone to flee to the Glittering World. Many floods occur in the oral stories; not all are related to Water Monster's revenge for child kidnapping. Lee, for example, shares the story of the Sun flooding the Earth out of anger. Lee, "Decolonizing the Navajo Nation," n.p.
32. Lapahie, "Shiprock Legend."
33. S. Green, "Ship Rock."
34. Morris, *From the Glittering World*, 39.
35. See "Commercial Film & Photography Permits," Navajo Nation Parks and Recreation, accessed July 11, 2023, https://navajonationparks.org/permits/commercial-film-photography/.
36. "**All areas on the Navajo Tribal Park locations are Closed to non-Navajos unless you have a valid permit issued by the Navajo Parks and Recreation Department or other delegated tribal authority. Failure to have a permit is considered trespassing on a Federal Indian Reservation and Person/Permittee will be cited to the fullest*

for infraction, per NN Code." "Backcountry Hiking & Camping Permits," Navajo Nation Parks and Recreation, accessed July 11, 2023. https://navajonationparks.org/permits/backcountry-hiking-camping/.
37. This is not specific to sacred sites on Navajo land. Historian Jared Farmer's expertise on sacred mountains, rocks, and geological sites on Turtle Island and internationally reveals that "across the world and throughout history, certain high points have signified holiness. The Aborigines of Australia have for millennia revered Uluru (Or Ayers Rock), the colossal red monolith in the center of their continent" (*On Zion's Mount*, 142).
38. Ethelou Yazzie and a great majority of Diné retell that Asdzą́ą́ Nádleehé (also called Yoolgai Asdzą́ą́ or White Shell Woman) is the sole mother of the Hero Twins. Zolbrod relates that the Hero Twins had two separate mothers, in fact two "Air Spirit People": Changing Woman and White Shell Woman (Asdzą́ą́ Nádleehé and Yoolgai Asdzą́ą́, respectively). Asdzą́ą́ Nádleehé became lonely and curious for companionship and resigned to find out if Jóhonaa'éí ("The One Who Rules the Day," or Sun) was equally lonely. She decided to attract Jóhonaa'éí's attention. She found a place high on flat rock and lay down for four days in a row, "face up, with her feet to the east and her legs spread comfortably apart. That way she could relax as she observed the sun make its path across the sky." Zolbrod, *Diné bahane'*, 181. After the fourth day, she became pregnant by Jóhonaa'éí with the Hero Twins, whom she bore after eight days of pregnancy.
39. L. Emerson, interview, *Reel Indian Pictures*.
40. L. Emerson, interview, *Reel Indian Pictures*.
41. L. Emerson, interview, *Reel Indian Pictures*.
42. In Zolbrod's version, the sisters Changing Woman and White Shell Woman each bore a child, and in the Navajo way of kinship relations, their children are considered siblings, so to call them twins is not inaccurate even if not birthed by the same mother.
43. Asdzą́ą́ Nádleehé withheld who fathered the Twins. As curious and growing young warriors, they demanded to know their father's identity and ultimately discovered it was Jóhonaa'éí (Sun). Asdzą́ą́ Nádleehé discouraged them from traveling to meet him. Through a series of trials and with the help of Na'ashjé'ii 'Asdzą́ą́ (Spider Woman), the Hero Twins prepared mentally and physically. Ethelou Yazzie praises Spider Woman as "one of the greatest women of all time. Today she could be a scientific or engineering genius. She could foresee events, know plans, understand the laws of nature. Spider Woman was able to interpret Natural Law and put it to use for the Navajo people" ("Navajo Wisdom and Traditions," 28). Na'ashjé'ii 'Asdzą́ą́ nourished the twins and equipped them each with a proper "hiinááh bits'os (magic eagle feather) for protection. . . . [She taught them] the proper chants and prayers to keep them from harm." Lee, "Decolonizing the Navajo Nation," n.p. They survived the dangerous journey to the Sun, Jóhonaa'éí, who initially refused to believe he fathered twins.
44. Zolbrod, *Diné bahane'*, 211.

45. The illustrated cover image of Johnny Rustywire's *Navajo Spaceships* (2006) is reflective of the N'da' (or Nidáá') that my dad and I attended.
46. Zolbrod, *Diné bahane'*, 231.
47. Rustywire, *Navajo Spaceships*, 3.
48. Rustywire, *Navajo Spaceships*, 3.
49. Kelley and Francis, *Navajo Sacred Places*, 69
50. Kelley and Francis, *Navajo Sacred Places*, 69.
51. Zolbrod, *Diné bahane'*, 232.
52. Lee, "Decolonizing the Navajo Nation," n.p.
53. Rustywire, *Navajo Spaceships*, 4.
54. Zolbrod, *Diné bahane'*, 233. After Naayéé Neezgháni kills the adult Tsé Nináhálééh, he spares the lives of the two monster hatchlings, making one of them into atsá, the eagle, and turning the other into na'ashjaa', an owl. Lee, "Decolonizing the Navajo Nation," n.p. Larry W. Emerson explains that atsá teaches us gratitude and "prayer," while na'ashjaa' "teaches us the difference between wisdom and foolishness" (interview, *Reel Indian Pictures*). Before sparing the owl's life, Naayéé Neezgháni said, "I won't kill you. If you were fully grown like your parents are I would.... But you are young. There is time for you to become something else: something useful to my people and to earth-surface people in the days to come, when men and women shall again increase in the land." Zolbrod, *Diné bahane'*, 235.
55. Denny and Lerma, "Diné Principles," 119.
56. L. Emerson, interview, *Reel Indian Pictures*. While most interpretations of twenty-first-century monsters align, there are minor differences: "The brothers returned home after killing all the monsters. They rested when they saw red smoke in the distance. They were curious as to what was causing the red smoke. They travelled to the smoke and found a hole in the ground. They looked inside and found several monsters resting. They quickly entered the place and attempted to kill them. Dichin Hastiih (hunger), Tę́'é'į́ Hastiih (poverty), Bił Hastiih (sleep), Yaa' Hastiih (lice man), and Sá̜ (old age) were hiding" (Lee, "Decolonizing the Navajo Nation," n.p.). These monsters pled for their continued existence, which the Hero Twins granted, as they were compassionate (Lee, "Decolonizing the Navajo Nation," n.p.). Another source reflects the following monsters: "Poverty, Old Age, Lice, and Hunger (or Death)" (McPherson, *Dinéjí Na'Nitin*, 217).
57. Becenti, "Dikos Ntsaaígíí dóódaa!"; Denetdale, "COVID-19"; Dooley, "Coronavirus"; Jones, "Navajo Nation"; Olinger, "#NavajoStrong"; Roessel, "COVID-19"; Rosenthal, Menking, and Begay, "Fighting"; Shone and O'Neal, "Navajo People." Prior to the COVID-19 pandemic, cultural anthropologist Maureen Trudelle Schwarz discussed the 1993 hantavirus epidemic on the Navajo Nation as "the mystery illness" and referenced Diné oral stories that metaphorized it as a monster.
58. Roessel, "COVID-19."
59. Dooley, "Coronavirus."
60. Rosenthal, Menking, and Begay, "Fighting."
61. Olinger, "#NavajoStrong."

62. I have endeavored to avoid gendering the Hero Twins in my analysis. If a direct quote genders the Warrior Twins as male brothers, I cite the original verbatim.
63. Olinger, "#NavajoStrong."
64. "Navajo Nation COVID-19 Dashboard. Navajo Nation Dikos Ntsaaígíí-19 (COVID-19)," Navajo Department of Health, Situation Report #663, January 4, 2022, https://www.ndoh.navajo-nsn.gov/COVID-19/Data.
65. "Navajo Nation Dikos Ntsaaígíí-19 (COVID-19)," Navajo Epidemiology Center, Situation Report #928, June 30, 2023, https://nec.navajo-nsn.gov/Projects/Infectious-Disease/COVID-19.
66. Lee, "Decolonizing the Navajo Nation," n.p.
67. Tsé Bit'a'í is one of many Indigenous landforms that have been othered and displaced in major motion pictures. Steven Spielberg staged Bear Lodge (popularly known as "Devils Tower") as a landmark recognizable to aliens in *Close Encounters of the Third Kind* (1977). Greg Mottola, director of *Paul* (2011), says he was the mastermind for designating Bear Lodge as the landmark in *Close Encounters*. Bear Lodge is also featured in *Paul*. In both movies, Bear Lodge was not dislocated out of Wyoming, but their origin stories were erased. The name "Devils Tower" is a landmark that has Indigenous storied roots that have been rendered moot. Bear Lodge is the English translation of a Lakota name. The Crow, Arapaho, Shoshone, Cheyenne, and Kiowa have their own names and stories for the landmark. Momaday remembers the Kiowa origin story of Bear Lodge: "When I was six months old my parents took me to Devil's [*sic*] Tower, Wyoming, which is called in Kiowa Tsoai, 'rock tree'" (Momaday, *The Names*, 42). Essentially, a boy transforms into a bear who chases his sisters who scramble into a tree. The bear uses its claws to try to climb it and makes the indentations that are visible on the landmark. Momaday's Kiowa name is Tsoai-talee, which means "Rock Tree Boy."
68. Shieber, "Netflix."
69. Teller, "Here's What New Mexico Officials."
70. Santos, *Epistemologies of the South*, 238.
71. The Internet Movie Database (IMDb.com) lists twenty-eight titles (fiction features, documentaries, and short films) that cast Tsé Bit'a'í, or Shiprock Peak, as a filming location. Internet Movie Database, "Filming Location Matching."
72. I deliberately target non-Diné filmmakers, but bell hooks's strong critique of white male filmmakers is requisite. See hooks, "artistic integrity: race and accountability," in *Reel to Real*.
73. Derby, "Rocks with Wings."
74. Gerew, "Shiprock."
75. Davis, "Jumanji."
76. Da, "'The Rock' Visits NM."
77. Beyond the scope of this book is the actual colonization of Mars, in particular by Navajo scientists. Notably, there is active admonishment by Diné medicine People. On March 11, 2021, NASA announced that "Perseverance rover['s first scientific focus] is a rock named 'Máaz'—the Navajo word for 'Mars.' The rover's

team, in collaboration with the Navajo Nation Office of the President and Vice President, has been naming features of scientific interest with words in the Navajo language" (Greicius, "NASA's Perseverance"). Articles such as Whelan, "Mapping Máaz"; Gohd, "NASA Honors"; and K. Allen, "Hataałii," soon followed.

78. Scholarship about land and landscape in film is sparse, and what exists does not address Indigenous presence (hence Indigenous stories). For example, Martin Lefebvre's *Landscape and Film* (2006) contains essays that reference Navajo land, focusing solely on the white gaze of Monument Valley, a John Ford "leitmotif" (114). Other studies that mostly ignore Indigenous perspectives are David Melbye's *Landscape Allegory in Cinema* (2010), Robert Fish's *Cinematic Countrysides* (2007), and Graeme Harper and Jonathan Raynor's *Cinema and Landscape* (2010). There are no scholarly books that address how Indigenous-storied lands inform film, whether by Indigenous or non-Indigenous filmmakers.

79. Slotkin's chapter summarizes Burroughs's life and literary, albeit racist, influences: "the imaginary history of Burroughs' 'Barsoom' (Mars) parallels [President Franklin] Roosevelt's account of the rise, decline, and rebirth of the great 'fighting races.' His work after 1916 was directly influenced by the work of two racialist historians: Madison Grant, *The Passing of the Great Race* (1916); and Theodore Lothrop Stoddard, *The Rising Tide of Color Against White World Supremacy* (1920) and *The Revolt Against Civilization* (1922)" ("Edgar Rice Burroughs," 198).

80. Slotkin, "Edgar Rice Burroughs," 204.

81. See "Famous Kin of Edgar Rice Burroughs," FamousKin.com, accessed May 5, 2016, www.famouskin.com/famous-kin-menu.php?name=12930+edgar+rice+burroughs.

82. Slotkin, "Edgar Rice Burroughs," 203.

83. In 1896, Burroughs unwillingly served as a soldier with the 7th U.S. Cavalry in Fort Grant, Arizona, after failing the entrance exam for West Point in 1895. Slotkin, "Edgar Rice Burroughs," 196.

84. I interpret this inclusion in the film as an attempt to mirror Burroughs's original characterization of John Carter, who "lived with the Sioux as a warrior among warriors." Slotkin, "Edgar Rice Burroughs," 203. As one who lives among an Indigenous People and culture, Carter presumably speaks their language.

85. Slotkin, "Edgar Rice Burroughs," 204.

86. Ryan, "Lynn Collins."

87. Slotkin, "Edgar Rice Burroughs," 206, 207.

88. Slotkin, "Edgar Rice Burroughs," 207. Deja Thoris (uncredited) makes a cameo appearance in the season opener of the 2020 HBO series *Lovecraft Country*. She appears from one of three UFOs and floats downward in a beam of light, with her arms spread wide. She has fire-engine-red skin and dons a gold bikini. Her long, black hair signals an Afro-Indigenous on-screen presence. She lands softly in front of Atticus Freeman, *Lovecraft Country*'s protagonist, and embraces him, whispering one inaudible word. The voice-over narration reveals this is a story of a young boy and his dream. He has fallen asleep reading Burroughs's hardcover *A*

Princess of Mars, and his dream conflates storylines from various sci-fi stories as well as with real-life wars and heroes. M. Green, "Sundown," 0:45–2:25.
89. In the final cut, the only scene in *John Carter* displacing Tsé Bit'a'í is at 59:10–59:14. The original trailer focused squarely on the monolith as "a world away," and it can be previewed on Disney+; however, a subsequent trailer excludes Shiprock Peak altogether.
90. Morris, *From the Glittering World,* 39.
91. "Best Geological Formation," USA Today 10Best, accessed January 1, 2017, https://www.10best.com/awards/travel/best-geological-formation/.
92. U.S. Route 666 was renamed Highway 491 in 2003. Locals referred to the stretch of road as "Devil's Highway" due to the many lives lost from head-on collisions and pedestrian hit-and-runs that were often because of the necessity of hitchhiking, like that of a late auntie of mine.
93. In 2015, Calgary adopted a new city slogan: "Be Part of the Energy." The former, dated slogan, "Heart of the New West," highlights the pitting of Western cowboy culture against diverse Indigenous cultures. This binary defines the genre of the Western, so it could explain why this image was predominantly featured for all passengers to behold.
94. Kestler-D'Amours, "This River."
95. Kestler-D'Amours, "This River."
96. Ahéhee' to Christine Harvey for providing family details. I am indebted to Leonie Pihama for connecting me to Christine and for all corrections and suggestions to the following text regarding te reo Māori (the Māori language). All errors remaining are mine alone.
97. Ahéhee' to Michelle Johnson Jennings, who facilitated the coordination and organization of this unforgettable and deeply resonate visit. Kia ora to all those involved with hospitality, chauffeuring, and hosting us: Moewai Aterea, Awhina Cameron, Ngaropi Cameron, Leoni Pihama, Cherryl Smith, and Rihi Tenana.
98. Moore, *Navajo Beadwork,* 179. In 2020, I was scheduled to teach a land-based course on the Big Island of Hawai'i, but it was canceled due to the pandemic. I had collaborated with Kanaka 'Ōiwi land and mountain protectors, community-engaged action warriors, scholars, and knowledge holders in the course's creation. Auntie Pua is a Mauna Kea ("white mountain") protector. Destroyers want to build another thirty-meter telescope (TMT) on the northern plateau of Mauna Kea, a storied and sacred place where Kanaka 'Ōiwi origin stories commence. As part of the Mauna Kea Ohana (family), Auntie Pua is driven by her obligation to protect her Mauna. See the *Standing Above the Clouds* website, https://www.standingabovetheclouds.com. Auntie Pua taught me stories of Mauna Kea, and in support of her and the Hawaiian Nation's ongoing fight against the desecration of their ancestral kin, I beaded and gifted her the necklace.

Chapter 2

1. *The Fourth Eye* by Brendan Hokowhitu and Vijay Devadas is influential: "As the first publication of its kind on Indigenous media in Aotearoa New Zealand . . . this

collection brings a fresh approach to the relatively distinct fields of Media Studies and Indigenous Studies" (xv). They adopt Arjun Appadurai's coinage of the mediascape (from the media landscape) (Appadurai, "Disjuncture and Difference"). I refrain from using the Indigenous mediascape because this chapter is only about film and television. The media they analyze includes newspapers, magazines, and billboards, in addition to film and television.

2. The growth of the field of Indigenous visual storytelling is expeditious. Indigenous film and television creatives' output span all genres, including dramas, comedies, rom-coms, and horror. On film courses I have developed, see Watchman, "Teaching Indigenous Film."

3. Grams helped care for the family farm on Old Farm Road (lane two) in Shiprock, and she enlisted us, her grandchildren. The primary caretakers were siblings Little Unc (as we knew him) Cato Sells (1906–98) and her auntie Ida Benally, a rug weaver and expert blue corn paperbread maker. My memories of planting seeds of corn, melons, squash, chiles, and other foods and medicines are only positive. It did not seem like work to pull weeds, play in the mud as we manipulated the irrigation system, or harvest. When not in the field, we also helped butcher sheep, and I still laugh at how my cousins and I would chase each other with the sheep intestines (before they were fully clean). In my analogy, I am fully aware that I exclude all the various plant varieties that sustained our People. I am settling with corn since it is a Diné food staple. In *Food Sovereignty the Navajo Way* (2018), Charlotte Frisbie observes, "The Navajos cultivated corn of many different colors: blue, white, and yellow were the main ones, but gray, black, red, and multicolored were also known" (163). 'Asdzáán Néézʼ (Tall Woman) informed Frisbie on the ceremonial uses of naadą́ą́' (corn) as well as provided a variety of recipes (168–73). 'Asdzáán Nééz's English name was Rose Mitchell (1874–1977).

4. Ben, "Corn Represents."

5. Salabye and Manolescu, "The Navajo Beginnings."

6. I have learned from the educational cornstalk philosophy created by Roger Begay. Because his educational tool is for "Diné conceptual learning," from infancy throughout all life stages to Elderhood, I do not replicate his model. Begay encourages educators to tailor their approaches to their subject areas; therefore, I use the cornstalk as an analogy. See Begay, "The Cornstalk Philosophy of Learning."

7. For film criticism and historicity about self-representations and of Indigenous-made filmmaking, see Barclay, *Our Own Image*; Cummings, *Visualities*; Cummings, *Visualities 2*; Mita, "The Soul and the Image"; and J. Smith, "Indigenous Insistence on Film."

8. For criticism about filmic representations *of* Indigenous Peoples, see P. Deloria, "Indian Wars, the Movie," in *Indians in Unexpected Places*; Aleiss, *Making the White Man's Indian*; P. Smith, *Everything You Know About Indians Is Wrong*; and Raheja, *Reservation Reelism*. Cree filmmaker Neil Diamond, in collaboration with Catherine Bainbridge and Jeremiah Hayes, released the documentary *Reel Injun* (2009), which offers a comprehensive and chronological trajectory on cinematic representations of Indigenous Peoples.

9. See Aleiss, "Native Americans"; Aleiss, "The Vanishing American"; and Bernd, "Voices in the Era of Silents."
10. P. Smith, *Everything You Know About Indians Is Wrong*, 37.
11. Because Angela Aleiss's *Making the White Man's Indian*, Philip J. Deloria's *Indians in Unexpected Places*, Joanna Hearne's *Native Recognition*, Michelle Raheja's *Reservation Reelism*, and IMDb reflect slightly different information, I reference the stats on the website created and maintained by Carewe's grandchildren, https://edwincarewe.com/biography/. Hearne has the most extensive biography of Carewe in *Native Recognition*.
12. Carewe is the first Indigenous filmmaker, but images *of* us appeared in 1894—not on the big screen but ironically through a peephole—through Thomas Edison's kinetoscopic moving images (P. Deloria, *Indians in Unexpected Places*, 73). Ian D. Skorodin's *Tushka* premiered in 1996 but is not recognized as "the first" Native American–directed feature film. Instead, critics acknowledge Chris Eyre's *Smoke Signals* (1998) as the first.
13. Alanis Obomsawin (Abenaki) has directed more than fifty-nine films since 1971.
14. Māori film is undeniably its own field. I mean no disrespect in highlighting only two foundational directors of Māori cinema. "New Zealand (NZ) On Screen: Iwi Whitiāhua," https://www.nzonscreen.com, has a large Māori database in several genres; "Maori Cinema," by Leo Koziol, https://mubi.com/lists/maori-cinema-of-new-zealand, includes non-Māori-directed films; "A Brief History of Māori Cinema," by Ngā Taonga: Sound & Vision, https://www.ngataonga.org.nz/blog/film/maori-cinema/, is an audiovisual archive that offers a concise cinematic history of Māori filmmaking since 1913; and Merata Mita's "The Soul and the Image" outlines Māori film and television up to 1992.
15. Mita is the first Indigenous woman to solo direct a full-length feature film, *Mauri* (1988). (An earlier film, *To Love a Māori*, was co-directed by a Māori filmmaker, Ramai Hayward, and her non-Indigenous husband, Rudall Hayward, in 1972.) Mita tirelessly advocated for Indigenous self-representation and is honored as a godmother of Indigenous film. From 1979, she directed and co-directed thirteen visual stories (features, shorts, documentaries, television shows, and a music video). *Saving Grace: Te Whakarauora Tangata* (2011) was posthumously released. From 1970, Barclay directed twenty visual stories (television shows, feature-length films, shorts, and documentaries) and is credited as subject, cinematographer, writer, or producer for eight others.
16. After Barclay's death, he was the subject of at least four other projects. See "Screenography," NZ Onscreen Iwi Whitiāhua, accessed July 11, 2023, https://www.nzonscreen.com/profile/barry-barclay/screenography.
17. Barclay's introduction of the category "Fourth Cinema" is not without heated debate and critique, which Jo Smith covers in "Indigenous Insistence."
18. Barclay, "Celebrating," 10.
19. Barclay cited eleven Indigenous-made feature films as of 2002; this would have increased if he included documentaries and shorts. M. Elise Marubbio and Eric L.

Buffalohead (Ponca) list forty-six total visual stories, made prior to 2002. Marubbio and Buffalohead, *Native Americans on Film*, 361–67. They identified ninety feature films, shorts, and documentaries by Indigenous creatives made from 2002 to 2013. This work testifies that Fourth Cinema creatives were thriving, and Barclay's promotion of the Fourth Cinema camera asserted that the "actions and relationships" of Indigenous Peoples continually restore since unapologetically taking the camera from the hands of those on the deck.

20. Dunlevy, "Obituary." The character Aila prompted Anishinaabe writer Ali Nahdee to create the Aila Test (inspired by the Bechdel Test), which she later revised to the Ali Nahdee Test. Essentially, there are three basic rules: (1) an Indigenous woman has to be the main character; (2) who does not fall in love with a white man; (3) who is not raped and does not die at any point in the story. See Nahdee, "My Statement."
21. See Masayesva, "Indigenous Experimentalism"; Raheja, *Reservation Reelism*, 18, 247, and note 31; and Barker, Introduction to *Postindian Aesthetics*.
22. Freeland, "We Need Diverse Voices."
23. An earlier concept, "intellectual sovereignty," was coined by Robert Warrior (Osage). See Kauanui and Warrior, "Robert Warrior"; and Warrior, *Tribal Secrets*.
24. Notable works include Black, *Picturing Indians*; Hearne, *Native Recognition*; Hokowhitu, "Te Kapa o Taika," which advances the concept of embodied sovereignty; Hokowhitu and Devadas, *The Fourth Eye*; Marubbio and Buffalohead, *Native Americans on Film*; Pavlik, Marubbio, and Holm, *Native Apparitions*, wherein they opt for "Indigenous Media Sovereignty"; Raheja, *Reservation Reelism*; Rickard, "Indigenous Visual Sovereignty"; Rickard et al., "Sovereignty: A Line in the Sand"; and J. Smith, "Indigenous Insistence on Film."
25. Steve Pavlik, M. Elise Marubbio, and Tom Holm say it best: "At its core, Indigenous media sovereignty represents the agency of Indigenous cultural survivance over a more than five-hundred-year period. In the last forty years or so, Indigenous people globally have claimed and refocused the communication technology that has been so devastating to their cultural sovereignty and identity over the last hundred years. They have done so against ongoing settler nation and dominant cultural forms of media representation, which, as mentioned, create ongoing colonial power structures, validate racial violence, and result in internalized colonialism and intergenerational trauma. Indigenous people have enacted Indigenous media sovereignty to uphold and proclaim their peoplehood; to control the representations of their people, their stories, and their cultural productions; and to enact decolonization—rights upheld by the United Nations in 2007" (*Native Apparitions*, 8).
26. Hokowhitu, "Theorizing Indigenous Media," 105.
27. J. Smith, "Indigenous Insistence on Film," 492.
28. Gorman, "Navajo Sovereignty," 149.
29. L. Emerson, "Diné Sovereign Action," 161.
30. L. Emerson, "Diné Sovereign Action," 161.

31. L. Emerson, "Diné Sovereign Action," 171.
32. Black, *Picturing Indians*, 30.
33. Lewis, "The New Navajo Cinema," 52.
34. Lewis, "The New Navajo Cinema," 50.
35. Lewis, "The New Navajo Cinema," 51.
36. *Thrivance: Journal of Indigenous Ways of Being, Knowing, and Doing*, accessed July 11, 2023, https://ipsonet.org/publications/open-access/thrivance/.
37. Launched in 1960, the Navajo Film and Media Commission was active throughout the 1970s. "Our History," Navajo Nation TV & Film, accessed March 8, 2023, https://www.navajonationtvandfilm.com.
38. "In 2019, legislation provided $100,000 for the newly created grant called Senator John Pinto Memorial Fund" (Gomez, "20 Native Filmmakers"). From this grant, twenty recipients were awarded $5,000 each. See the list of awardees and their projects: "Senator John Pinto Memorial Fund Information," New Mexico Legislature, accessed March 8, 2023, https://www.nmlegis.gov/handouts/IAC%2010 1620%20Item%204%20Senator%20John%20Pinto%20Memorial%20Fund%20 information%20for%20committee.pdf.
39. See "Native and Indigenous Storytellers: Apply for Grants Up to $25K via the New Short Documentary Fund," Sundance Institute, April 25, 2018, https://www.sun dance.org/blogs/program-spotlight/native-and-indigenous-storytellers-apply -grants-up-to-25k-short-documentary-fund. Also, the Cultural Survival website has an extensive resource list for "Indigenous Film and Video Makers," last updated May 7, 2010: https://www.culturalsurvival.org/publications/cultural -survival-quarterly/resources-indigenous-film-and-video-makers.
40. Worth and Adair, "Navajo Filmmakers"; Worth and Adair, *Through Navajo Eyes*.
41. Worth and Adair, "Navajo Filmmakers," 33.
42. Worth and Adair, *Through Navajo Eyes*, 264–66.
43. While Worth and Adair designate these films "full-length," I consider them shorts.
44. Lewis, *Navajo Talking Picture*, 126–33; Lewis, "The New Navajo Cinema"; Raheja, *Reservation Reelism*, 156; and Pack, "Constructing 'The Navajo,'" discuss the 1966 research project and specifically comment on Worth and Adair's work. The Penn Museum website Navajo Film Themselves, https://www.penn.museum /sites/navajofilmthemselves/, is a comprehensive resource that includes background information, screening history, and other relevant information about the filmmakers. Notably, there is a link to purchase a DVD of the Diné films: https:// penn-museum-shop.myshopify.com/products/navajo-film-themselves-1.
45. Worth and Adair, *Through Navajo Eyes*, 128.
46. Penn Museum website, Navajo Film Themselves.
47. Lewis, *Navajo Talking Picture*, 50.
48. Lewis, *Navajo Talking Picture*, 65.
49. Lewis, *Navajo Talking Picture*, 4. Lewis writes that Curtis's *Yebechai Dance* was "early cinema" (released in 1906); however, the Library of Congress lists a photographic still print titled "Yebichai War Gods," created in 1904. See "Yebichai War

Gods," Library of Congress, accessed July 11, 2023, https://www.loc.gov/pictures/item/90713932/.
50. Lewis, *Navajo Talking Picture*, 3.
51. Ahéhee' to Uncle Casey Watchman for the translation.
52. Marcus, "Dark Winds Q&A."
53. McFarland, "Empowering 'Dark Winds'"; Oxendine, "Chickasaw Producer"; Tangcay, "'Dark Winds'"; "Dark Winds," Wikipedia, last modified February 16, 2023, 17:59, https://en.wikipedia.org/wiki/Dark_Winds.
54. Tangcay, "'Dark Winds.'"
55. See, for example, Melanie Yazzie (Diné) and Elena Ortiz (Ohkay Owingeh), "Dark Winds; Shame on You!," October 24, 2022, in "The Red Power Hour," *The Red Nation Podcast*, YouTube video, 1:13:27, https://youtu.be/giK1cKXiduA.
56. Krisst, "'Dark Winds.'"
57. Innes, "Wait a Second," 440.
58. On Dinétics, see Sam, "Jake Skeets Interview."
59. Cummings, "Visualities of Desire," 101 (my emphasis).
60. Cummings, "Visualities of Desire," 103, 104.
61. Landry, *The Official Magazine*, 37.
62. Cummings, "Visualities of Desire," 107.
63. Innes, "Wait a Second," 441.
64. Gonzales, "Full Interview."
65. Landry, "Humanity and Complexity," C1.
66. Landry, "Humanity and Complexity," C3.
67. Landry, "Humanity and Complexity," C3. Montoya's observation was based strictly on the films that were screened at the time. This is not to suggest that Diné filmmakers only restory creation narratives. Diné visual storytelling is diverse and spans all genres, much like Diné critical work. Montoya, for example, is working on a monograph that focuses on Diné environmental racism, and her work is Diné centered and grounded in finding ways to heal Diné lands for our futures.
68. Belin, *From the Belly*, 75.
69. I suggest Googling "film festivals" for the most updated URLs. Some are ImagineNative, the American Indian Film Festival, Dreamspeakers, LA Skins Fest, Māoriland Film Festival, and the National Museum of the American Indian Film and Media. The University of British Columbia also has a comprehensive list of film festivals: "Aboriginal Films and Filmmakers," University of British Columbia, updated January 11, 2023, https://guides.library.ubc.ca/aboriginalfilmmakers/festivals.
70. I suggest Googling "Indigenous film institutes" for the most updated information. Some are the Adam Beach Film Institute, the American Indian Film Institute, Māoriland Productions, the Ngā Pakiaka Incubator Program, and the Indigenous Program at the Sundance Institute.
71. Lewis, "The New Navajo Cinema," 52.
72. Michelle Good (Cree from Red Pheasant First Nation) published "Cultural Pillagers," in *Truth Telling* (2023), which uses the same analogy for invasive species.

73. Select filmographies and resource lists include Indigenous-content films (films made by non-Indigenous creatives). See, for example, Black, *Picturing Indians*; Knopf, *Decolonizing the Lens of Power*; Leuthold, *Indigenous Aesthetics*; Marubbio and Buffalohead, *Native Americans on Film*; Pearson and Knab, *Reverse Shots*; and the National Film Board of Canada (website), accessed March 8, 2023, https://www.nfb.ca. There is an online database of eighty-seven creatives on the Kin Theory website, under "creator search": https://www.kintheory.org/member-search (last modified December 20, 2021). Raheja also lists thirteen contemporary directors and their various genres. Raheja, *Reservation Reelism*, 281n7.
74. McCue and Barton, "Influential Filmmakers," 2:59–3:04
75. Wente, "Hi Sheila, thanks for bringing this up."
76. J. Smith, "Indigenous Insistence on Film," 490.
77. Justice, *Why Indigenous Literatures Matter*, 9.
78. See Andersen, *"Métis"*; Leroux, *Distorted Descent*; Sturm, *Becoming Indian*; TallBear, *Native American DNA*.
79. Indigenous Screen Office, "ISO Statement."
80. Tailfeathers, "We Trust Artists."
81. Gosnell-Myers, "White Privilege."
82. See Vizenor's entertaining book review, "The Pretend Indians."
83. Rickard, "Indigenous Visual Sovereignty," 1:26:15–1:26:39.
84. Tuck and Yang, "Decolonization," 6.
85. Tuck and Yang, "Decolonization," 3.
86. Tuck and Yang, "Decolonization," 10.
87. Tuck and Yang, "Decolonization," 10.
88. Tuck and Yang, "Decolonization," 13.
89. Justice, *Why Indigenous Literatures Matter*, 169.
90. Tuck and Yang, "Decolonization," 13.
91. The October 2022 allegation about Turpel-Lafond, reported by Geoff Leo, presents a mountain of research and evidence that divided Elders and community leaders. See Leo, "Disputed History." In September 2022, another case was reported; see Cyca, "The Curious Case of Gina Adams." On October 27, 2023, Leo, Roxanna Woloshyn, and Linda Guerriero also published a damning exposé, "Who Is the Real Buffy Sainte-Marie?" https://www.cbc.ca/newsinteractives/features/buffy-sainte-marie.
92. P. Smith, *Everything You Know About Indians Is Wrong*, 41.
93. The Native American Media Alliance (https://nama.media/) supports Indigenous creatives with professional development opportunities and is a resource for the industry to turn to for recruiting Indigenous talent. One of the professional development programs they offer is a Native American Showrunners program, which began in 2020.
94. Stine, "'We Are the Original Stewards of This Land.'"
95. She also has producer and writer credits for other non-Indigenous-content shows. Teller Ornelas has written about her clan affiliations in the *Hollywood Reporter* and the *New York Times* (see Teller Ornelas, "Donald Trump Would

Make a Terrible Navajo"; and Teller Ornelas, "Indigenous People's Long Road to Visibility in Hollywood").
96. Miller, "Sierra Teller Ornelas."
97. Miller, "Sierra Teller Ornelas."
98. All episodes are included in the Internet Movie Database, or IMDb.com. An exhaustive survey of Indigenous presence on U.S. television is not possible, but noteworthy examples include Alaqua Cox (Menominee and Mohican) who is the first Indigenous woman to be cast in a lead role as a Marvel television character, starring as Echo in Disney+'s *Hawkeye* and the spinoff show *Echo*. *Dexter: New Blood* premiered in 2021 and features a running theme of Missing and Murdered Indigenous Women and Girls (MMIWG). It is set near a fictional Seneca reserve and showcases Seneca language and spirituality, with consultation by Caleb G. Abrams (Onöndowa'ga:', Seneca). There is a TV show in development under the collaboration of Bird Runningwater and Ava DuVernay. See "'Sovereign,' the First Native TV Drama, in Development at NBC," October 28, 2020, https://nativenewsonline.net/arts-entertainment/nbc-greenlights-sovereign-the-first-native-tv-drama. North of the Medicine Line, APTN has included Indigenous on-screen presence for over two decades.
99. Black's *Picturing Indians* (2020) addresses Diné extras on pages 167 and 170. Additionally, the *Navajo Times* article "Chicago Gets a Taste of Greyhills" (June 17, 1993) references Norman Brown as a Navajo filmmaker.

Chapter 3

1. A variation of this chapter was previously published: Watchman, "Reel Restoration in *Drunktown's Finest*." Portions are also reflected in Watchman and Innes, "Transforming Toxic Indigenous Masculinity." Ahéhee' to Sydney Freeland, MorningStar Angeline, Carmen Moore, and Jeremiah Bitsui for your feedback on early drafts of this chapter.
2. I embrace Raheja's challenge to approach film analysis "through the lens of a particular Indigenous epistemic knowledge" (*Reservation Realism*, 148). The epistemic knowledge and lens I use is hózhǫ́. The epistemological and philosophical distinctness of hózhǫ́ is addressed in Lee, *Diné Perspectives*.
3. Tapahonso, "Singing in Navajo," 40.
4. Barber, *The Canadian Oxford Dictionary*, s.v. "reel."
5. Aleiss, *Making the White Man's Indian*; Bataille and Silet, "The Indian in American Film"; Bataille and Silet, *Images of American Indians on Film*; Bataille and Silet, *The Pretend Indians*; Bird, *Dressing in Feathers*; Black, *Picturing Indians*; Boyd, "An Examination"; Buscombe, *"Injuns!"*; Friar and Friar, *The Only Good Indian*; Hearne, *Native Recognition*; Hilger, *From Savage to Nobleman*; Howe, Markowitz, and Cummings, *Seeing Red*; Kilpatrick, *Celluloid Indians*; Marubbio, *Killing the Indian Maiden*; Marubbio and Buffalohead, *Native Americans on Film*; Pavlik, Marubbio, and Holm, *Native Apparitions*; Price, "The Stereotyping"; Raheja, *Reservation Realism*; Rollins and O'Connor, *Hollywood's Indian*; Singer, *Wiping the War Paint*.
6. In "The New Navajo Cinema," Lewis looks at the work of Diné filmmakers Lowe, Becker, and Klain. He identifies "the preservation or restoration of familial ties,

cultural continuity, Native language, individual wellness, and tribal land" as crucial to their stories (57).
7. I was unable to procure the late 1980s segment or transcript despite numerous attempts to contact ABC.
8. Skeets, "Drunktown."
9. Wissot, "Director Sydney Freeland."
10. "Interview with Sydney Freeland," Vision Maker Media, accessed September 27, 2016, http://www.visionmakermedia.org/listen/sydney-freeland (page discontinued).
11. Dry Lake (real-life Gallup) is located along I-40, between two sacred mountains: Dookʼoʼoosłííd (our westerly mountain) and Tsoodził (our southerly mountain).
12. Visual sovereignty has been grappled with by several creatives and in dialogue with the scholarly community. Pavlik, Marubbio, and Holm advance Indigenous media sovereignty: "The term invokes using media from a Native perspective at the community, pan-tribal, national, and international levels to effect change and represent Native people from their perspective, with their stories, and through their voices. It is nothing less than the creative right to produce media across genres and cinematic approaches" (*Native Apparitions*, 10). Another succinct definition of visual sovereignty is defined by Hearne as "an expansive framework that creates a critical space to privilege a range of Indigenous aesthetic strategies and access to traditionality in a political world" (*Native Recognition*, 15). Hearne considers previous work done by Jolene Rickard, Beverly Singer, Michelle H. Raheja, Steven Leuthold, and Randolph Lewis.
13. Raheja, *Reservation Reelism*, 149.
14. See, for example, Watchman and Innes, "Transforming Toxic Indigenous Masculinity."
15. This is like the opening montage of *Skins*, directed by Chris Eyre (Cheyenne and Arapaho). In *Skins*' montage, the handheld camera technique takes the perspective of being inside a vehicle and focuses on what passers-by witness while traveling through the fictional Beaver Creek Indian Reservation. While it does not open with a montage, *The Exiles*, by Kent MacKenzie, follows relocated Indigenous youth in the Bunker Hill neighborhood of Los Angeles through documentary-style techniques (employing a handheld camera, voice-over narration, and archival footage).
16. In Chief Manuelito's time, runners were messengers during war, which Tiana Bighorse reminds us: "In every group there should be a runner. There always has to be somebody on hand to take a message to where the warriors are. They do it in relay on horse or on foot" ("Chosen to be a Leader," 71). A runner's purpose was valuable to Diné survival, which is beyond the scope of my analysis for this film.
17. I begin my book with Diné protocol and include this mantra in chapter 1.
18. Jerome Jeffery Clark (Diné) offers an exceptionally nuanced analysis (or rehearsal) and theory making of this same montage in the fourth chapter of his dis-

sertation. He shared his work for the Yale Group for the Study of Native America Lunch Talk on March 8, 2021, called "Border Town (Im)possibilities: Rehearsing Diné Life and Death in the Nááhwíílbiihí Story and *Drunktown's Finest*." Clark's talk exemplifies Diné epistemologies to answer Nizhoni's pleading question based on his theory of ch'íhonít'i' ("a way out"). Ch'íhonít'i' is a technique specific to Diné weavers that is sometimes called the weaver's path or a spirit line that serves to let the spirit of creativity, good energy, and thoughts out of the tapestry. This teaching was gifted by Na'ashjé'ii Asdzą́ą́; coupled with Diné kinship practices, Clark argues that Diné should not get locked into settler colonial ideas that counter valuable and complex Diné teachings, namely that Diné should stay and not leave, as lamented by Nizhoni's query. Clark, "Seeking Life."

19. Kelley and Francis, *A Diné History of Navajoland*, 6.
20. Tapahonso, "Singing in Navajo," 39.
21. Solis, "An Interview with 'Drunktown's Finest' Writer/Director Sydney Freeland."
22. J. P. Richardson, "Beggar to a King," recorded October 16, 1957, track 1 on Jape Richardson and the Japetts, *Beggar to a King*, Mercury Starday 71219X45, 45 rpm; Wingate Valley Boys, performers, "Beggar to a King," track 6 on *The Wingate Valley Boys*, Indian Arts of America R-3001, 1927, 33⅓ rpm. Other country singers have performed this song, including Hank Snow and George Jones.
23. Momaday, *The Man Made of Words*, 124.
24. Skeets's poem "Drunktown" also mirrors this description.
25. Denetdale, "'Drunktown's Finest.'"
26. *Drunktown's Finest* does not mention the prevalence of basketball as a healthy outlet on reservations. Some films engage this: Netflix released a six-part docuseries, *Basketball or Nothing* (2019), directed by Matt Howley; and Chris Eyre's *Edge of America* (2003) is based on the documentary *Rocks with Wings* (2001), by Rick Derby.
27. The inmates' ethnicities are unknown. Gallup (Dry Lake) is ethnically diverse. It is home to Diné, Hopi, Zuni, brown Mexicans, and non-Indigenous settlers from South Asia, so to label them as "drunk *indians*" like *20/20* did would be erroneous and racist.
28. I borrow "Navajo aesthetic" from Beverly Singer, who applies it to visual media (*Wiping the War Paint*, 34). Anthropologists used Navajo aesthetic to scrutinize Navajo arts and crafts, such as weaving or painting. Here, Navajo aesthetic incorporates the land, animals, the People, arts, and crafts that offer a Diné gaze.
29. Landry, "Humanity and Complexity," C3.
30. McPherson, *Dinéjí Na'Nitin*, 152.
31. Denetdale, *Reclaiming Diné History*, 134–37. Asdzą́ą́ Nádleehé was created by the Diyin Diné'é (Holy People) and fostered by First Woman and First Man (supernatural beings that embodied human form). Asdzą́ą́ Nádleehé was raised on Ch'ool'í'í (Gobernador Knob), which is a sacred inner mountain within the four sacred mountains. Four days after her birth, she grew into a young woman, marked by her first menses, which led to the first Kinaaldá, or puberty ceremony.

32. Toledo-Benalli, "Kinaaldá." Kinaaldá running builds strength and endurance, as the runner must run farther than she ran the day before. Eulynda Jean Toledo-Benalli asserts that running connects the Kinaaldá to the spiritual realm. A critical component of a Kinaaldá is that the girl grinds corn for much of the time, which keeps the mind focused, allowing clean thoughts and speech. It also teaches generosity, as the corn being ground will be used to bake the alkaan, a six-foot round cake baked underground overnight.
33. Not a direct quotation, but summarizing Farella, *The Main Stalk*, 32–36.
34. This spelling of Naát'áanii Nez Mean's name mirrors how he spells it on X (formerly known as Twitter).
35. Whitman (Euchi-Muscogee Creek) has a long career as a photographer, artist, and actor.
36. Nizhoni Smiles is also the name of a family dentist and orthodontist in Shiprock, New Mexico, and St. Michaels, Arizona.
37. Freeland revealed that this accident stems from reality. A horse was struck and killed by a person driving while on meth. Graver, "'Drunktown's Finest.'"
38. Raheja, *Reservation Reelism*, 152.
39. Lewis, "The New Navajo Cinema," 57.
40. Kelley and Francis, *Navajo Sacred Places*, 17–18.
41. I was featured in the 1995 edition of Women of the Navajo.
42. While the correct way to ask is "Há'áát'íísh adóone'é nílí?" the film reflects a spoken form of the question that sounds like "Há't'ííshdóone'é?"
43. Hearne, *Native Recognition*, 14.
44. Coomes, "Calendar."
45. VirileGrow is sildenafil citrate, commonly known as Viagra.
46. For reports of the controversy, see Peters, "'Legacy of Exiled Ndnz.'"
47. This is not to say that she was denied participation in any Kinaaldá, as there are puberty ceremonies for both males and females, according to the stories. I am not aware of Kinaaldá ceremonies for nádleeh.
48. Zolbrod, *Diné bahane'*, 60. Hastiin Harmon's version is shared below.
49. Zolbrod, *Diné bahane'*, 374n37.
50. Werito, "Understanding Hózhǫ́," 27–29.
51. hooks, *Reel to Real*, 215 (my emphasis).
52. The centuries-long influence of fundamentalist Christianity and paternal ideologies that invaded Indigenous communities is a well-oiled machine and deeply internalized. Hateful and ignorant accounts continue to circulate that reflect homophobic and violent views; for example, Hastiin Béésh\ligai's rendering in "The Separation of Males & Females." Freeland's film reflects these ideologies through the beating of Eugene and through Felixia's desperation to leave.
53. C. Allen, *Blood Narrative*, 161 and 185. I extend Allen's thinking into my analysis.
54. Wissot, "Director Sydney Freeland."
55. Thomas, "Navajo Cultural Constructions," 156.

Notes to Pages 101–111

56. While Thomas provides detailed tables that delineate and explain the complex Navajo gender categories in his chapter, I reference the gender distinctions as he narrates them in Nibley's documentary.
57. Denetdale, "Carving Navajo National Boundaries," 293–94.
58. Healthy Nations Initiative, "Northwest New Mexico," 46.
59. Email correspondence with EiRena Begay, September 25, 2015.
60. Email correspondence with Begay.
61. Denetdale, "'Drunktown's Finest.'"
62. Watchman and Innes, "Transforming Toxic Indigenous Masculinity," 137.
63. Denetdale, "'Drunktown's Finest.'"

Chapter 4

1. Not all of Lowe's works are listed on IMDb; several short films are on his Vimeo site, https://vimeo.com/blackhorselowe/videos.
2. Lewis, "The New Navajo Cinema," 53.
3. Hearne and Schlachter, "'Pockets Full of Stories,'" 267.
4. Barclay, "Celebrating Fourth Cinema," 11.
5. Kelley and Francis, *Navajo Sacred Places*, 2.
6. Marjorie Beaucage, personal conversation, February 26, 2022.
7. Piatote, "Sonic Sovereignty," 4.
8. Piatote, "Sonic Sovereignty," 7.
9. Robinson, *Hungry Listening*, 62.
10. Robinson analyzes "The Report" by Diné composer Raven Chacon (Pulitzer Prize in Music, 2022). Chacon commissioned Lowe to direct the video that accompanies the composition in 2015. This project enlists firearms that are deployed to a musical score; because I was unable to procure the full video, I am unable to comment on Robinson's analysis. I see intersections (based solely on the one-minute excerpt on Vimeo) with my work on land, sky, sound, silence, and hane'tonomy, but it is—for now—beyond the scope of my study.
11. Robinson, *Hungry Listening*, 2–3.
12. Robinson, *Hungry Listening*, 3.
13. Robinson, *Hungry Listening*, 8, 11.
14. Robinson, *Hungry Listening*, 15.
15. Kuhn and Westwell, *A Dictionary of Film Studies*, s.v. "Diegesis."
16. Geiger and Rutsky, "Glossary of Critical Terms," 1068.
17. Geiger and Rutsky, "Glossary of Critical Terms," 1078.
18. Bordwell, "Diegetic Theories of Narration," 16.
19. Bordwell, *Meaning Making*, 8.
20. Baldick, *The Oxford Dictionary of Literary Terms*, s.v. "diegesis."
21. Barry, *Beginning Theory*, 231.
22. Austin, *Navajo Courts*; Cook, "The Creation of the Navajo People"; Jacobsen and Bowman, "Don't Even Talk to Me"; Yazzie, *Navajo History*.

23. Morris, *From the Glittering World*, 47.
24. Yazzie, *Navajo History*, 74. Alice Cook's father passed down k'éí origin stories. Their family version differs slightly from Yazzie's account. They agree that Changing Woman created Clans from her body, but they differ in what part of Changing Woman's body the Clans were formed: "She took *chxiin*, outer skin layers from: Her right hand to make the *Tótsohnii* clan; Her left hand to make the *Honágháahnii* clan; Her left breast to make the *Kinyaa'áanii* clan; and the back of her neck to make the *Tódích'íi'nii* clan." Cook, "The Creation of the Navajo People."
25. Yazzie, *Navajo History*, 74.
26. A story about a pet mountain lion and its relationship with the Tódich'íi'nii (contradicting Yazzie's story) is in Salabye and Manolescu, "The Navajo Beginnings of Corn." Klopfenstein's decade-long-plus apprenticeship of learning the stories offers a slightly different version regarding the guardians, whom he also calls pets. He does not list the Bitter Water as being watched over by bull snakes—he says "Big Snakes"—and instead of the Mud Clan having porcupines as guardians, he says they have hummingbirds (Dahiitíhí). Klopfenstein, "The Early Part."
27. Justice Raymond D. Austin offers a different origin story of k'éí, which also reflects two different Clans from this version. See Austin, *Navajo Courts and Navajo Common Law*, 145. He adds another version in 145n6, expanding the origin story of the four original Clans. Ethelou Yazzie documented that instead of scepters, they carried canes made of white shell, turquoise, and obsidian (*Navajo History*, 80). A fourth cane, likely of abalone, was not mentioned. Cook also relates there were four staffs, but her version departs from both Austin's and Yazzie's in terms of which Clan carried which staff. In the end, what is consistent across stories is that the canes were used to source the various waters and mud found on Navajo land.
28. Hearne and Schlachter, "'Pockets Full of Stories,'" 273.
29. Raheja, *Reservation Reelism*, 216.
30. Lewis, "The New Navajo Cinema," 58.
31. Hearne and Schlachter, "'Pockets Full of Stories,'" 274 (my emphasis).
32. Klopfenstein, "The Early Part."
33. Marubbio and Buffalohead, *Native Americans on Film*, 17.
34. Hearne and Schlachter, "'Pockets Full of Stories,'" 274–75.
35. Hearne and Schlachter, "'Pockets Full of Stories,'" 266.
36. See Hearne, "Remembering Smoke Signals."
37. Hearne and Schlachter, "'Pockets Full of Stories,'" 275. In Ford's *The Searchers*, Monument Valley was staged as Texas, and his work was largely responsible for popularizing southwest (Diné) landscapes as the Wild West.
38. Ahéhee' to my cousin Ryan (Rion) Manus for drawing my attention to Metallica's video, directed by Wayne Isham. Alanis Morissette filmed "Live in the Navajo Nation," which features several areas on the Navajo Nation but specifically White House Ruin in Canyon de Chelly. "Live" elevates the beauty of Diné Bikéyah that attracts media attention.

39. Momaday believed "that only in *dine bizaad*, the Navajo language, . . . can this place [Monument Valley] be described, or even indicated in its true character" (*The Names*, 69). The Navajo-language name is Tsé Bii' Ndzisgaii, which means "valley of the rocks," to describe the picturesque beauty of red, elegant rock formations. Because Ford staged the area as the undescriptive "American West" in his Westerns, Tsé Bii' Ndzisgaii has been eclipsed and erased. The attention to Diné Bikéyah brought Ford fame, with a popular lookout bearing his name, John Ford Point. Paul Chaat Smith points out that "John Ford, the king of westerns, set his most famous movies about Indians in Monument Valley, a landscape that might be described as Martian, to contrast the alienness of the land with the flimsy covered wagons and lonely outposts. Often the Indians seemed alien as well, but they seemed to belong there, while the Americans looked like intruders, or tourists" (*Everything You Know About Indians Is Wrong*, 49). The comparison of Tsé Bii' Ndzisgaii and Dinétah as Martian alien land displaces Navajo land's storied autonomy and aesthetic magnificence, and is epistemicide.
40. Piatote, "Sonic Sovereignty," 8.
41. Kahn-John and Koithan, "Living in Health," 27.
42. Yazzie, "Navajo Wisdom and Traditions," 12. Yazzie's sources (predominantly from the Rough Rock area in the early seventies) attribute our current world as the Fourth World. She writes: "It was not until the People moved into the Fourth World that they learned to discuss things and cooperate with one another. Dissatisfaction with evil and suffering, led the People in our history to seek a means to lift themselves up to a world of better conditions" ("Navajo Wisdom and Traditions," 11).
43. Lowe, "Blackhorse Lowe," 0:38–0:47.
44. She draws out John's name as *Jo-oo-ohn*. When enunciated as such, it becomes a derogatory term that is intended to offend fluent Diné bizaad speakers, which is another reflection of hóchxǫ́.
45. Denetdale, *Reclaiming Diné History*, 31.
46. Quoted in Johnson, *Navajo Stories of the Long Walk Period*, 266.
47. For example, Houston Wood quotes Eric D. Snider's review of *5th World*—"rather than introducing anything as revolutionary as, say, a plot, Lowe gives us endless shots of desert landscapes and blue skies"—revealing Snider's outsider status and unfamiliarity with Diné stories. Snider, quoted in Wood, "Dimensions of Difference," 46n12.
48. L. Emerson, "Diné Sovereign Action," 178.
49. Lester, "The Emergence Story." The next world in this context is the Fifth World. The quote about stones, wood, and feathers is from Lester but he attributes the monsters to being born in the Fourth World.
50. Tuyuc, "In NYC."

Chapter 5

1. The Tłı̨chǫ Yatıì words (and Wıìlıìdeh Yatı̀, which is a dialect of Tłı̨chǫ Yatıì) for "story" are godi, gondi, hondi. Because the authors I introduce speak variants of

Dene (or Doné, Dǫne), specifically Dënesųłıné, Tłıchǫ Yatıì, and Wıìlıìdeh Yatı, I only reference these Dene languages. I will use the specific word if speaking only of that Nation's Dene language: in the context of speaking only about Dënesųłıné, I say honi; in the context of Tłıchǫ or Wıìlıìdeh, I write hondi, and in the context of Diné (Navajo), I say hane'. If generalizing or metaphorizing about story, narrative, or wisdom in general, I have chosen the rather cumbersome honi/hondi/hane'. When speaking in general about all Dene People, I simply write Dene. The Tłıchǫ word for Dene People is Doné, Dǫ, or Dǫne. As languages revive, spelling varies; case in point, there are many ways I have seen Dënesųłıné spelled.
2. Tapahonso, "Singing in Navajo," 74.
3. LeSage, Drybones-Foliot, and Simpson, *Ndè Sıì Wet'aɂà: Northern Indigenous Voices on Land, Life, & Art* (2022), exemplifies emergent Dene literary talent.
4. Explained in the preface and repeated here: The four sacred mountains are storied as created by the Diyin Diné'é, to demarcate Diné traditional territory. Beginning with the east mountain: Tsisnaajiní (also Sisnaajiní or Mount Blanca) in San Luis Valley, Colorado; then turning to the south is Tsoodził (Mount Taylor), northeast of Grants, New Mexico; turning to the west is Dook'o'oosłíí́d (San Francisco Peaks), near Flagstaff, Arizona; and the north sacred mountain is Dibé Ntsaa (Mount Hesperus of the La Plata Mountains) in southwestern Colorado. There are also two inner sacred mountains, Dził Ná'oodiłii (Huerfano Mountain) and Ch'ool'í'í (Gobernador Knob).
5. I begin in the East, which is how Diné thought is organized, and go in the direction of the sun.
6. I embrace correction here, if I have omitted anyone or have erred.
7. "Around the Northwest Territories, there are different language groups. There's North Slavey, South Slavey, Gwich'in, Mountain, Hare, Inuvialuit, and Yellowknife. There's Métis—they have their own language, called Michif. There's Chipewyan, of course, and there's Northern Cree." Van Camp and Muro, "Living," 302.
8. Van Camp, *Gather*, 76.
9. Justice, *Why Indigenous Literatures Matter*, 186.
10. On restorying as theory, Cherokee scholar Christopher B. Teuton devised an original model through gagoga stories. He writes, "The continuing process of restorying orality and oral literature—and thus reclaiming how Indigenous oral expressions are conceptualized and entextualized—depends on defining these expressive practices in specific cultural terms, histories, and contexts" ("Indigenous Orality and Oral Literatures," 170).
11. Macdougall, "How We Know," 236, 262n14.
12. Macdougall has also discussed Métis kinscapes with Nicole St. Onge for Metis Talks 2015.
13. Justice, *Why Indigenous Literatures Matter*, 197. He continues that kinscapes are "legible and interpretable relations to land—particularly the allotment maps—and thus the cartographic extension of the concept" (262). Goeman says borders exemplify "spatial violence" (*Mark My Words*, 21).

14. Baker, review of *Why Indigenous Literatures Matter*.
15. Justice, *Why Indigenous Literatures Matter*, 34.
16. Behchokǫ̀ means "Big Knife" and replaced the name Rae-Edzo.
17. Erasmus, "We the Dene," 177.
18. "February Is Indigenous Languages Month!," Yellowknife Education District No. 1, accessed March 17, 2023, https://www.ykl.nt.ca/_ci/p/3399. Blondin gives a comprehensive overview of each law in *My Life in the Sahtu*, 5–7.
19. Blondin, *Yamoria the Lawmaker*, 78.
20. Campbell, "The Hero of the Dine."
21. Campbell, "The Hero of the Dine."
22. Blondin, "Amìi Yamozha ne?," 84.
23. Blondin, *Yamoria the Lawmaker*, 70.
24. Blondin says Yamoria's sibling is a brother named Yamoga. The names Sazea and Yamória (as names of Yamozha's siblings) come from Freeman, "A Traditional Tlicho Story."
25. Innes, *Elder Brother*, 38.
26. Campbell, "The Hero of the Dine."
27. Van Camp, "How Stories Connect Us," 7:50–7:57.
28. Innes, *Elder Brother*, 23–24.
29. Denetdale, "The Value of Oral History," 80.
30. Innes, *Elder Brother*, 24.
31. The novel opens with two poetic epigraphs about sky and earth by two poets, "Stars Answer" by Moe Clark (Métis) and "Terra Nuillius [*sic*]" by Jordan Abel (Nisga'a). Katłià, *Land-Water-Sky*, 3–5. Their words at once birth and give voice to land, water, and sky, and can be read as a formal welcome to Katłià's stories.
32. Leslie Marmon Silko vividly wove imagery into her works, and she challenged outsiders about the literary conceptualization of landscape: "So long as the human consciousness remains *within* the hills, canyons, cliffs, and the plants, clouds, and sky, the term *landscape*, as it has entered the English language, is misleading. 'A portion of territory the eye can comprehend in a single view' does not correctly describe the relationship between the human being and his or her surroundings" (*Yellow Woman*, 27; Silko, "Landscape," 265).
33. Katłià, *Land-Water-Sky*, 4.
34. Katłià, *Land-Water-Sky*, 5.
35. Katłià, *Land-Water-Sky*, 8.
36. Katłià, *Land-Water-Sky*, 4.
37. Katłià, *Land-Water-Sky*, 10.
38. Katłià, *Land-Water-Sky*, 85.
39. Katłià, *Land-Water-Sky*, 173.
40. Katłià, *Land-Water-Sky*, 85.
41. Katłià, *Land-Water-Sky*, 15–16. Yat'a's celestial birth, discovery, and ceremonial welcome to the world resemble the origins of Asdzą́ą́ Nádleehé (Changing

Woman) from Diné oral traditions. An Elder "saw the sky light up and heard a baby's cry. Clouds covered the sky, and an unexplainable mist fell over the valley. The Elder blindly followed the sound of the cry, feeling her way through the fog until she spotted a small flailing movement atop a large boulder at the peak of the ridge.... The Elder picked the child up ... wondered who the child could have belonged to as she looked around for any sign of her parents, but all she could see was a spark of lighting through the mist." Katłjà, *Land-Water-Sky*, 14–15.

42. Katłjà, *Land-Water-Sky*, 21.
43. Katłjà, *Land-Water-Sky*, 174.
44. Helm, *The People of Denendeh*, 278.
45. Tłı̨chǫ Dene creative (transdisciplinary artist, composer, and musician) Casey Koyczan goes by the performance name Nàhgą. This name evolved from his previous incarnation as "The Bushman NT" in honor of the stories of "the spirit of the woods." Casey Koyczan, "NAHGA—Featured Artist," interview, *Breakout West* (blog), June 19, 2017, https://breakoutwest.ca/blog/nahga-featured-artist.
46. Katłjà, *Land-Water-Sky*, 60.
47. In Richard Van Camp's short story "The Fleshing," the Wheetago is allegorized (restoried) as the tar sands. The Wheetago's storied origins are not Dene but have come from the Cree- and Algonquian-speaking Nations. Stories traveled, encouraging cross-cultural sharing of intellectual and material resources. The fleshing of Denendeh has transformed Dene land into the tar sands, which is congruent with the fleshing of the town bully (named Dean) who is actively transforming into the Wheetago. They are monstrous destroyers, and their presence is not restorative, directly contrary to Dene laws.
48. Katłjà *Land-Water-Sky*, 16.
49. Katłjà, *Land-Water-Sky*, 86.
50. Katłjà, *Land-Water-Sky*, 77.
51. Lois Elizabeth Edge, a beadworker and educator, is quoted in Lussier, "Law with Heart and Beadwork," 298.
52. Gray, "Beads," 5.
53. Jamie Billette (Dene), creator of Beaded Blends, is a seasoned beadworker and specializes in feather work. Her grandmother's traditional Dene beadwork (of moss bags, mukluks, and mittens), which reflects the aesthetic of the land and depicts floral and berry designs, is her inspiration. Willis Janvier, *Dene Yati* podcast, March 16, 2021, https://fb.watch/lKRBr77F-6/?startTimeMs=16000&mibextid=v7YzmG.
54. Lussier, "Law with Heart and Beadwork," 276, 277. For example, Haudenosaunee wampum belts inscribe law and governance using white shell tubular beads (wampum), made of quahog clam shells. They are also admired for their unique technique of raised beadwork.
55. Katłjà, *Land-Water-Sky*, 166.
56. Katłjà, *Land-Water-Sky*, 8, 88.

57. Morritt-Jacobs, "N.W.T. Author."
58. Justice, *Why Indigenous Literatures Matter*, 210–11.
59. Van Camp, *Gather*, 31. His website, http://richardvancamp.com, is regularly maintained, and as of July 2023, he has published twenty-seven books in twenty-seven years. His website is comprehensive and includes his publications, awards, and links to other sites about his work. Hanson's chapter "Being Able to Tell Stories from the North," in *Literatures, Communities, and Learning*, 31–40, is a rich and humorous conversation with Van Camp.
60. Van Camp also restories taboo topics or traumatic events that could be triggering, with jaw-busting humor, because laughter is also medicine. "Why Ravens Smile to Little Old Ladies as They Walk By" and "Dogrib Midnight Runners" are laugh-out-loud funny, yet they comment on Elder vaginas and suicide. Such stories recall the kitchen-table conversations that Aunties have, which are punctuated with blushes, yelps, and wicked cackling that prompt tears of joy—to command literary Indigenous erotica *and* healing narratives with humor is laudable. His arsenal of published literary arts is the balm for all the oratory that was silenced by colonial onslaught and is waiting to be recovered.
61. Van Camp, "The Fleshing," 31.
62. Van Camp, "The Fleshing," 33.
63. Tenille K. Campbell, A Poet Photographer (website), accessed July 11, 2023, https://www.tenillecampbell.com.
64. T. Campbell, *nedí nezu̧*, 119.
65. T. Campbell, *nedí nezu̧*, 120.
66. Cree bead artist Ruth Cuthand beads diseases and viruses that Indigenous People were infected with. Her work is exhibited as *Beads in the Blood* (2021), the *Covid-19 Mask Series* (2020), the *Trading Series* (2010), and the *Surviving Series* (2010). These beaded pieces restory the narrative of succumbing to invasive diseases, as they are an homage to continual Indigenous survival. Another beadwork project that confronts colonialism is the beaded *Indian Act* (2002) exhibit created by Nadia Myre. She "denounced the discriminatory and exclusionary nature of this law . . . to subvert and re-appropriate the legislative text. White beads replace the words on the first 56 pages of the Act, rendering it null and void." "1876: Reopening History," 150 Years | 150 Works: Canadian Art as Historical Act, VMC, last modified April 2, 2018, https://150ans150oeuvres.uqam.ca/en/artwork/1876-indian-act-by-nadia-myre/#description.
67. Quoted in Threlfall, "Beadwork as Resistance."
68. Rodriguez, "Beading Is Medicine."
69. Woody, "Rosette," 109.
70. Ellen K. Moore writes, "Navajo beadwork has never been systematically studied and is rarely acknowledged by outsiders. . . . It has appeared primarily in the second half of the twentieth century and has become a phenomenon only in a little more than the past decade" (*Navajo Beadwork*, 5).

71. Moore, *Navajo Beadwork*, 8.
72. Moore, *Navajo Beadwork*, xvii.
73. On northern lights, see Barton, "Legends of the Northern Lights"; Boivin, *I Will See You Again*; "Legends of the Aurora"; Van den Berg, "Dene Photographer"; and Ward, "There Is Little Research."
74. Van Camp, *Gather*, 16.
75. Personal communication, February 21, 2022. The Dënesųłıné translation of Yati, as he spells it, means "word." The various meanings of Yatié are from Fabien et al., "Dëne Dédliné Yatié." For neighboring speakers of Tłįchǫ Yatiì, the word *Yati* is a direct cognate; see Saxon and Siemens, *Tłįchǫ Yatiì Enįhtł'è*.
76. Janvier's Diné guests: TJ Warren (Red Mesa, AZ), March 3, 2021; Geraldine Begay, March 28, 2021; Josiah Tsosie, May 3, 2021; and Tyrell Descheny (a weaver), November 1, 2021. One Tsuut'ina Nation guest, Brent Dodginghorse (former WHL player and band councillor), appeared on February 2, 2021. As Dene language is prioritized, I have not been able to understand some of the invited guests, particularly Darryl McDonald (Fon Du Lac, SK), April 4, 2021, whose topic was specifically on Dënesųłiné stories. Janvier commands the podium as an engaging host, but on January 21, 2022, he found himself in the guest seat, invited to appear on a Diné show called the *Cheíí Begay Show*.
77. Warren explains that stories about Indigenous Peoples crossing the Bering Strait have been disproven but did not offer any sources. Simon Ortiz, an Acoma, Keres-speaking thinker, says of the Bering Strait: "Indian people have disputed this non-Indian contention, which to them is intended to demean and denigrate their indigenous [sic] identity by implying that their origin was elsewhere and away from their Native American world. Further, Indian people have seen this as an attempt to undermine their claims to the land they have always known as theirs and which is absolutely associated with their cultural identity" (*Speaking for the Generations*, xiii).
78. Butler, "Navajo Nation."
79. Manywounds, "'It's Almost Biblical.'"
80. Tsuut'ina Gunaha Institute (website), accessed March 12, 2023, https://www.tsuutinagunahainstitute.com.
81. Todd, "Alberta Teacher"; "Request for Expression of Interest Submision [sic] Guidelines—Aboriginal Language Initiative Third Party Delivery Organization," Department of Canadian Heritage, Government of Canada, accessed July 1, 2023, https://www.canada.ca/en/canadian-heritage/services/funding/aboriginal-peoples/expression-interest-third-party.html.
82. "Our Story," Horse Lake First Nation, accessed October 15, 2022, http://horselakefn.ca/our-story/.
83. Redvers, *Fireweed Poems*, 103.
84. Hanson, *Literatures, Communities, and Learning*, 130.

85. Originally quoted in Merelda Potter's podcast, *Roadside Attractions*, "Episode 32: An Interview with Author Tenille Campbell," June 4, 2018, https://www.skroadsideattractions.com/summer-2018/interview-tenille-campbell. The website http://skroadsideattractions.com is no longer accessible.

Conclusion

1. Yazzie, "Navajo Wisdom and Traditions," 3.
2. Jim, "Na'azheeh/Hunting," 143.
3. Basso, *Wisdom Sits in Places*, 38.
4. Charley, "The Legacy of Uranium."
5. See, for example, the documentaries *Black Rock* (Trifa and Romer, 2019) and *Uranium* (Del Seronde, 2010).
6. Kelley and Francis, *Navajo Sacred Places*, 127.
7. Trifa and Romer, "Black Rock," 2:49–2:59.
8. Werito, "Understanding Hózhǫ́," 34.

BIBLIOGRAPHY

Aleiss, Angela. *Making the White Man's Indian: Native Americans and Hollywood Movies*. Westport, Conn.: Praeger, 2005.

Aleiss, Angela. "Native Americans: The Surprising Silents." *Cineaste* 21, no. 3 (Summer 1995): 34–35.

Aleiss, Angela. "'The Vanishing American': Hollywood's Compromise to Indian Reform." *Journal of American Studies* 25, no. 3 (December 1991): 467–72.

Allen, Chadwick. *Blood Narrative: Indigenous Identity in American Indian and Maori Literary and Activist Texts*. Durham, N.C.: Duke University Press, 2002.

Allen, Krista. "Hataałii: Use of Navajo on Mars 'Disrespectful.'" *Navajo Times*, March 25, 2021. https://www.navajotimes.com/ae/culture/hataalii-use-of-navajo-on-mars-disrespectful/.

Andersen, Chris. *"Métis": Race, Recognition, and the Struggle for Indigenous Peoplehood*. Vancouver: University of British Colombia Press, 2014.

Anderson, Brendan. "Enemy Slayer: A Navajo Oratorio—Preview." Vimeo, 2008. Accessed July 11, 2023. https://vimeo.com/679299.

Appadurai, Arjun. "Disjuncture and Difference in the Global Cultural Economy." *Theory, Culture, & Society* 7, nos. 2–3 (1990): 295–310.

Austin, Raymond D. *Navajo Courts and Navajo Common Law: A Tradition of Self-Governance*. Minneapolis: University of Minnesota Press, 2009.

Baker, Carleigh. Review of *Why Indigenous Literatures Matter*, by Daniel Heath Justice. *Quill and Quire*, March 3, 2018. www.quillandquire.com/review/why-indigenous-literatures-matter/.

Baldick, Chris. *The Oxford Dictionary of Literary Terms*. 4th ed. Oxford: Oxford University Press, 2015.

Barber, Katherine, ed. *The Canadian Oxford Dictionary*. 2nd ed. Oxford: Oxford University Press, 2005.

Barclay, Barry. "Celebrating Fourth Cinema." *Illusions: A New Zealand Magazine of Film, Television, and Theatre Criticism* 35 (July 2003): 7–11.

Barclay, Barry. *Our Own Image: A Story of a Maori Filmmaker*. Minneapolis: University of Minnesota Press, 2015.

Barker, Debra K. S. Introduction to *Postindian Aesthetics: Affirming Indigenous Literary Sovereignty*, edited by Debra K. S. Barker and Connie A. Jacobs, 3–12. Tucson: University of Arizona Press, 2022.

Barry, Peter. *Beginning Theory: An Introduction to Literary and Cultural Theory*. New York: Palgrave, 2002.

Barton, Katherine. "Legends of the Northern Lights." CBC News, December 10, 2019. https://newsinteractives.cbc.ca/longform/legends-of-the-northern-lights.

Basso, Keith H. *Wisdom Sits in Places: Landscape and Language Among the Western Apache*. Albuquerque: University of New Mexico Press, 1996.

Bataille, Gretchen M., and Charles L. P. Silet. *Images of American Indians on Film: An Annotated Bibliography*. New York: Garland, 1985.

Bataille, Gretchen M., and Charles L. P. Silet. "The Indian in American Film: A Checklist of Published Materials on Popular Images of the Indian in the American Film." *Journal of Popular Film* 5, no. 2 (1976): 171–82.

Bataille, Gretchen M., and Charles L. P. Silet, eds. *The Pretend Indians: Images of Native Americans in the Movies*. Ames: Iowa State University Press, 1980.

Bay, Michael, dir. *Transformers*. Hollywood, Calif.: Paramount Pictures, 2007.

Beavers, John. "The Bell Route." *Sewanee Mountain Messenger*, May 30, 2018. http://www.sewaneemessenger.com/headlines/?post_id=727&title=%E2%80%8Bthe-bell-route.

Becenti, Arlyssa. "Dikos Ntsaaígíí dóódaa! Nation Musters Defense Against Covid-19." *Navajo Times*, March 12, 2020. https://www.navajotimes.com/reznews/dikos-ntsaaigii-doodaa-nation-musters-defense-against-covid-19/.

Bedonie, Hosteen, et al. *Álchíní Bá Hane'*. Vol. 1 of *Naaltsoos Naaki Góne' Yilts' iłígíí* [Navajo children's literature]. Edited by Edmund L. Ciccarello. Albuquerque: Native American Materials Development Center, 1984.

Bééshłigai, Hastiin. "The Separation of Males & Females." *Leading the Way: The Wisdom of the Navajo People*, April (T'ą́ą́chil) 2016.

Begay, Roger. "The Cornstalk Philosophy of Learning." Judicial Branch of the Navajo Nation Peacemaking Program, Window Rock, Ariz., 2007. https://courts.navajo-nsn.gov/Peacemaking/corntext.pdf.

Belin, Esther G. *From the Belly of My Beauty*. Tucson: University of Arizona Press, 1999.

Belin, Esther G., Jeff Berglund, Connie A. Jacobs, and Anthony K. Webster, eds. *The Diné Reader: An Anthology of Navajo Literature*. Tucson: University of Arizona Press, 2021.

Ben, Galen. "Corn Represents the Journey of Life." *Leading the Way: The Wisdom of the Navajo People, Harvest*, October (Ghąąjį') 2017.

Bernd, Christina Gish. "Voices in the Era of Silents: An American Indian Aesthetic in Early Silent Film." *Native Studies Review* 16, no. 2 (2005): 39–76.

Bighorse, Tiana. "Chosen to Be a Leader." In *The Diné Reader: An Anthology of Navajo Literature*, edited by Esther G. Belin, Jeff Berglund, Connie A. Jacobs, and Anthony K. Webster, 66–77. Tucson: University of Arizona Press, 2021.

Bird, S. Elizabeth, ed. *Dressing in Feathers: The Construction of the Indian in American Popular Culture*. Boulder, Colo.: Westview Press, 1996.

Black, Liza. *Picturing Indians: Native Americans in Film, 1941–1960*. Lincoln: University of Nebraska Press, 2020.

Blondin, George. "Amìi Yamozha ne? (Who Is Yamozha?)." In *Tłı̨chǫ Whaèhdǫ̀ǫ̀ Godiì Ełexè Whela (A Collection of Tłı̨chǫ Stories from Long Ago)*, 83–87. Behchokǫ̀: Tłı̨chǫ Government, 2018. https://tlicho.ca/sites/default/files/2018Collectionof TlichoStories.pdf.

Blondin, George. "I Still Am in Love with the Land. I Am Still in Love with My History." In *In the Words of Elders: Aboriginal Cultures in Transition*, edited by Peter Kulchyski, Don McCaskill, and David Newhouse, 377–413. Toronto: University of Toronto Press, 1999.

Blondin, George. *My Life in the Sahtu*. Ottawa: Royal Commission on Aboriginal Peoples, 1993. https://publications.gc.ca/collections/collection_2016/bcp-pco/Z1-1991-1-41-14-eng.pdf.

Blondin, George. *Yamoria the Lawmaker: Stories of the Dene*. Edmonton: NeWest Press, 1997.

Boivin, Lisa. *I Will See You Again*. Winnipeg: HighWater Press, 2020.

Bordwell, David. "Diegetic Theories of Narration." In *Narration in the Fiction Film*, 16–26. Madison: University of Wisconsin Press, 1985.

Bordwell, David. *Meaning Making: Inference and Rhetoric in the Interpretation of Cinema*. Cambridge, Mass.: Harvard University Press, 1989.

Boyd, Julia. "An Examination of Native Americans in Film and the Rise of Native Filmmakers." *The Elon Journal of Undergraduate Research in Communications* 6, no. 1 (2015): 105–13.

Brown, Michael. "800-Year-Old Moccasin Fragment Suggests Dene Ancestors Migrated Farther South than Previously Thought." *Folio: Society, Culture, and Research* (University of Alberta), March 10, 2021. https://www.ualberta.ca/folio/2021/03/800-year-old-moccasin-fragment-suggests-dene-ancestors-migrated-farther-south-than-previously-thought.html.

Burroughs, Edgar Rice. *A Princess of Mars*. Chicago: A. C. McClurg, 1912.

Buscombe, Edward. *"Injuns!" Native Americans in the Movies*. London: Reaktion Books, 2006.

Butler, Joshua Lavar. "Navajo Nation Invited to Canadian Dene Gathering." *Navajo Hopi Observer*, July 21, 2005. https://www.nhonews.com/news/2005/jul/21/navajo-nation-invited-to-canadian-dene-gathering/.

Camp, Margaret. "'Legend of Shiprock'—Revealing History of the Navajo." *The American Indian* ("A Publication That Reflects the True Character of the American Indian"), 1929.

Campanelli, Stephen, dir. *Indian Horse*. Toronto: Elevation Pictures, 2017.

Campbell, Daniel. "The Hero of the Dene: A Herculean Myth That Served as a Map, a Unifier and an Inspiration." *Up Here: The Voice of Canada's Far North*, April 1, 2015. https://uphere.ca/articles/hero-dene.

Campbell, Tenille K. *#IndianLovePoems*. Winnipeg: Signature Editions, 2017.
Campbell, Tenille K. *nedí nezú: good medicine poems*. Vancouver: Arsenal Pulp Press, 2021.
Casey, Edward S. *The Fate of Place: A Philosophical History*. Oakland: University of California Press, 2013.
Chamberlin, J. Edward. *If This Is Your Land, Where Are Your Stories? Finding Common Ground*. New York: Alfred A. Knopf, 2003.
Charley, Perry H. "The Legacy of Uranium in the Shiprock Community." *Shiprock Magazine: A Publication of Shiprock Historical Society Inc.*, 2012.
Clark, Jerome Jeffery. "Seeking Life: Diné Storytelling as Power, Imagination and Future-Making." PhD diss., Arizona State University, 2021.
Clifford, Arnold. "Dzil Nah Oh Diilthii Doh Jonah Bah Haan Neeh: Central Mountain and Sun Tales." *Shiprock Magazine: A Publication of Shiprock Historical Society Inc.*, 2015.
Cook, Alice. "The Creation of the Navajo People & the Clans." *Leading the Way: The Wisdom of the Navajo People, Clan Migration Stories*, October (Ghąąjį') 2013.
Coomes, Jessica. "Calendar Featuring Navajo Women Hot Seller. Modest Poses May Help Launch Careers for Some." *Arizona Republic*, October 12, 2006.
Correll, J. Lee, Editha L. Watson, and David M. Brugge. "Navajo Bibliography with Subject Index. Revised Edition." Research Report No. 2. Office of Education, Navajo Parks and Recreation, U.S. Department of Health, Education, and Welfare, 1969.
Cummings, Denise K., ed. *Visualities: Perspectives on Contemporary American Indian Film and Art*. East Lansing: Michigan State University Press, 2011.
Cummings, Denise K., ed. *Visualities 2: More Perspectives on Contemporary American Indian Film and Art*. East Lansing: Michigan State University Press, 2019.
Cummings, Denise K. "Visualities of Desire in *Shimásání* and *Sami Blood*." In *Visualities 2: More Perspectives on Contemporary American Indian Film and Art*, edited by Denise K. Cummings, 97–126. East Lansing: Michigan State University Press, 2019.
Cyca, Michelle. "The Curious Case of Gina Adams." *Maclean's*, September 6, 2022. https://www.macleans.ca/longforms/the-curious-case-of-gina-adams-a-pretendian-investigation/.
Da, Royal. "'The Rock' Visits NM: 'Thank You to the Good People of This Area.'" KOAT 7 Action News, April 29, 2019. https://www.koat.com/article/the-rock-thanks-four-corners-area-in-instagram-video/27290766.
Davis, Ron. "Jumanji Sequel Brings the Rock, Kevin Hart to New Mexico." *Albuquerque Business First*, April 30, 2019. https://www.bizjournals.com/albuquerque/news/2019/04/30/jumanji-sequel-brings-the-rock-kevin-hart-to-new.html.
Deloria, Philip J. *Indians in Unexpected Places*. Lawrence: University Press of Kansas, 2004.
Deloria, Vine, Jr. *Red Earth, White Lies: Native Americans and the Myth of Scientific Fact*. Golden, Colo.: Fulcrum, 1997.
Dempsey, Marilyn. "Ti' Dine Bizaad be yadeillti' dooleel! Let's go speak Navajo!" *Navajo Times*, December 10, 2009, C-7. Navajo Times Publishing Co., Inc.

Denetclaw, Pauly. "Data Shows Huge Reduction in Diné Speakers." *Navajo Times*, November 16, 2007. https://navajotimes.com/reznews/data-shows-huge-reduction-in-dine-speakers/.
Denetdale, Jennifer Nez. "COVID-19 on the Navajo Nation: One of Many Monsters." Kitatipithitamak Mithwayawin: Indigenous-Led Countermeasures to Coronavirus (COVID-19) and Other Pandemics Then, Now, and Into the Future. Updated, 2020. https://covid19indigenous.ca/elementor-3504/.
Denetdale, Jennifer Nez. "Carving Navajo National Boundaries: Patriotism, Tradition, and the Diné Marriage Act of 2005." *American Quarterly* 60, no. 2 (2008): 289–94.
Denetdale, Jennifer Nez. "Chronology of Important Dates in Diné Political and Literary History." In *The Diné Reader: An Anthology of Navajo Literature*, edited by Esther G. Belin, Jeff Berglund, Connie A. Jacobs, and Anthony K. Webster, 363–70. Tucson: University of Arizona Press, 2021.
Denetdale, Jennifer Nez. "'Drunktown's Finest' Papers Over Border Town Violence and Bigotry." *Indian Country Media Network*, January 27, 2015, updated September 12, 2018. https://indiancountrytoday.com/archive/drunktowns-finest-papers-over-border-town-violence-and-bigotry.
Denetdale, Jennifer Nez. "Nation to Nation: 09 Bad Acts/Bad Paper." Smithsonian-NMAI, September 23, 2014. YouTube video, 16:58. https://www.youtube.com/watch?v=5Qiv5gE5UNo.
Denetdale, Jennifer Nez. *Reclaiming Diné History: The Legacies of Chief Manuelito and Juanita*. Tucson: University of Arizona Press, 2007.
Denetdale, Jennifer Nez. "The Value of Oral History on the Path to Diné/Navajo Sovereignty." In *Diné Perspectives: Revitalizing and Reclaiming Navajo Thought*, edited by Lloyd L. Lee, 68–82. Tucson: University of Arizona Press, 2014.
Denny, Avery, and Michael Lerma. "Diné Principles of Good Governance." In *Navajo Sovereignty: Understandings and Visions of the Diné People*, edited by Lloyd L. Lee, 103–29. Tucson: University of Arizona Press, 2017.
Derby, Rick, dir. *Rocks with Wings*. Shiprock Productions and Oregon Public Broadcasting, 2001.
Derby, Rick. "Rocks with Wings." *Shiprock Magazine: A Publication of Shiprock Historical Society Inc.*, 2012.
Diné College. "Diné College Principles." Accessed July 11, 2023. www.dinecollege.edu/about_dc/about-dc/.
Dooley, Sunny. "Coronavirus Is Attacking the Navajo 'Because We Have Built the Perfect Human for It to Invade.'" *Scientific American*, July 8, 2020. https://www.scientificamerican.com/article/coronavirus-is-attacking-the-navajo-because-we-have-built-the-perfect-human-for-it-to-invade/.
Dreese, Donelle N. *Ecocriticism: Creating Self and Place in Environmental and American Indian Literatures*. New York: Peter Lang, 2002.
Dunlevy, T'Cha. "Obituary: Mikmaq Filmmaker Jeff Barnaby Fought Indigenous Stereotypes." *Montreal Gazette*, October 14, 2022. https://montrealgazette.com/entertainment/local-arts/obituary-mikmaq-filmmaker-jeff-barnaby-fought-indigenous-stereotypes.

Eagletail, Hal. "Indigenous Language Lesson: Tsuut'ina Nation." Calgary Public Library, December 23, 2019. YouTube video, 1:40. https://www.youtube.com/watch?v=iuoUF0n90iU.

Edge, Lois Elizabeth. "My Grandmother's Moccasins: Indigenous Women, Ways of Knowing and Indigenous Aesthetic of Beadwork." PhD diss., University of Alberta, 2011.

Emerson, Larry W. "Diné Culture, Decolonization, and the Politics of Hózhǫ́." In *Diné Perspectives: Revitalizing and Reclaiming Navajo Thought*, edited by Lloyd L. Lee, 49–67. Tucson: University of Arizona Press, 2014.

Emerson, Larry W. "Diné Sovereign Action: Rejecting Colonial Sovereignty and Invoking Diné Peacemaking." In *Navajo Sovereignty: Understandings and Visions of the Diné People*, edited by Lloyd L. Lee, 160–78. Tucson: University of Arizona Press, 2017.

Emerson, Larry W. Interview by Ramona Emerson. *Reel Indian Pictures*. Vimeo, August 27, 2017. https://vimeo.com/230398845.

Emerson, Ramona. *Shutter*. New York: Soho Press, 2022.

Erasmus, Georges. "We the Dene." In *Dene Nation: The Colony Within*, edited by Mel Watkins, 177–81. Toronto: University of Toronto Press, 1977.

Fabien, Lawrence, Tommy Unka, Christine Fabien, Harvey Mandeville, Denise McKay, Freddie King, Henry Calmut, and Mary Jane Beaulieu, Elders Committee. "Dëne Dëdliné Yatié: ʔerehtłʼíscho. Denínu Kųę́ Yatié." South Slavey Divisional Education Council, Northwest Territories, 2012. http://www.ssdec.nt.ca/ablang/ablanguage/chiptionary/Chipewyan%20Dictionary.pdf.

Farella, John. R. *The Main Stalk: A Synthesis of Navajo Philosophy*. Tucson: University of Arizona Press, 1984.

Farmer, Jared. *On Zion's Mount: Mormons, Indians, and the American Landscape*. Cambridge, Mass.: Harvard University Press, 2008.

Fast, Robin Riley. "The Land Is Full of Stories: Navajo Histories in the Work of Luci Tapahonso." *Women's Studies* 36, no. 3 (2007): 185–211.

Fish, Robert, ed. *Cinematic Countrysides*. Manchester: Manchester University Press, 2007.

Fonseca, Felicia, and Mike Schneider. "Native Americans Fret as Report Card Released on 2020 Census." *Navajo-Hopi Observer*, March 10, 2022. https://www.nhonews.com/news/2022/mar/10/native-americans-fret-report-card-released-2020-ce/.

Freeland, Sydney. "We Need Diverse Voices Telling All Types of Stories—Not Just Their Own." *Time Magazine*, March 12, 2018. https://time.com/5179714/sydney-freeland-diversity-hollywood-representation/.

Freeman, Dave. "A Traditional Tlicho Story." *Notes from the Trail* (blog), Wilderness Classroom, March 25, 2011. https://wildernessclassroom.org/a-traditional-dene-story/.

Friar, Ralph, and Natasha Friar. *The Only Good Indian . . . : The Hollywood Gospel*. Hollywood: Drama Book Specialists, 1972.

Frisbie, Charlotte. *Food Sovereignty the Navajo Way: Cooking with Tall Woman*. Albuquerque: University of New Mexico Press, 2018.

Geiger, Jeffrey, and R. L. Rutsky, eds. "Glossary of Critical Terms." In *Film Analysis: A Norton Reader*, 1061–87. 2nd ed. New York: W. W. Norton, 2013.

Gerew, Gary. "Shiprock Having Another Monumental Moment." *Albuquerque Business First*, March 28, 2013. https://www.bizjournals.com/albuquerque/blog/morning-edition/2013/03/shiprock-appears-in-host-movies.html.

Glotfelty, Cheryll, and Harold Fromm, eds. *The Ecocriticism Reader: Landmarks in Literary Ecology*. Athens: University of Georgia Press, 1996.

Goeman, Mishuana. *Mark My Words: Native Women Mapping Our Nations*. Minneapolis: University of Minnesota Press, 2013.

Gohd, Chelsea. "NASA Honors Navajo Language on Mars with Perseverance Rover Rock Names." *Space*, March 15, 2021. https://www.space.com/mars-navajo-language-perseverance-rover.

Gomez, Adrian. "20 Native Filmmakers Receive Sen. John Pinto Grants." *Albuquerque Journal*, July 13, 2020.

Gonzales, Antonia. "Full Interview | 'Shutter': Behind Diné Author's Debut Novel." *New Mexico in Focus*, September 2, 2022. YouTube video, 18:39. https://www.youtube.com/watch?v=3SCEGcwCcW8.

Gorman, Collen. "Navajo Sovereignty Through the Lens of Creativity, Imagination, and Vision." In *Navajo Sovereignty: Understandings and Visions of the Diné People*, edited by Lloyd L. Lee, 139–59. Tucson: University of Arizona Press, 2017.

Gosnell-Myers, Ginger. "White Privilege, False Claims of Indigenous Identity and Michelle Latimer." *The Tyee*, December 23, 2020. https://thetyee.ca/Opinion/2020/12/23/White-Privilege-False-Claims-Indigenous-Michelle-Latimer/.

Graver, David. "'Drunktown's Finest' Director Sydney Freeland on Growing Up Navajo and Trans." Vice Media, February 22, 2015. http://www.vice.com/en/article/xd5n54/trans-and-navajo-drunktowns-finest-999.

Gray, Malinda Joy. "Beads: Symbols of Indigenous Cultural Resilience and Value." MA thesis, University of Toronto, 2017.

Green, Misha, writer. "Sundown." *Lovecraft Country*. Season 1, episode 1. Directed by Yann Demange. Aired August 16, 2020, on Home Box Office.

Green, Stewart. "Ship Rock: What to Know About This Sacred Navajo Peak in New Mexico." TripSavvy, April 18, 2018, updated May 17, 2022. https://www.liveabout.com/facts-about-shiprock-756148.

Greicius, Tony. "NASA's Perseverance Mars Rover Mission Honors Navajo Language." NASA, March 11, 2021. https://www.nasa.gov/feature/jpl/nasa-s-perseverance-mars-rover-mission-honors-navajo-language.

Grey, Mark (composer), Laura Tohe (lyricist), and Michael Christie (conductor). *Enemy Slayer: A Navajo Oratorio*. Recorded at Symphony Hall, Phoenix, Arizona, on February 7 and 9, 2008. Naxos Records, March 2009. https://www.naxos.com/CatalogueDetail/?id=8.559604.

Griffin, Angela. "Handicraft Museum a Work of Art." *Asheville Citizen-Times*, May 28, 1989, 13.

Hanson, Aubrey Jean. *Literatures, Communities, and Learning: Conversations with Indigenous Writers*. Waterloo: Wilfrid Laurier University Press, 2020.

Harper, Graeme, and Jonathan Rayner, eds. *Cinema and Landscape: Film, Nation and Cultural Geography*. Chicago: University of Chicago Press, 2010.

Healthy Nations Initiative. "Northwest New Mexico Fighting Back." In *Grantee Programs 1994–2002*, 46–53. Aurora: University of Colorado Anschutz Medical Campus, 2016. https://coloradosph.cuanschutz.edu/docs/librariesprovider205/past-work/healthy_nations_initiative_grantees_accomplishments.pdf?sfvrsn=eb3cl4b9_2.

Hearne, Joanna. *Native Recognition: Indigenous Cinema and the Western*. Albany: State University of New York Press, 2012.

Hearne, Joanna. "Remembering Smoke Signals: Interview with Chris Eyre and Sherman Alexie." *Free Library* 29, no. 3 (2010). https://www.thefreelibrary.com/Remembering+Smoke+Signals%3A+interviews+with+Chris+Eyre+and+Sherman . . . -a0247034914.

Hearne, Joanna, and Zack Schlachter. "'Pockets Full of Stories': An Interview with Sterlin Harjo and Blackhorse Lowe." In *Native Americans on Film: Conversations, Teaching, and Theory*, edited by M. Elise Marubbio and Eric L. Buffalohead, 265–87. Lexington: University Press of Kentucky, 2013.

Helm, June. *The People of Denendeh: Ethnohistory of the Indians of Canada's Northwest Territories*. Iowa City: University of Iowa Press, 2000.

Helms, Ed, Michael Schur, and Sierra Teller Ornelas, creators. *Rutherford Falls*. Universal City, Calif.: Universal Television, 2021–22.

Hilger, Michael. *From Savage to Nobleman: Images of Native Americans in Film*. Lanham, Md.: Scarecrow Press, 1995.

Hokowhitu, Brendan. "Te Kapa o Taika: A Commentary on *Boy*." In "Taika Waititi's *Boy*," edited by Jo Smith and Ocean Ripeka Mercier, special issue, *New Zealand Journal of Media Studies* 13, no. 1 (2012): 108–19.

Hokowhitu, Brendan. "Theorizing Indigenous Media." In *The Fourth Eye: Māori Media in Aotearoa New Zealand*, edited by Brendan Hokowhitu and Vijay Devadas, 101–23. Minneapolis: University of Minnesota Press, 2013.

Hokowhitu, Brendan, and Vijay Devadas, eds. *The Fourth Eye: Māori Media in Aotearoa New Zealand*. Minneapolis: University of Minnesota Press, 2013.

hooks, bell. *Reel to Real: Race, Sex, and Class at the Movies*. London: Routledge, 1996.

Howe, LeAnne, and Padraig Kirwan. *Famine Pots: The Choctaw-Irish Gift Exchange, 1847–Present*. East Lansing: Michigan State University Press, 2020.

Howe, LeAnne, Harvey Markowitz, and Denise K. Cummings, eds. *Seeing Red: Hollywood's Pixeled Skins: American Indians and Film*. East Lansing: Michigan State University Press, 2013.

Howley, Matt, dir. *Basketball or Nothing*. Los Gatos, Calif.: Netflix, 2019.

Iñárritu, Alejandro González, dir. *Amores Perros*. Mexico City: Nu Vision, 2000.

Indigenous Screen Office. "ISO Statement Regarding Indigenous Identity." December 18, 2020. http://www.iso-bea.ca/iso-statement-regarding-indigenous-identity/.

Innes, Robert Alexander. *Elder Brother and the Law of the People: Contemporary Kinship and Cowessess First Nation*. Winnipeg: University of Manitoba Press, 2013.

Innes, Robert Alexander. "Elder Brother as Theoretical Framework." In *Sources and Methods in Indigenous Studies*, edited by Chris Andersen and Jean M. O'Brien, 135–42. New York: Routledge, 2016.

Innes, Robert Alexander. "'Wait a Second. Who Are You Anyways?': The Insider/Outsider Debate and American Indian Studies." *American Indian Quarterly* 33, no. 4 (2009): 440–61.

Internet Movie Database. "Filming Location Matching, 'Shiprock, New Mexico, USA.'" Accessed March 5, 2023. www.imdb.com/search/title/?locations=Shiprock%2C+New+Mexico%2C+USA.

Isham, Wayne, dir. "Metallica: I Disappear." Filmed in Monument Valley, April 13, 2000. Released May 4, 2000. YouTube video, 4:28. https://youtu.be/nYSDC3cHoZs.

Jacobs, Sue-Ellen, Wesley Thomas, and Sabine Lang, eds. *Two-Spirit People: Native American Gender Identity, Sexuality, and Spirituality*. Urbana: University of Illinois Press, 1997.

Jacobsen, Kristina, and Shirley Ann Bowman. "'Don't Even Talk to Me if You're Kinya'áanii [Towering House]': Adopted Clans, Kinship, and 'Blood' in Navajo Country." *Journal of the Native American and Indigenous Studies Association* 6, no. 1 (2019): 43–76.

Jim, Rex Lee. "Na'azheeh/Hunting." In *The Diné Reader: An Anthology of Navajo Literature*, edited by Esther G. Belin, Jeff Berglund, Connie A. Jacobs, and Anthony K. Webster, 133–44. Tucson: University of Arizona Press, 2021.

Joe, Eugene B. "Shiprock Historical Society." *Shiprock Fair Magazine: 100th Anniversary; A Presentation by Shiprock Historical Society*, 2011.

Johnson, Broderick H., ed. *Navajo Stories of the Long Walk Period*. Tsaile: Navajo Community College Press, 1973.

Jones, Dustin. "Navajo Nation Combats a New 'Monster': Coronavirus." National Public Radio, November 11, 2020. https://www.npr.org/2020/11/11/934012040/navajo-nation-combats-a-new-monster-coronavirus.

Justice, Daniel Heath. *Why Indigenous Literatures Matter*. Waterloo: Wilfrid Laurier University Press, 2018.

Kahn-John, Michelle, and Mary Koithan. "Living in Health, Harmony, and Beauty: The Diné (Navajo) Hózhó Wellness Philosophy." *Global Advances in Health and Medicine* 4, no. 3 (2015): 24–30.

Kasden, Jake, dir. *Jumanji: The Next Level*. Culver City, Calif.: Sony Pictures Releasing, 2019.

Katłįà. *Land-Water-Sky: Ndè-Ti-Yat'a*. Halifax: Roseway, 2020.

Kauanui, J. Kēhaulani, and Robert Warrior. "Robert Warrior on Intellectual Sovereignty and the Work of the Public Intellectual." In *Speaking of Indigenous Politics: Conversations with Activists, Scholars, and Tribal Leaders*, edited by J. Kēhaulani Kauanui, 328–42. Minneapolis: University of Minnesota Press, 2018.

Kelley, Klara, and Harris Francis. *A Diné History of Navajoland*. Tucson: University of Arizona Press, 2019.

Kelley, Klara Bonsack, and Harris Francis. *Navajo Sacred Places*. Bloomington: Indiana University Press, 1994.

Kestler-D'Amours, Jillian. "This River in Canada Is Now a 'Legal Person.'" *Al Jazeera*, April 3, 2021. http://www.aljazeera.com/news/2021/4/3/this-river-in-canada-now-legal-person.

Kilpatrick, Jacquelyn. *Celluloid Indians: Native Americans and Film*. Lincoln: University of Nebraska Press, 1999.

King, Farina. *The Earth Memory Compass: Diné Landscapes and Education in the Twentieth Century*. Lawrence: University Press of Kansas, 2018.

Klopfenstein, Adair. "The Early Part of the Clan Migration." *Leading the Way: The Wisdom of the Navajo People, Clan Migration Stories*, October (Ghą́ąjį́) 2013.

Knopf, Kerstin. *Decolonizing the Lens of Power: Indigenous Films in North America*. Amsterdam: Rodopi, 2008.

Kovach, Margaret. *Indigenous Methodologies: Characteristics, Conversations, Contexts*. Toronto: University of Toronto Press, 2009.

Krisst, Rima. "'Dark Winds' Hears Critics: Director Says TV Series Will 'Course-Correct' for Accuracy." *Native News Online*, June 30, 2022. https://nativenewsonline.net/arts-entertainment/dark-winds-hears-critics-director-says-tv-series-will-course-correct-for-accuracy.

Kuhn, Annette, and Guy Westwell, eds. *A Dictionary of Film Studies*. Oxford: Oxford University Press, 2012.

Landry, Alysa. "Humanity and Complexity: 'Diné Spotlight' to Show Accurate Picture of What It Really Means to Be Native." *Navajo Times: Diné bi Naaltsoos*, March 26, 2015. https://navajotimes.com/ae/arts/humanity-and-complexity/.

Landry, Alysa. "The Official Magazine Northern Navajo Nation Fair: Celebrating 100 Years of Tradition * Harvest * Healing." *Shiprock Fair Magazine: 100th Anniversary; A Presentation by Shiprock Historical Society*, 2011.

Landry, Alysa. "Shiprock Historical Society Is a 'Storehouse of History' for Navajo Nation." *Indian Country Today*, February 6, 2015, updated September 13, 2018. http://www.indiancountrytoday.com/archive/shiprock-historical-society-is-a-storehouse-of-history-for-navajo-nation.

Lapahie, Harrison, "Shiprock Legend." Reprinted as "Ship Rocked in New Mexico," by Denise Beebower Sloan, Beebower Productions. http://www.beebower.com/ship-rocked-in-new-mexico/.

Lee, Lloyd L. "Decolonizing the Navajo Nation: The Lessons of the Naabaahii." Convention program article. 42nd Annual National Indian Education Association (NIEA) Convention & Tradeshow, Albuquerque, October 27–30, 2011. https://files.eric.ed.gov/fulltext/ED528280.pdf.

Lee, Lloyd L. *Diné Perspectives: Revitalizing and Reclaiming Navajo Thought*. Tucson: University of Arizona Press, 2014.

Lee, Lloyd L., ed. *Navajo Sovereignty: Understandings and Visions of the Diné People*. Tucson: University of Arizona Press, 2017.

Lefebvre, Martin, ed. *Landscape and Film*. New York: Routledge, 2006.

"Legends of the Aurora." Spectacular Northwest Territories. https://spectacularnwt.com/story/legends-aurora.

Leo, Geoff. "Disputed History." *CBC News*, October 12, 2022. https://www.cbc.ca/newsinteractives/features/mary-ellen-turpel-lafond-indigenous-cree-claims.

Léonetti, Jean-Baptiste, dir. *Beyond the Reach*. Santa Monica, Calif.: Lionsgate, 2015.

Leroux, Darryl. *Distorted Descent: White Claims to Indigenous Identity*. Winnipeg: University of Manitoba Press, 2019.

LeSage, Kyla, Thumlee Drybones-Foliot, and Leanne Betasamosake Simpson. *Ndè Sı̀ı̀ Wet'aʔà: Northern Indigenous Voices on Land, Life, & Art*. Winnipeg: ARP Books, 2022.

Lester, Emery. "The Emergence Story." *Leading the Way: The Wisdom of the Navajo People, Winter Stories*, December (Niłch'itsoh) 2011.

Leuthold, Steven. "An Indigenous Aesthetic? Two Noted Videographers: George Burdeau and Victor Masayesva." *Wicazo Sa Review* 10, no. 1 (Spring 1994): 40–51.

Leuthold, Steven. *Indigenous Aesthetics: Native Art, Media, and Identity*. Austin: University of Texas Press, 1998.

Lewis, Randolph. *Navajo Talking Picture: Cinema on Native Ground*. Lincoln: University of Nebraska Press, 2012.

Lewis, Randolph. "The New Navajo Cinema: Cinema and Nation in the Indigenous Southwest." *The Velvet Light Trap: A Critical Journal of Film & Television*, no. 66 (Fall 2010): 50–61.

Linford, Laurance D. *Navajo Places: History, Legend, Landscape*. Salt Lake City: University of Utah Press, 2000.

Lowe, Blackhorse. "Blackhorse Lowe on '5th World.'" Sundance Institute, February 26, 2009. YouTube video, 2:11. https://www.youtube.com/watch?v=cPAuZ3Pus6k.

Lussier, Danielle. "Law with Heart and Beadwork: Decolonizing Legal Education, Developing Indigenous Legal Pedagogy, and Healing Community." PhD diss., University of Ottawa, 2021.

Macdougall, Brenda. "How We Know Who We Are: Historical Literacy, Kinscapes, and Defining a People." In *Daniels v. Canada: In and Beyond the Courts*, edited by Chris Andersen and Nathalie Kermoal, 233–68. Winnipeg: University of Manitoba Press, 2021.

Macdougall, Brenda, and Nicole St. Onge. "Kinscapes: Using the Digital Humanities to Track an In Situ Plains Metis Nation." Métis Talks, Rupertsland Institute, Edmonton, Alberta, November 17, 2015. https://www.rupertsland.org/2015/11/10/metis-talks/.

MacKenzie, Kent, dir. *The Exiles*. Harrington Park: Milestone Films, 2008.

Manywounds, Livia. "'It's Almost Biblical': First Nation Leaders in Calgary to Organize International Dene Reunification Event." *CBC News*, March 2, 2019. https://www.cbc.ca/news/canada/calgary/calgary-dene-first-nation-reunification-meeting-1.5040316.

Marcus, Laura E. "Dark Winds Q&A—Director Chris Eyre on Why Zahn McClarnon Is the Perfect Joe Leaphorn." *AMC Talk* (blog), AMC, June 21, 2022. https://www.amc.com/blogs/dark-winds-q-and-a-director-chris-eyre-on-why-zahn-mcclarnon-is-the-perfect-joe-leaphorn--1054503.

Martinez, Nixon. "Bringing the Sacred Mountains to the Fifth World." *Leading the Way: The Wisdom of the Navajo People, Winter Stories*, January (Ya Niłt'ees) 2016.

Martinez, Nixon. "Changing Woman from Birth to Puberty." *Leading the Way: The Wisdom of the Navajo People, Diné Mothers*, May (T'ą́ą́tsoh) 2016.

Marubbio, M. Elise. *Killing the Indian Maiden: Images of Native American Women in Film*. Lexington: University Press of Kentucky, 2006.

Marubbio, M. Elise, and Eric L. Buffalohead. *Native Americans on Film: Conversations, Teaching, and Theory*. Lexington: University Press of Kentucky, 2013.

Masayesva, Victor. "Indigenous Experimentalism." In *Magnetic North: Canadian Experimental Video*, edited by Jenny Lion, 228–39. Minneapolis: University of Minnesota Press, 2000.

Matthews, Washington. *Navajo Legends*. New York: Houghton Mifflin, 1897.

McCue, Duncan, and Rosemary Barton. "Influential Filmmakers React to State of Indigenous Film in Canada." CBC's *The National*, 2018. https://www.cbc.ca/player/play/1260514371552.

McFarland, Melanie. "Empowering 'Dark Winds' Navajo Women: 'As Native People, Our Continuing Existence Is a Radical Act.'" *Salon*, July 4, 2022. https://www.salon.com/2022/07/04/dark-winds-maya-rose-dittloff-native-women-autonomy/.

McPherson, Robert S. *Dinéjí Na'Nitin: Navajo Traditional Teachings and History*. Boulder: University Press of Colorado, 2012.

Melbye, David. *Landscape Allegory in Cinema: From Wilderness to Wasteland*. New York: Palgrave Macmillan, 2010.

Metcalfe, Jessica Z., John W. Ives, Sabrina Shirazi, Kevin P. Gilmore, Jennifer Hallson, Fiona Brock, Bonnie J. Clark, and Beth Shapiro. "Isotopic Evidence for Long-Distance Connections of the AD Thirteenth-Century Promontory Caves Occupants." *American Antiquity* 86, no. 3 (2021): 526–48.

Meyer, Stephenie. *The Host*. Boston: Little, Brown, 2008.

Miller, Stuart. "Sierra Teller Ornelas on the Roots of 'Rutherford Falls.'" *New York Times*, April 21, 2021.

Mita, Merata. "The Soul and the Image." In *Film in Aotearoa New Zealand*, edited by Jonathan Dennis and Jan Bieringa, 36–54. Wellington: Victoria University Press, 1992.

Momaday, N. Scott. *The Man Made of Words: Essays, Stories, Passages*. New York: St. Martin's, 1997.

Momaday, N. Scott. *The Names: A Memoir*. Tucson: University of Arizona Press, 1976.

Moore, Ellen K. *Navajo Beadwork: Architecture of Light*. Tucson: University of Arizona Press, 2003.

Morissette, Alanis. "Live in the Navajo Nation." *Music in High Places*. Chatsworth, Calif.: Image Entertainment, 2002. YouTube video, 52:48. https://youtu.be/4VZNwQ4FFls.

Morris, Errol, dir. *The Dark Wind*. Burbank, Calif.: New Line Cinema, 1991.

Morris, Irvin. *From the Glittering World: A Navajo Story*. Norman: University of Oklahoma Press, 1997.

Morritt-Jacobs, Charlotte. "N.W.T. Author Reimagines Dene Legends in New Novel Land-Water-Sky / Ndè-Ti-Yat'a." APTN National News, October 16, 2020. https://www.aptnnews.ca/national-news/n-w-t-author-reimagines-dene-legends-in-new-novel-land-water-sky-nde-ti-yata/.

Mottola, Greg, dir. *Paul*. Hollywood, Calif.: Universal Pictures, Netflix, 2011.

Nabokov, Peter. *Where the Lightning Strikes: The Lives of American Indian Sacred Places*. London: Penguin Books, 2006.

Nahdee, Ali. "My Statement on The Ali Nahdee Test." *Ali Nahdee Blog*, April 14, 2022. https://alinahdee.wordpress.com/2022/04/14/my-statement-on-the-ali-nahdee-test/.

Neskahi, Art. "Allen Neskahi, Sr., Emma Atcitty Neskahi and Allan Neskahi, Jr." *Shiprock Magazine: A Publication of Shiprock Historical Society Inc.*, 2012.

Nibley, Lydia, dir. *Two-Spirits*. New York City: Cinema Guild, 2009.

Niccol, Andrew, dir. *The Host*. Hollywood, Calif.: Open Road Films and Universal Pictures, 2013.

Olinger, Jonathan, dir. "#NavajoStrong / Diné Bidziil / Navajo Nation COVID-19 Call for Support." Protect the Sacred, May 6, 2020. YouTube video, 1:40. https://www.youtube.com/watch?v=cPm2h4yiZ8I.

Ortiz, Simon ed. *Speaking for the Generations: Native Writers on Writing*. Tucson: University of Arizona Press, 1998.

Owen, Roz, dir. *Trouble in the Garden*. Toronto: White Eagle Entertainment, 2018.

Oxendine, Chez. "Chickasaw Producer Graham Roland Brings Navajo Detective Story to AMC." *Tribal Business News*, June 6, 2022. https://tribalbusinessnews.com/sections/arts-and-culture/13924-chickasaw-producer-graham-roland-brings-navajo-detective-story-to-amc.

Pack, Sam. "Constructing 'The Navajo': Visual and Literary Representation from Inside and Out." In "The Secular Past, the Mythic Past, and the Impending Future," special issue, *Wicazo Sa Review* 15, no. 1 (Spring 2000): 137–56.

Pavlik, Steve, M. Elise Marubbio, and Tom Holm. *Native Apparitions: Critical Perspectives on Hollywood's Indians*. Tucson: University of Arizona Press, 2017.

Pearson, Wendy Gay, and Susan Knabe, eds. *Reverse Shots: Indigenous Film and Media in an International Context*. Waterloo: Wilfrid Laurier University Press, 2015.

Peters, Pamela J. "'Legacy of Exiled Ndnz' and the Film That Inspired My Work 'The Exiles.'" December 12, 2017. http://www.pamelajpeters.com/2017/12/12/legacy-of-exiled-ndnz-and-the-film-that-inspired-my-work-the-exiles/.

Piatote, Beth. "Sonic Sovereignty in D'Arcy McNickle's *The Surrounded*." Unpublished manuscript, April 8, 2014. Copy in author's possession.

Price, John A. "The Stereotyping of North American Indians in Motion Pictures." *Ethnohistory* 20, no. 2 (1973): 153–71.

Raheja, Michelle H. *Reservation Reelism: Redfacing, Visual Sovereignty, and Representations of Native Americans in Film*. Lincoln: University of Nebraska Press, 2010.

Redvers, Tunchai. *Fireweed Poems*. Cape Croker: Kegedonce Press, 2019.

Rickard, Jolene. "Indigenous Visual Sovereignty." Power Institute, October 5, 2020. YouTube video, 1:30:12. https://www.youtube.com/watch?v=aGOUJbGK2o0.

Rickard, Jolene, George Longfish, Zig Jackson, Pamela Shields Carroll, Ron Carraher, and Hulleah Tsinhnahjinnie. "Sovereignty: A Line in the Sand." In "Strong Hearts: Native American Visions and Voices," special issue, *Aperture*, no. 139 (Summer 1995): 50–59.

Robinson, Dylan. *Hungry Listening: Resonant Theory for Indigenous Sound Studies*. Minneapolis: University of Minnesota Press, 2020.

Rodriguez, Jeremiah. "'Beading Is Medicine': Intricate Map Connects Indigenous Artists Across Canada, U.S." CTV News, April 7, 2021. https://www.ctvnews.ca/lifestyle/beading-is-medicine-intricate-map-connects-indigenous-artists-across-canada-u-s-1.5378292.

Roessel, Mary Hasbah. "COVID-19 Ravaging the Navajo Nation." Medscape, June 9, 2020. https://www.medscape.com/viewarticle/932019.

Rollins, Peter C., and John E. O'Connor, eds. *Hollywood's Indian: The Portrayal of the Native American in Film*. Lexington: University Press of Kentucky, 1998.

Rosenthal, E. Lee, Paige Menking, and Mae-Gilene Begay. "Fighting the COVID-19 Merciless Monster: Lives on the Line—Community Health Representatives' Roles in the Pandemic Battle on the Navajo Nation." *Journal of Ambulatory Care Management* 43, no. 4 (2020): 301–5.

Rustywire, Johnny. *Navajo Spaceships: Star Mountain & Rez Memories: Stories of the Native Born and Life on Indian Land*. Phoenix: Canyon Press, 2006.

Ryan, Mike. "Lynn Collins, 'John Carter' Star, Cried While Reading the Script (in a Good Way)." *Huffington Post*, March 9, 2012. https://www.huffpost.com/entry/lynn-collins-john-carter_n_1335311.

Salabye, John E., Jr., and Kathleen Manolescu. "The Navajo Beginnings of Corn." *Leading the Way: The Wisdom of the Navajo People*, May (T'ááts'oh) 2009.

Salabye, John E., Jr., and Kathleen Manolescu. "Universal Center: *Habeedí*." *Leading the Way: The Wisdom of the Navajo People*, November (Niłch'its'ósí) 2011.

Sam, Sean. "Jake Skeets Interview." *LIGEIA Magazine*, Fall 2019. https://www.ligeiamagazine.com/fall-2019/jake-skeets-interview/.

Santos, Boaventura de Sousa. *Epistemologies of the South: Justice Against Epistemicide*. London: Routledge, 2014.

Santos, Boaventura de Sousa, Joao Arriscado Nunes, and Maria Paula Meneses. "Opening up the Canon of Knowledge and Recognition of Difference." In *Another Knowledge Is Possible: Beyond Northern Epistemologies*, vii–xxix. London: Verso, 2007.

Sapochnik, Miguel, dir. *Finch*. Cupertino, Calif.: Apple Original Films, 2021. Apple TV+.

Saxon, Leslie, and Mary Siemens, eds. *Tłı̨chǫ Yatıì Enı̨htł'è: A Dogrib Dictionary*. Rae-Ezo, NWT: Dogrib Divisional Board of Education, 1996. https://tlicho.ca/sites/default/files/A_Dogrib_Dictionary.pdf.

Shieber, Jonathan. "Netflix Commits $1 Billion to Make New Mexico Home to One of the World's Largest Studios." TechCrunch, November 23, 2020. https://www.techcrunch.com/2020/11/23/netflix-commits-1-billion-to-make-new-mexico-home-to-one-of-the-worlds-largest-studios/.

Shone, Colton, and Nathan O'Neal. "How the Navajo People Are Using Culture to Fight Back Against 'Covid Monster.'" Center for Health Journalism, USC Annenberg, September 15, 2020. https://www.centerforhealthjournalism.org/fellowships/projects/how-navajo-people-are-using-culture-fight-back-against-covid-monster.

Silko, Leslie Marmon. "Landscape, History, and the Pueblo Imagination." In *The Ecocriticism Reader: Landmarks in Literary Ecology*, edited by Cheryll Glotfelty and Harold Fromm, 264–75. Athens: University of Georgia Press, 1996.

Silko, Leslie Marmon. *Yellow Woman and a Beauty of the Spirit*. New York: Simon & Schuster, 1996.

Singer, Beverly R. *Wiping the War Paint off the Lens: Native American Film and Video*. Minneapolis: University of Minnesota Press, 2001.

Skeets, Jake. "Drunktown." *Spilled Milk Magazine*, no. 8 (2018). Reprinted by Poets.org. https://poets.org/poem/drunktown.

Skeets, Jake. "The Other House: Musings on the Diné Perspective of Time." *Emergence Magazine*, April 29, 2020. https://emergencemagazine.org/essay/the-other-house/?fbclid=IwAR1asyC2czzN01N_pkye-TzPSLHlfAHcyqe5I5cxY2ZxSOv-CbVnCI87Oe4.

Slotkin, Richard. "Edgar Rice Burroughs: The Virginian in Outer Space, 1911–1925." In *Gunfighter Nation: The Myth of the Frontier in Twentieth-Century America*, 195–211. New York: Athenaeum, 1992.

Smith, Jo. "Indigenous Insistence on Film." In *Routledge Handbook of Critical Indigenous Studies*, edited by Brendan Hokowhitu, Aileen Moreton-Robinson, Linda Tuhiwai-Smith, Chris Andersen, and Steve Larkin, 488–500. New York: Routledge, 2020.

Smith, Paul Chaat. *Everything You Know About Indians Is Wrong*. Minneapolis: University of Minnesota Press, 2009.

Solis, Jose. "An Interview with 'Drunktown's Finest' Writer/Director Sydney Freeland." Stage Buddy Online, March 23, 2015. https://stagebuddy.com/film/interview-drunktowns-finest-writerdirector-sydney-freeland.

Spielberg, Steven, dir. *Close Encounters of the Third Kind*. Culver City, Calif.: Columbia Pictures, 1977.

Stanton, Andrew, dir. *John Carter*. Burbank, Calif.: Walt Disney Pictures, 2012.

Starlight, Bruce. "Bruce Starlight Speaks Tsuut'ina." *First Words*, January 7, 2019. Produced by CBC Radio. Podcast. MP3 audio, 7:02. https://www.cbc.ca/radio/unreserved/first-words-bruce-starlight-speaks-tsuut-ina-1.4975805.

Stine, Allison. "'We Are the Original Stewards of This Land': 'Spirit Rangers' Boss on Imagining Native Park Rangers." *Salon*, October 10, 2022. https://www.salon.com/2022/10/10/spirit-rangers-netflix-indigenous-native-karissa-valencia/.

Sturm, Circe. *Becoming Indian: The Struggle over Cherokee Identity in the Twenty-First Century*. Santa Fe, N.Mex.: School for Advanced Research Press, 2011.

Tailfeathers, Elle-Máijá. "We Trust Artists Like Michelle Latimer to Avoid Harming Indigenous People." NOW Toronto, December 21, 2020. https://www.nowtoronto.com/movies/michelle-latimer-indigenous-identity/.

TallBear, Kim. *Native American DNA: Tribal Belonging and the False Promise of Genetic Science*. Minneapolis: University of Minnesota Press, 2013.

Tangcay, Jazz. "'Dark Winds' Writer Billy Luther on Native Representation: 'We Didn't Need to Explain Everything, We Just Showed It.'" *Variety*, July 25, 2022. https://variety.com/2022/tv/news/dark-winds-billy-luther-amc-1235324747/.

Tapahonso, Luci. *Blue Horses Rush In*. Tucson: University of Arizona Press, 1997.

Tapahonso, Luci. *A Radiant Curve*. Tucson: University of Arizona Press, 2008.

Tapahonso, Luci. *Sáanii Dahataał: The Women Are Singing*. Tucson: University of Arizona Press, 1993.

Tapahonso, Luci. "Singing in Navajo, Writing in English: The Poetics of Four Navajo Writers." *Culturefront* 2, no. 2 (1993): 36–41, 74–75.

Teller, Chris. "Here's What New Mexico Officials and Leaders Have Said About Netflix's Planned Expansion in Albuquerque." *Albuquerque Business First*, November 23, 2020. https://www.bizjournals.com/albuquerque/news/2020/11/23/nm-leaders-react-netflix-planned-expansion.html.

Teller Ornelas, Sierra. "Donald Trump Would Make a Terrible Navajo." *New York Times*, December 2, 2017.

Teller Ornelas, Sierra. "Indigenous People's Long Road to Visibility in Hollywood (Guest Column)." *Hollywood Reporter*, January 30, 2019.

Teller Ornelas, Sierra. "Rutherford Falls Creator Talk with Sierra Ornelas." VIFF, January 24, 2022. YouTube video, 1;05:05. https://www.youtube.com/watch?v=gKfFSLPN2us.

Teuton, Christopher. "Indigenous Orality and Oral Literatures." In *The Oxford Handbook of Indigenous American Literature*, edited by James H. Cox and Daniel Heath Justice, 167–75. Oxford: Oxford University Press, 2014.

Thomas, Wesley. "Navajo Cultural Constructions of Gender and Sexuality." In *Two-Spirit People: Native American Gender Identity, Sexuality, and Spirituality*, edited by Sue-Ellen Jacobs, Wesley Thomas, and Sabine Lang, 156–73. Urbana: University of Illinois Press, 1997.

Threlfall, John. "Beadwork as Resistance." *University of Victoria Fine Arts* (blog), July 21, 2021. https://finearts.uvic.ca/research/blog/2021/07/21/beadwork-as-resistance/.

Todd, Zoe. "Alberta Teacher Races to Save Dying Indigenous Language Before Time Runs Out." CBC News, November 13, 2017. https://www.cbc.ca/news/canada/edmonton/alberta-beaver-language-victoria-wanihadie-indigenous-1.4394156.

Tohe, Laura. *Enemy Slayer: A Navajo Oratorio*. Music by Mark Grey. Naxos, 2009. https://www.naxos.com/sharedfiles/PDF/8.559604_sungtext.pdf.

Tohe, Laura. "Hwéeldi Bééhániih: Remembering the Long Walk." *Wicazo Sa Review* 22, no. 1 (2007): 77–82.

Tohe, Laura. "Within Dinétah the People's Spirit Remains Strong." In *The Diné Reader: An Anthology of Navajo Literature*, edited by Esther G. Belin, Jeff Berglund, Connie A. Jacobs, and Anthony K. Webster, 126–30. Tucson: University of Arizona Press, 2021.

Toledo-Benalli, Eulynda Jean. "Kinaaldá: Diné Women Knowledge." PhD diss., University of New Mexico, 2003.

Trifa, Geordie, and Pieter Romer. "Black Rock." CBC Short Docs, June 7, 2019. YouTube video, 27:04. https://www.youtube.com/watch?v=iOq9fEHKRMs.

Tuck, Eve, and K. Wayne Yang. "Decolonization Is Not a Metaphor." *Decolonization: Indigeneity, Education, & Society* 1, no. 1 (September 8, 2012): 1–40.

Tuyuc, Genesis. "In NYC, Native American Students Celebrate Indigenous Films, Filmmakers." *Indian Country Today* Media Network Online, November 30, 2015, updated September 13, 2018. https://indiancountrytoday.com/archive/in-nyc-native-american-students-celebrate-indigenous-films-filmmakers.

Van Camp, Richard. "Dogrib Midnight Runners." In *The Moon of Letting Go and Other Stories*, 19–29. Winnipeg: Enfield and Wizenty, 2009.

Van Camp, Richard. "The Fleshing." In *Godless but Loyal to Heaven: Stories*, 18–42. Winnipeg: Enfield and Wizenty, 2013.

Van Camp, Richard. *Gather: Richard Van Camp on the Joy of Storytelling*. Regina: University of Regina Press, 2021.

Van Camp, Richard. "How Stories Connect Us: Richard Van Camp and Friends." The Word on the Street Toronto. Streamed live on September 17, 2021. YouTube video, 1:06:07. https://www.youtube.com/watch?v=C8PH7pR7zI0.

Van Camp, Richard. "Why Ravens Smile to Little Old Ladies as They Walk By . . ." In *Troubling Tricksters: Revisioning Critical Conversations*, edited by Deanna Reder and Linda M. Morra, 95–98. Waterloo: Wilfrid Laurier University Press, 2010.

Van Camp, Richard, and Junko Muro. "Living in a Time for Celebration: An Interview with Richard Van Camp." In *Across Cultures / Across Borders: Canadian Aboriginal and Native American Literatures*, edited by Paul DePasquale, Renate Eigenbrod, and Emma LaRocque, 297–311. Peterborough: Broadview Press, 2010.

Van den Berg, Amy. "Dene Photographer Captures the Spirit of the Northern Lights." *Broadview*, November 19, 2020. https://broadview.org/ryan-dickie-northern-lights/.

Vizenor, Gerald. *Fugitive Poses: Native American Indian Scenes of Absence and Presence*. Lincoln: University of Nebraska Press, 1998.

Vizenor, Gerald. *Native Liberty: Natural Reason and Cultural Survivance*. Lincoln: University of Nebraska Press, 2009.

Vizenor, Gerald. "The Pretend Indians: Images of Native Americans in the Movies by Gretchen Bataille; Charles Silet." *Film Quarterly* 34, no. 4 (Summer 1981): 36.

Vizenor, Gerald. *Survivance: Narratives of Native Presence*. Lincoln: University of Nebraska Press, 2008.

Ward, Terry. "There Is Little Research to Back Reports of Northern Lights Sounds. So What Are People Hearing?" CNN Travel, April 1, 2021. https://www.cnn.com/travel/article/northern-lights-aurora-borealis-sounds-reports-scn/index.html.

Warrior, Robert. *Tribal Secrets: Recovering American Indian Intellectual Traditions*. Minneapolis: University of Minnesota Press, 1995.

Watchman, Renae. "Reel Restoration in *Drunktown's Finest*." *Journal of the Native American and Indigenous Studies Association* 7, no. 2 (2020): 29–54.

Watchman, Renae. "Teaching Indigenous Film Through an Indigenous Epistemic Lens." In "How We Teach Indigenous Literatures," edited by Michelle Coupal and Deanna Reder, special issue, *Studies in American Indian Literatures (SAIL)* 34, nos. 1–2 (September 2022): 112–34.

Watchman, Renae, and Robert Alexander Innes. "Transforming Toxic Indigenous Masculinity: A Critical Indigenous Masculinities and Indigenous Film Studies Approach to *Drunktown's Finest*." In *Visions of the Heart: Issues Involving Indigenous Peoples in Canada*, edited by Gina Starblanket and David Long with Olive Patricia Dickason, 126–41. Oxford: University of Oxford Press, 2020.

Wente, Jesse (@jessewente). "Hi Sheila, thanks for bringing this up, it's an interesting point. It's obviously an Indigenous story, no question there. However, I think to call it an Indigenous film erodes our narrative sovereignty and undermines Indigenous screen storytellers. Here's why. 1/19." Twitter, April 15, 2018, 5:39 a.m. https://twitter.com/jessewente/status/985482818393341953.

Werito, Vincent. "Understanding Hózhǫ́ to Achieve Critical Consciousness: A Contemporary Diné Interpretation of the Philosophical Principles of Hózhǫ́." In *Diné Perspectives: Revitalizing and Reclaiming Navajo Thought*, edited by Lloyd L. Lee, 25–38. Tucson: University of Arizona Press, 2014.

Whelan, Catherine. "Mapping Máaz: NASA Uses Navajo Language to Name Features on Mars." National Public Radio, March 12, 2021. https://www.npr.org/2021/03/12/976641201/mapping-maaz-nasa-uses-navajo-language-to-name-features-on-mars.

Wilcox, Meg. "7 Names for Calgary, Before It Became Calgary." CBC Radio Canada, December 3, 2015. https://www.cbc.ca/news/canada/calgary/calgary-names-elbow-1.3345967.

Wissot, Lauren. "Director Sydney Freeland Discusses *Drunktown's Finest*." *Filmmaker Magazine Online*, January 23, 2014. https://filmmakermagazine.com/83510-director-sydney-freeland-discusses-drunktowns-finest/#.YyxwvS0r3oo.

Wood, Houston. "Dimensions of Difference in Indigenous Film." In *Native Americans on Film*, edited by M. Elise Marubbio and Eric L. Buffalohead, 35–57. Lexington: University Press of Kentucky, 2013.

Woody, Elizabeth. "Rosette." In *The Diné Reader: An Anthology of Navajo Literature*, edited by Esther G. Belin, Jeff Berglund, Connie A. Jacobs, and Anthony K. Webster, 105–9. Tucson: University of Arizona Press, 2021.

Worth, Sol, and John Adair. "Navajo Filmmakers." *American Anthropologist* 72, no. 1 (February 1970): 9–34.

Worth, Sol, and John Adair. *Through Navajo Eyes: An Exploration in Film Communication and Anthropology*, with a new introduction, afterword, and notes by Richard Chalfen. Albuquerque: University of New Mexico Press, 1997.

Wyllie, Julian. "NEH Grants Back Pubmedia Film on Reconstruction-Era Armed Conflict, Biography of Author Julia Alvarez." *Current* Online, August 17, 2022. https://current.org/2022/08/neh-grants-back-pubmedia-film-on-reconstruction-era-armed-conflict-biography-of-author-julia-alvarez/.

Yazzie, Ethelou. *Navajo History*. Many Farms, Ariz.: Navajo Community College Press, 1971.

Yazzie, Ethelou. "Navajo Wisdom and Traditions." Paper presented at the International Conference on the Unity of the Sciences, New York, November 27, 1975. https://files.eric.ed.gov/fulltext/ED124366.pdf.

Younging, Gregory. *Elements of Indigenous Style: A Guide for Writing by and About Indigenous Peoples*. Edmonton: Brush Education, 2018.

Zolbrod, Paul G. *Diné bahane': The Navajo Creation Story*. Albuquerque: University of New Mexico Press, 1984.

SELECTED INDIGENOUS FILMOGRAPHY

Sample feature-length fiction, shorts, and documentaries. Several are not cited, as this is intended to be a glimpse at the ongoing growth of Indigenous creative work. Visual media that have been cited and were made by non-Indigenous directors are found in the general bibliography.

Anderson, Mike (Diné), dir. *Old Antelope Lake*. Philadelphia: Penn Museum, 1966.
Angeline, Morningstar (Diné, Chippewa, Blackfeet, Shoshone, and Latinx), and Ajuawak Kapashesit (Anishinaabe/Cree), dirs. *Seeds*. Morningstar Media, 2022.
Barclay, Barry (Ngāti Apa), dir. *Ngāti*. Auckland: Pacific Films, 1987.
Barnaby, Jeff (Mi'gmaq), dir. *Blood Quantum*. Toronto: Elevation Pictures, 2019.
Barnaby, Jeff, dir. *Rhymes for Young Ghouls*. Montreal: Les Films Séville, 2013.
Becker, Nanobah (Diné), dir. *The 6th World: An Origin Story*. San Francisco: Independent Television Service, 2012.
Benally, Razelle Wiyakaluta (Diné), dir. *War Cries*. 2019.
Benally, Susie (Diné), dir. *A Navajo Weaver*. Philadelphia: Penn Museum, 1966.
Bowman, Arlene (Diné), dir. *Navajo Talking Picture*. New York: Women Make Movies, 1986.
Carr, Lena (Diné), dir. *Kinaalda: Navajo Rite of Passage*. New York: Women Make Movies, 2000.
Cegielski, Christopher Nataanii (Diné), dir. *Bloodlines*. 2015. https://www.nataanii cegielski.com/work/bloodlines.
Clah, Al (Diné), dir. *Intrepid Shadows*. Philadelphia: Penn Museum, 1966.
De La Rosa, Shonie (Diné), and Andee De La Rosa (Diné). *Mile Post 398*. Kayenta: Sheephead Films, 2007.
De La Rosa, Shonie and Chris Kientz *AH-HOS-TEEND "Retired."* Las Cruces: Running Dog Lackey Productions; Kayenta: Sheephead Films, 2017.
Del Seronde, Sarah (Diné), dir. *Metal Road*. 2017.
Del Seronde, Sarah, dir. *Sa'ah*. Columbia, S.C.: National Educational Telecommunications Association (NETA Productions), 2005.

Del Seronde, Sarah, dir. *U: Uranium*. 2010. Executive Productions: First Nations Development Institute, Seventh Generation Fund, Western Action Mining Network, Navajo Waters Documentary.

Deer, Tracey (Mohawk), dir. *Beans*. Toronto: Mongrel Media, 2021.

Deer, Tracey dir. *Club Native*. Montreal: National Film Board of Canada, 2008.

Diamond, Neil (Cree), Catherine Bainbridge, and Jeremiah Hayes, dirs. *Reel Injun: The Trail of the Hollywood Indian*. Montreal: Rezolution Pictures, 2009.

Emerson, Ramona (Diné), dir. *The Last Trek*. 2006.

Emerson, Ramona, and Kelly Byars (Choctaw and Chickasaw), dirs. *The Mayors of Shiprock*. Santa Fe: New West Media Foundation, 2017.

Eyre, Chris (Cheyenne and Arapaho), dir. *Edge of America*. Hollywood, Calif.: Paramount Pictures, 2003.

Eyre, Chris, dir. *Skins*. Century City, Calif.: First Look Pictures, 2002.

Eyre, Chris, dir. *Skinwalkers*. Arlington: PBS Pictures, 2002.

Eyre, Chris, dir. *Smoke Signals*. Los Angeles: Miramax, 1998.

Freeland, Sydney (Diné), dir. "Aunt Ida's 90th Birthday." *Rutherford Falls*, season 1, episode 3, April 22, 2021.

Freeland, Sydney, dir. *Drunktown's Finest*. Tulsa: Indion Entertainment Group, 2015.

Freeland, Sydney, dir. "Episode #1.7." *Star Trek: Strange New Worlds*, June 16, 2022.

Freeland, Sydney, dir. *Hoverboard*. 2012.

Freeland, Sydney, dir. "NDN Clinic." *Reservation Dogs*, season 1, episode 2, August 9, 2021.

Freeland, Sydney, dir. "Negotiations." *Rutherford Falls*, season 1, episode 6, April 22, 2021.

Freeland, Sydney, dir. "Skoden." *Rutherford Falls*, season 1, episode 8, April 22, 2021.

Freeland, Sydney, dir. "Terry Thomas." *Rutherford Falls*, season 1, episode 4, April 22, 2021.

Freeland, Sydney, dir. "What About Your Dad?" *Reservation Dogs*, season 1, episode 4, August 23, 2021.

Harjo, Sterlin (Seminole/Muscogee Creek), dir. *Barking Water*. Tulsa: Indion Entertainment Group, 2009.

Harjo, Sterlin, dir. *Four Sheets to the Wind*. Century City, Calif.: First Look Studios, 2007.

Harjo, Sterlin, and Taika Waititi (Māori, Te Whānau-ā-Apanui), creators. *Reservation Dogs*. Miami: FXP, 2021–present.

Hayward. Ramai (Māori), and Rudall Hayward. *To Love a Māori*. New Zealand: Rudall & Ramai Hayward Film Productions, 1972.

Howard, Stacy (Diné), dir. *Amásání*. 2017.

Hoyungowa, Jake (Diné), dir. *Nihigaal bee Iina—Tsoodził to Doko'o'osliid: Journey for Existence*. Flagstaff: Paper Rocket Productions, 2016.

Kahn, Alta (Diné), dir. *Second Weaver*. Philadelphia: Penn Museum, 1966.

Klain, Bennie (Diné), dir. *Weaving Worlds*. Lincoln: Vision Maker Media, 2008.

Klain, Bennie, dir. *Yada Yada*. Toronto: Vtape, 2002.

Kunuk, Zacharias (Inuk), dir. *Atanarjuat: The Fast Runner.* Toronto: Igloolik Isuma Productions, Inc., 2001. Distributed by Odeon Films.
Lowe, Blackhorse (Diné), dir. *Chasing the Light.* 2014.
Lowe, Blackhorse, dir. "Come and Get Your Love." *Reservation Dogs,* season 1, episode 5, August 30, 2021.
Lowe, Blackhorse, dir. *5th World.* Fifth World: Blackhorse Lowe LLC; Mesa: PBR Streetgang, 2005.
Lowe, Blackhorse, dir. *Fukry.* Fifth World: Blackhorse Lowe LLC, 2019.
Lowe, Blackhorse, dir. *Shimásání.* Fifth World: Blackhorse Lowe LLC, 2009.
Lowe, Blackhorse, dir. *Shush.* Fifth World: Blackhorse Lowe LLC, 2004.
Lowe, Blackhorse, dir. "Stay Gold Cheesy Boy." *Reservation Dogs,* season 2, episode 7, September 7, 2022.
Lowe, Blackhorse, dir. "This Is Where the Plot Thickens." *Reservation Dogs,* season 2, episode 8, September 14, 2022.
Lowe, Blackhorse, dir. "Uncle Brownie." *Reservation Dogs,* season 1, episode 3, August 16, 2021.
Luther, Billy (Diné), dir. *Frybread Face and Me.* Tulsa: Indion Entertainment Group, 2023.
Luther, Billy, dir. *Miss Navajo.* Hollywood, Calif.: World of Wonder Productions; San Francisco: ITVS International, 2007.
Masayesva, Victor, Jr. (Hopi), dir. *Imagining Indians.* Watertown: Documentary Educational Resources, 1992.
Mita, Merata (Ngāti Pikiao, Ngāi Te Rangi), dir. *Mauri.* New Zealand: Awatea Films, 1988.
Mita, Merata, dir. *Patu!* New Zealand: Awatea Films, 1983.
Mita, Merata, dir. *Saving Grace: Te Whakarauora Tangata.* New Zealand: StanStrong and Ora Digital, 2011.
Montoya, Teresa (Diné), dir. *Doing the Sheep Good.* 2013.
Nelson, Johnny (Diné), dir. *The Navajo Silversmith.* Philadelphia: Penn Museum, 1966.
Nelson, Johnny, dir. *The Shallow Well.* Philadelphia: Penn Museum, 1966.
Peters, Pamela (Diné), dir. *Legacy of Exiled NDNZ.* 2014. https://vimeo.com/323394336.
Roland, Graham (Chickasaw), creator and executive producer. *Dark Winds.* New York: AMC Networks, 2022.
Seschillie, Donavan (Diné), dir. *The Rocket Boy.* Flagstaff: Paper Rocket Productions, 2015.
Singer Beverly R. (Diné), dir. *Hózhó of Native Women.* New York: Women Make Movies, 1997.
Skorodin, Ian D. (Choctaw), dir. *Tushka.* 1996.
Taylor, Drew Hayden (Ojibwe), and Paul Kemp, dirs. *The Pretendians. The Passionate Eye,* CBC Television, September 29, 2022.
Tome, Shaandiin (Diné), dir. *hashtł'ishnii* [mud]. 2018. http://www.shaandiin.com/mud-film.

Trifa, Geordie, and Pieter Romer (Nisga'a), dirs. *Black Rock*. 2019. https://www.youtube.com/watch?v=iOq9fEHKRMs.

Tso, Ivey Camille Manybeads (Diné), dir. *Powerlands*. 2022. https://powerlands.org.

Tso, Ivey Camille Manybeads, dir. *The TV*. 2010.

Tsosie, Mary Jane, and Maxine Tsosie (Diné), dirs. *The Spirit of the Navajo*. Philadelphia: Penn Museum, 1966.

Valencia, Karissa (Santa Ynez Chumash), creator. *Spirit Rangers*. Los Angeles: Netflix Animation, 2022–present.

Yazzie, Rhianna (Diné), dir. *Dodging Bullets*. Minneapolis: Fahrenheit Productions, 2015.

Yazzie, Rhianna, dir. *A Winter Love*. Minneapolis: A Winter Love Productions & Navajo Playwright Films, 2022.

INDEX

Note: Page numbers in *italics* indicate illustrations.

adoption, 74–75, 88–89, 95, 96, 136, 138. *See also* Smiles, Nizhoni (character)
alcoholism, xvi, 35, 79, 83, 88–89, 101–2. See also *Drunktown's Finest*
alkaan (corn cake, Kinaaldá cake), 15–16, 96, 98, 179n32
'ałk'idą́ą́' jiní (a long time ago, they said), 6, 13–16, 151, 161n46
Allison, Corey, 113, 119–20, 122
Àma (character), 134–39
Andrei (character), 112, 115–17, *116*, 123–24
Angeline, MorningStar, 78, 79, 81, 86, 88–89, 96
appropriation, 42–43, 45–46, 71–75
A Princess of Mars (1912), 41–42
Aria (character), 112, 115–17, *116*, 118, 123–24, *124*, 183n44
Asdzą́ą́ Nádleehé (Changing Woman), 32, 63, 87–88, 111, 118, 123, 124, 166n38, 179n31
audience, 30, 61, 62, 67, 69, 108, 151
Auntie (character played by Carmelita B. Lowe), 111–12, 120, 122

Barclay, Barry, 53–54, 106, 172n15
Barnaby, Jeff, 54
Basso, Keith H., 18–19, 26–27, 153, 165n5
beadwork, 7, 49, 138–39, 141–44, 187n54, 187n66, 187n70

Beaucage, Marjorie, 107
beauty, 92–94, 96–97. *See also* hózhǫ́
Becker, Nanobah, 51, 58, 67–68, 90, 152
bé'ézhóó' (Diné hairbrush), *66*, 66–67
Begay, EiRena, 101–2
Belin, Esther G., 68
Benally, Susie, 58–60, *60*
Bitsui, Jeremiah, 79, 86, 88, 94–95, 97–98
Blondin, George, 126, 134, 141, 185n24
blood quantum, 74
Blood Quantum (2019), 54
Blue Bird flour, 65–66
Boivin, Lisa, 147
Bordwell, David, 109–10
Bosque Redondo. *See* Hwéeldi
Bowman, Arlene, 61
Burroughs, Edgar Rice, 41–42, 44, 169n83

Campbell, Tenille K., 141, 147, 148, 154
Carewe, Edwin, 53, 172n11, 172n12
Carter, John (character), 42–44, 169n84
Case, Pua, 49, 170n98
Casey, Edward S., 19, 163n75
Chee, Jim (character), 62, 77
Chee, Melvatha R., 150
Clan affiliations, xv, 91, 94–95, 110–14, 118–22, 144, 157n2
Clans, xv, 110–11, 157n4, 181n24, 182n27
Clements, Marie, 148–49

Clifford, Arnold, 17–18
commodification, 45–46, 49
corn (naadą́ą́), 24, 51–53, 68, 96, 171n3, 171n6, 179n32
Cousin-Brother John (character), 113, 119–20
COVID-19, 35–37, 167n57
coyote stories, 7, 15, 162n58, 165n31
Cummings, Denise K., 65–67
Curtis, Edward, 61, 174n49

Dahtı̨ (character), 134–35, 136–37, 139
Dark Winds (2022), 63–64
Deèyeh (character), 134–35, 136, 138–39
Deloria, Vine Jr., 5, 74
Dene, xviii, xx–xxi, 28–30, 128
Dene languages, 128, 134–35, 144–48, 183n1, 184n7
Dene Nation, 127–28, 159n14
Denendeh, xviii, *xx*, 21, *129*
Denetdale, Jennifer Nez, 11, 18, 24, 83–84, 102, 121–22, 134
Dene Yati podcast, 144–45
Dickson, Heather, 141
diegesis, 108–10
Diné (The People, also Náhookah Diné or Bilá' ashdla'), 24, 28–30, 128
Diné aesthetics (Dinétics), 14–15, 55, 65
Diné Bahane' (1984), 7, 19, 96, 163n74, 166n38
Diné Bikéyah (Navajo land), restrictions, 37–38, 165n36. See also Dinétah
Diné bizaad (Navajo language): Dene languages and, 144–45; in film and television, 62, 63, 68, 92–93, 106, 111–12, 120–21, 183n44; in music and literature, 10–11, 135, 152; in scholarly work, 5–6; speakers, 6, 27, 92–93, 165n20
Diné diegesis, 21, 105–25
Dinétah (Land of the People), *xix*, xviii, *xx*, 15, 17, 18, 78, 105. See also Diné Bikéyah
disease, 35–37, 167n57, 187n66
dislocation, 23, 37–44, 168n67, 170n89, 182n39. See also displacement

displacement, 19, 24–25. See also dislocation; Hwéeldi; Long Walk
Doing the Sheep Good (2013), 68
Dǫne Nàowo (Dene laws, Yamoria Law), 126–27, 131–36
Dooley, Sunny, 35
Drunktown's Finest (2014) (*see also* Freeland, Sydney): cinematic techniques, 79–87, *81*; as Diné-centered hane', 20–21, 102, 103, 152; hóchx̨ǫ́ in, 79, 86–87, 183n44; k'é relations in, 91–96; Kinaaldá in, 87–88, *103*, 103–4; running in, 87–91

Eagletail, Fred, 28, 130
Eagletail, Hal, 28, 165n22
Earl's Family Restaurant, 84
Elders (*see also* grandparents; k'é; matriarchs): in film, 88, 95–99, 101, 107, 111–12, 116, 118–20, 122–23; filmmakers, 52, 58–60, *60*; in literature, 135–40; as roots, 4, 52, 126, 131–32, 145, 159n6
Elephant's Feet formation, 114, *116*, 117
Emerson, Larry W., xv, 3, 32, 56, 123, 157n2
Emerson, Ramona, 67
epistemicide, xviii, 9, 23–25, 45–46, 49, 100, 103, 158n13
epistemologies, Indigenous, 4–8
Erasmus, Georges, 25, 131
Eyre, Chris, 62, 115

5th World (2005), 21, 105–7, 110–23, 152, 183n47. See also Lowe, Blackhorse
Fifth World. See Glittering World
film, Indigenous: approaches, 54–55, 70, 71, 177n6, 178n15; audience for, 64, 113–14; evolution, 51–69, 171n2, 172n12; support for, 58, 174n38, 176n92
film festivals, 67–69, 175n69
Ford, John, 116–17, 182n37
Fort Sumner. See Hwéeldi
four sacred mountains, 15, 17–18, 147, 158n12, 162n65, 179n31, 184n4. See also Dinétah

Index

Fourth Cinema, 54, 106, 172n19
Fourth World, 15, 124–25, 183n42. *See also* Hajíínéí hane'
Francis, Harris, 15–16, 81, 91, 107, 152
Freeland, Sydney, 55, 76, 77, 79, 80, 82, 85–86. See also *Drunktown's Finest*

Gallup, 20, 79, *81*, 81–82, 83, 101–2, 178n11, 179n27
Glittering World, 15, 28–29, 105. *See also* Hajíínéí hane'
Goeman, Mishuana, 16–17
Gordon, Kiowa, 88
Gosnell-Meyers, Ginger, 72
grandparents, xvi–xvii, 11, 22, 74, 91, 93, 95, 100. *See also* Manus, Sylvia Allen

Hajíínéí hane' (emergence stories), 7, 14–16, 28–30, 63, 68, 145, 161n48, 161n49, 162n54, 165n31. *See also* hane'; kéyah
Halfe, Louise Bernice, 143–44
hane' (story, narrative, wisdom) (*see also* Hajíínéí hane'; honi): Dene honi and, 144–45, 152–53; dismissed, 29–30, 122–23, 165n28; explained, 6–13, 122–23, 160n17; ignorance of, 88–89, 95, 96; as imbricated with kéyah, 15–20, 26–27, 107, 114–17, 126, 162n65, 164n14; jiní in, 81, 103; in material culture, 22, 85–86, 138–39, 141–44, 187n54; modern media and, 151–52; sharing, 9–10, 11–13, 159n6; temporalities, 33–34, 107, 108
hane'tonomy, 20, 26, 52, 57, 75, 135, 150
Harvey, Christine, 48–49
Hearne, Joanna, 79, 93, 106, 114–15
Hengst, Kathy (author's auntie Coddy), 9, 45
Hero Twins: gender, 36, 168n62; hane' about, 27, 98, 162n65, 166n38, 166n42, 166n43; modern restorying, 10–11, 32, 36, 167n56

Hillerman, Tony, 61–64, 67, 77
hitchhiking, 83–84, 85, 112, 115–17, *116*, 120, 170n92
hóchxǫ́ (disharmony), 21, 79, 88–90, 101–2, 117–22, 183n44
Hokowhitu, Brendan, 56
Holy People (Diyin Diné'é), 10, 13, 15, 78, 81, 87, 105, 107, 114, 115, 162n53, 179n31. *See also* Hajíínéí hane'
homecoming, 13, 90, 178n18
homophobia, 88–90, 98–100, 180n52
honi (story/stories), 28, 126–27, 131–34, 136, 138, 144–45, 152–53
hooghan (ceremonial home), xxi, 33, 65, 78, 101, 103, 159n17
hózhǫ́ (to strive for harmony, beauty, balance, peace, and happiness), 3–4, 10–11, 78–79, 96–97, 131–32, 155
humor, Indigenous, 54, 55, 62, 65, 76, 117, 118, 148, 187n60
Hwéeldi (place of suffering/survival), 9–13, 19

identity, Indigenous, 42–43, 71–75. *See also* Clan affiliations; k'é
Imagining Indians (1992), 61–62
incest, 91, 94, 119–22
indians, 85, 158n8
Indigenous people in non-Indigenous film, 42–43, 53, 61–62, 70, 77, 172n12
Innes, Robert Alexander, 8, 19, 64–65, 90, 134

Jackson, Lisa, 69–70
Janvier, Willis, 144–45, 188n76
Jim, Rex Lee, 6, 8, 152
jiní (they say), 81, 103. *See also* 'ałk'idą́ą́' jiní
Joe, Eugene B., 9, 24
John, Felixia (character), 86–87, 89–90, 92–96, 98–99
John, Grandma Ruth (character), 95, 96, 101
John, Hastiin Harmon (character), 88, 95, 97–99

John Carter (2012), 23, 40–44, 170n89
Jóhonaa'éí (Sun), 32, 35, 166n38, 166n43
Justice, Daniel Heath, 8, 74, 128–29, 130

Kahn, Alta, 58–59, *59*, *60*
Katłįà (Catherine Lafferty), 134–40, 148
k'é (matrilineal kinship), 57, 63, 80, 91–96, 110–14
k'éí (Clanship). *See* Clan affiliations; Clans
Kelley, Klara, 15–16, 81, 91, 107, 152
kéyah (land): compared with Dene ndè, 135; dislocation, 168n67 (*see also* Tsé Bii' Ndzisgaii; Tsé Bit'a'í); as imbricated with hane', 15–20, 26–27, 107, 114–17, 126, 162n65, 164n14; in Indigenous film, 65, 114–17, *116*, 169n78, 183n47; Indigenous relations with, 6, 16–20, 153–54, 163n69, 185n32
Kinaaldá, 15–16, 66, 87, 94, 95–96, 179n31, 179n32, 180n47; in film and television, 63, 87–88, 98, *103*, 103–4
kinscapes, 130, 141–44, 184n13
Klain, Bennie, 58, 67, 90
Knoki, LivA'ndrea, 112, 115–17, *116*, 118, 123–24, *124*, 183n44
Kovach, Margaret, 5, 8, 25

land. *See* kéyah; ndè
Land-Water-Sky: Ndè-Ti-Yat'a (2020), 134–40, 185n31
languages, Indigenous (*see also* Dene languages; Diné bizaad): in film and television, 63, 68, 92–93, 106, 111–12, 120–21; revitalization, 5–6, 10–11, 128, 134–35, 146–48, 165n20
Lapahie, Harrison, 30–31
Lee, Lloyd L., 34–35, 37
Lewis, Randolph, 57–58, 61, 68, 90, 106, 113–14
Long Walk, 11–13, 19, 25, 76
Lowe, Blackhorse (see also *5th World*; *Shimásání* [2009]): cinematography, 10, 21, 58, 76, 106, 111–13, 119, 183n47; family, 113; landscape in his films, 114–17, *116*, 183n47; use of sound and silence, 106–8, 111–13, 119–25
Luther, Billy, 63–64, 92

Manus, Sylvia Allen (Grams, author's maternal grandmother), xvi, xvii–xviii, xx, 22, 26–27, 38, *39*, *44*, 44–45, 95–96, 171n3
Māori, 53–54, 170n1, 172n14, 172n15
Mars (Máaz), 40–44, 168n77, 182n39
Martinez, Fred, 100
Maryboy, Luther "Sick Boy" (character), 79, 86, 88, 94–95, 97–98
Masayesva, Victor, Jr., 61–62
masculinity, 87, 90, 97–98, 101, 119–20
matriarchs (*see also* Elders; k'é; women): in Dene culture, 138, 139, 141, 148; in Indigenous film, 91–96, 99, 101, 103–4, 111–12, 120, 122; land features as, 32, 48, 49; in non-Indigenous stories, 42, 43–44; scholarly colleagues, 11
Means, Naát'áanii Nez, 88
Means, Tatanka, 40
migration accounts, 27–29, 130, 188n77
Miss Navajo (2007), 63, 92
Mita, Merata, 53, 172n15
Momaday, N. Scott, 18, 19, 24–25, 90
monsters, 35–37, 167n56, 167n57. *See also* Nąąhgą; Naayéé
Montoya, Teresa, 68
Monument Valley. *See* Tsé Bii' Ndzisgaii
Moore, Carmen, 86–87, 89–90, 92–96, 98–99
Morris, Irvin, 14, 17, 30, 31, 45–46, 105, 110–11, 162n59
mountains, 15, 18, 48–49, 127, 158n12, 162n56, 170n98, 184n4

Nąąhgą (bushman shapeshifter), 137–38, 139
Naat'áanii Néez (town of Shiprock), xvi, 24–25

Naayéé (monsters), 32–37, 124–25, 167n56, 167n57. *See also specific monsters*
Naayéé Neezgháni (Protector), 32, 34–35, 162n54, 167n54. *See also* Hero Twins
Nabahe, Reginald, 34, 159n6
Nabokov, Peter, 29–30, 165n28
Nadene (Apache), 12–13, 18–19, 26–27, 41–44, 153
nádleeh (third gender), 99–101, 162n57. *See also* John, Felixia (character)
Navajo Nation offices and agencies, 37–38, 58, 165n36
Navajos Film Themselves, 58–61, *59, 60,* 174n44
Navajo Talking Picture (1986), 61
ndè (land), 134–36
Neskahi, Allan, Jr., xviii, xx–xxi
Neskahi, Arlie, xxi
Neskahi, Art, xvii, xx
Nihimá (our mother). *See* Tsé Bit'a'í
nizhóni, 96–97. *See also* hózhǫ́; Smiles, Nizhoni

Olver, Toni, 95, 96, 101
oral tradition. *See* hane'; honi; saad
Owen, Roz, 70–71

Paul, Sharnell, 94
permits, 37–38, 165n36
personhood of landforms, 22, 48
Piatote, Beth, 106, 107–8
pipes, 28, 29, 145
poverty, 35, 82–84, 167n56
powwows, xviii, xx–xxi, 165n22
pretendians, 20, 71–75
Protect the Sacred movement, 36

Raheja, Michelle H., 79, 80, 113
Redford, Robert, 61–62, 78
Redvers, Tunchai, 147–48
relationality, xviii, 63, 71, 113, 125, 128, 130, 141. *See also* Clan affiliations; Clans; k'é
Reservation Dogs, 76, 106

reservation life, 35, 87–90, 98–100
resource extraction, 140–41, 153–54
restorying/restoration, 5–6, 79–80, 128–31, 134, 154–55, 184n10
Rhymes for Young Ghouls (2013), 54
Rickard, Jolene, 56, 73
Robinson, Dylan, 106, 108
Rocks with Wings (2001), 38–39, *39*
running, 80, 87–91, 96, 98, *103,* 103–4, 178n16, 179n32
Rutherford Falls, 76

saad (knowledge, language, voice), 7–8, 21, 111, 113, 126
Sa'ąh Naagháí Bik'eh Hózhǫ́ǫ́n, 6, 52, 121, 123
Sandoval, Ron (author's stepfather), 153–54
scholarship, Indigenous, 4–6, 8–13, 19–20
science fiction, 39–44, 68, 151, 169n88
Sells, Angie (author's great auntie), 38, *39*
sheep, 66, 85, 92, 117, 119, 120, 171
Shimásání (2009), 65–67, *66,* 106
Shiprock (town), xvi, 24–25
Shiprock Historical Society, 9, 24
Shiprock Lady Chieftains, 38–39, *39*
Shiprock Peak. *See* Tsé Bit'a'í
Shutter (2022), 67
Silentwalker, Sheldon, 112, 115–17, *116,* 123–24
Silko, Leslie Marmon, 90, 163n69, 164n14, 185n32
Sinclair, Raven, 70–71
Singer, Ryan, 151
Sixth World, 68, 152
Sizèh (character), 135, 137, 139
Skeets, Jake, 14–15, 55, 79
sky (yá, yat'a), 105, 115, 135, 137, 143–44, 185n32, 185n41. *See also* Jóhonaa'éí; sunrise
Slotkin, Richard, 41–42, 44
Smiles, Nizhoni (character), 78, 79, 81, 86, 88–89, 96

Smith, Jo, 56, 70
Smith, Paul Chaat, 75, 182n39
sound and silence, 55, 65, 82, 106–10
sovereignty, 55–57, 173n25, 178n12
sovereignty, sonic. *See* sound and silence
Starlight, Bruce, xviii, xx–xxi, 145–46
stories. *See* hane'; honi
sunrise, 53, 80–81, 87, 91
survivance, 159n18; through hane' and honi, 17, 22, 28, 48, 126–27, 142–43, 147–48; Indigenous film and, 65–66, 68, 173n25; landforms as reminders of, 13, 17, 22, 48

tádídíín (corn pollen), 53, 81, 91
Tailfeathers, Elle-Máijá, 72
Tapahonso, Luci, xi–xiii, 3, 7–8, 9–10, 12–13, 22, 78–79, 81, 91, 126
Taranaki Maunga, 48–49
television, Indigenous, 7, 20, 51–53, 56, 63–64, 75–77, 171n2, 177n97
Teller Ornelas, Sierra Nizhoni, 76, 176n94
The 6th World (2012), 68
Thomas, Wesley, 100–101
Thompson, Larry, 92–94
Tłı̨chǫ (Dogrib), 127, 135–36
Tó Bájísh Chíní (Peacemaker), 32. *See also* Hero Twins
Tohe, Laura, 9–11, 12, 14, 17, 105
tourism, 46, 84, 86
Trail of Tears, xvi–xvii
transgender people, 87, 94, 96, 100, 147–48. *See also* Freeland, Sydney
transphobia, 88–89, 90, 94, 98–100
Trimble, Sabina, 146
Trouble in the Garden (2018), 70–71
Tsé Bii' Ndzisgaii (Valley of the Rocks, Monument Valley), 31, 114; as site for non-Indigenous film, 61, 116–17, 169n78, 182n37, 182n38, 182n39
Tsé Bit'a'í (Winged Rock, Rock with Wings, Wings of Rock, Shiprock Peak), 23–25, 164n5, 164n6; author's relationship with, xvi, 20, 26–27, 40–41, 45–47, *47*, 150–51; climbing, 31–32; commercialization of, 45–46; dislocated and othered, xvii–xviii, 20, 23, 37–44, 150, 168n71, 170n89; Indigenous depictions, 19, 22, 36, 45, *45*, 48–49, 115, 123, 125, 151; personhood status for, 48; photographs, *23*, 45–47, *47*
Tsé Nináhálééh (Bird Monsters), 32–35, 115, 151, 167n54
tsiiyééł (Diné hair bun), *66*, 66–67, 88, 123, *124*
Tsuut'ina First Nation, xviii, 27–28, 145–46
Tsuut'ina language, 27–28, 146
Tuck, Eve, 73–75
Two-Spirits (2009), 100–101

Uncle (character played by Larry A. Lowe), 111–12, 120, 122

Van Camp, Richard, 8, 128, 133–34, 140–41, 186n47, 186n59, 187n60

Wanihadie, Victoria, 146–47
Warren, TJ (Terry James), 144–45
warriors, 36, 54, 97–98, 132–33, 135–37. *See also* Hero Twins
Watchman, Katherine Mae Keedah (author's paternal grandmother), xvi, 22
Watchman, Lewison R. (Daddy Lew), xvi, 26, 32–33, 62, 154
water (tó, ti), as theme, 83, 134–35
weaving, 22, 86, 108, 142–43, 178n18
Wente, Jesse, 69–70
Werito, Vincent, 3–4, 26, 97
wheetago, 137–38, 140–41, 186n47
Whitman, Richard Ray, 88, 95, 97–99
Wingate Valley Boys, 82
winter storytelling, 7, 8, 9, 28
women, Indigenous (*see also* Asdzą́ą́ Nádleehé; Kinaaldá; matriarchs): in Indigenous film and television, 36, 54,

63, *66*, 66–67; place in Diné culture, 63, 76, 99, 101, 118, 124–25; Western views of, 44, 61, 92–94, 118–20
Women of the Navajo (WON), 92–94, 180n41
Woody, Elizabeth, 142–43

Yamoria/Yamozha, 132–34, 185n24. *See also* Dǫne Nàowo
Yang, K. Wayne, 73–75

Yat'a (character), 137–38, 185n41
Yazzie, Ethelou, xv, 3, 111, 151, 161n49, 162n53, 165n31, 166n38, 183n42
Yoolgai Asdzą́ą́ (White Shell Woman), 166n38, 166n42
Young, Allie, 36, 37
Younging, Gregory, 13

Zoe, John B., 139
Zolbrod, Paul G., 7, 19, 96, 163n74, 166n38

ABOUT THE AUTHOR

Tódich'íi'nii éínishłį dóó Kinya'áanii báshíshchíín. Tsalagi éí da shichei dóó Táchii'nii éí da shinálí. Naat'áanii Nééz déé' íiyisí naashá. Hamilton, Ontario, Canada, di shighaan.

Renae Watchman, PhD (Diné), is Bitter Water, born for Towering House, Bird Clan (Cherokee Nation of Oklahoma), and Red Running Through the Water. An associate professor of Indigenous studies at McMaster University, she teaches Indigenous literatures and Indigenous film. Dr. Watchman co-edited *Indianthusiasm: Indigenous Responses* with Hartmut Lutz and Florentine Strzelczyk.